THE
COMING
INFORMATION
AGE

COMMUNICATIONS

George Gerbner and Marsha Siefert, Editors

The Annenberg School of Communications

University of Pennsylvania, Philadelphia

Third Edition

THE COMING INFORMATION AGE

AN OVERVIEW OF TECHNOLOGY, ECONOMICS, AND POLITICS

WILSON P. DIZARD, JR.

Longman
New York & London

P
92
.U5
D5
1989

The Coming Information Age, third edition
An Overview of Technology, Economics, and Politics

Longman Inc., 95 Church Street, White Plains, N.Y. 10601

Associated companies:
Longman Group Ltd., London
Longman Cheshire Pty., Melbourne
Longman Paul Pty., Auckland
Copp Clark Pitman, Toronto
Pitman Publishing Inc., New York

Executive editor: Gordon T. R. Anderson
Production editor: Marie-Josée A. Schorp
Cover design: Susan J. Moore
Cover photo: Section of a wafer of megabit memory chips. Each rectangular chip
measures 2/5 by 3/5 inches and can store over a million bits of information.
Reproduced with permission of AT&T Archives.
Text art: K&S Graphics
Production supervisor: Kathleen M. Ryan

Library of Congress Cataloging-in-Publication Data

Dizard, Wilson P.
    The coming information age: an overview of technology, economics, and politics /
    Wilson P. Dizard. — 3rd ed.
    p.   cm. — (Communications)
    Bibliography: p.
    Includes index.
    ISBN 0-8013-0305-2
    1. Communication — United States. I. Title. II. Series: Communications
(Annenberg School of Communications (University of Pennsylvania))
P92.U5D5 1989
001.51′0973—dc19   88-20939
                                                 CIP

ISBN 0-8013-0305-2

89 90 91 92 93 94 9 8 7 6 5 4 3 2 1

For Lynn

Contents

Preface

This expanded third edition incorporates the many new developments that have occurred recently in our evolving information age society. The pace of these changes has been such that a new edition is necessary less than four years after a heavily revised second edition was issued.

In the earlier editions, I set out to describe the political, social, and technological factors that are converging to form the pattern of the new information age. That is still my purpose. We need to understand this convergence before we can deal effectively with the problems and opportunities facing us in the new age.

The most dramatic changes are taking place in technology. The key element here is the ubiquitous semiconductor chip. It embodies the power of the information age comparable to the role of the steam engine in the industrial era. The nineteen eighties saw a *massification* of semiconductor technology in ways that no one could have predicted earlier. One is reminded of the estimate made by IBM executives in the 1950s to the effect that about 50 computers would serve all the world's needs for the forseeable future.

One current IBM product is, in fact, a good example of the pace of change. The firm's second-generation personal computer, first marketed in 1987, has eight times the computational power of its original 1980 model. The eighties have seen similar leaps in such technologies as fiber optics, satellites, and superconductivity, all of which have outstripped earlier predictions about their development.

Technology has also been a factor in reshaping longstanding economic patterns. The breakup of AT&T in 1984 was the signal for a massive restructuring of the communications sector, a process that has not yet run its course. The introduction of the newer technologies has often been accelerated by start-up entrepreneurs, challenging established industrial giants. Another consequence of this change has been the globalization of production and marketing of communications goods and services. Japanese and European firms are now major competitors in a sector where the United States has been dominant heretofore.

Important as they are in themselves, technology and economic issues are dependent for their effectiveness on political decisions about the form and direction of American society in the evolving information age. In this new environment, our basic strength is a commitment to First Amendment guarantees of open information access for everyone. In its 18th-century form, the First Amendment refers only to speech and the press. This has been extended over two centuries to other channels of expression, e.g., radio and television. The task now is to assure similar rights of access to information in computers and other microelectronics-based resources.

Despite the global erosion of its economic and technological leadership, the United States is still the test-bed for this evolution. Nowhere else is there as much experimentation with new forms of electronic democracy in an evolving information society.

This experimentation is all to the good. But, as I suggested in the original preface to this work, we also need a more articulate consensus about goals and actions in our new information-rich society. In addition to better planning mechanisms, we can also use, in Nigel Calder's phrase, "all the fallibility we can get ... to preserve the absolute unpredictability and total improbability of our connected minds." This is a lovely paradox, and a saving one. In the final analysis, our ability to adapt the powerful new communications and information machines to these intensely human qualities will be the best measure of our success in the new age.

I want to thank the many individuals who, in different ways, have helped me with the original book and its revisions. A special tribute is due to the late Ithiel de Sola Pool of the Massachusetts Institute of Technology, a friend and professional colleague over many years. The title of his last book, *The Technologies of Freedom*, summarizes all of what I have tried to document in this work. He was a formidable defender of the principle that the new information and communications technologies would be of value only to the degree that they expand the range of informed dialogue between individuals. It was a principle he defended with consummate skill throughout his career as a teacher and writer.

I must also acknowledge the assistance of my colleagues at the Center for Strategic and International Studies and at Georgetown University's School of Foreign Service. The staff of the university's Lauinger library was, as always, patient with my requests for documentation of the elusive fact and the fragile idea. My four sons — John, Stephen, Wilson, and Mark — provided useful comments.

Finally, a special acknowledgement to Lynn, who brought to my efforts the invaluable chemistry of loving interest and informed criticism.

Wilson Dizard

THE
COMING
INFORMATION
AGE

CHAPTER 1

The Information Age

Of all the changes taking place in our time, none has more profound effects than the new ways in which we communicate with one another. For the first time in human history, there is a realistic prospect of communications networks that will link everyone on earth. The familiar telephone will provide the basic connection for most people as well as for an increasing array of computers and other information resources. There are still large gaps in this prospect, particularly in Third World countries. Nevertheless, the United Nations' goal of a telephone within an hour's walk of every village should be realized early in the next century.

There are no historical precedents to guide us through this momentous change in how we deal with one another. No one knows the ultimate effects of this new order of instantaneous links. Most predictions tend to stress the advantages of what is usually described as "bringing people closer together." This is undoubtedly a positive gain, although there is a dark side to the picture, given the destablizing factors brought about by the fragmentation of old patterns of personal and tribal isolation.

What is clear is that we need to understand more accurately the implications of these changes. In particular, this involves a better awareness of the converging technological, economic and political forces that are at work in this environment, the *information age*. This book is an interim report on these developments. Interim, because we are only in the first stages of the new age. Despite the swift pace of developments in recent years, it pales before the changes we will see in the years leading up to the new century and beyond.

"Information age" is an inadequate phrase for these complex events. It is a cliché, useful for tagging a set of ideas. The concept has, as we shall see, already reached a stage where there are contentious challenges to the very idea that there is an information age. This is, of course, all to the good. Some of the early simplicities about the wonders of the new era have already been heavily modified, or discarded, by later realities.

Nevertheless, something important is happening out there. And, by and large, it is happening in the United States first. The Europeans, Japanese and others are closing in, but ours is the first country to have completed the three-stage shift from an agricultural society to an industrial one, to a society whose primary economic and social activities are the production, storage and distribution of information.

Despite the relative decline of American world power in recent years, the United States remains the primary incubator of the ideas and techniques that are shaping the global information environment. The technologies of the information age were largely developed here, and they are usually applied here first. Americans lead the world in the *range* of their experimentation in this field. By and large, we still have the edge, but it is often a temporary one. The rapid diffusion of new ideas and techniques on a global basis is one of the hallmarks of the new age.

The research breakthrough made in a California laboratory shows up very quickly on production lines in Cologne and Osaka, often in an improved version. Technological isolationism — the kind that led Chinese emperors to decapitate subjects who sold secrets to outsiders — is no longer possible or desirable. America's comparative lead in high technology is a continuing national asset in the transition to the new information environment. Our lasting influence will, however, be measured more by our ability to adapt this technology in ways that enrich the prospects for more advanced forms of democracy.

The rush to identify the new information age has resulted in a wide array of adjectival clichés such as George Lichtheim's *post*-bourgeois, Rolf Dahrendorf's *post*-capitalist, Amitai Etzioni's *post*-modern, Kenneth Boulding's *post*-civilized, Herman Kahn's *post*-economic, Sidney Ahlstrom's *post*-Protestant, Lewis Feuer's *post*-ideological, and Roderick Seidenberg's *post*-historic societies. Richard Barnet adds a pragmatic note with his contribution: *post*-petroleum society. Most of these descriptions have been left at the *post* by a phrase popularized almost two decades ago by Harvard sociologist Daniel Bell: the *post*-industrial society. The common prefix of all these labels suggests an autumnal quality to our age, a sense of ending. Neither Bell not the other future watchers have projected a grand design of what is to come, either out of intellectual prudence or simply out of awe at the many contentious prospects available.[1]

Nevertheless, each of them assigns great significance to the prospects examined here — the evolution of a more complex information and communications environment. They may approach the phenomenon from varying perspectives and draw different conclusions, but they share a sense of its importance. Professor Bell, in particular, put the information factor at the center of the concept of the post-industrial society. The result, he suggested, has been a seismic shift of the economy from goods production to information-based services, with professionals and technicians replacing business entrepreneurs as the preeminent social class.

His analysis was based, in part, on research carried out in the mid-sixties by Fritz Machlup, a Princeton University economist. Machlup's work was a groundbreaking attempt to define the role of information activities in the American economy. He looked at what he called "the knowledge industries" — an umbrella phrase covering the educational system, the media, libraries, research institutes, and other information-intensive activities traditionally identified as parts of the services sector. His conclusion was that these activities were, collectively, the largest segment of the economy, accounting for over 40 percent of the work force and about one-third of the annual gross national product. Moreover, he concluded, the knowledge industries had become the major economic growth areas.[2] Professor Machlup's work gave statistical underpinning to Dr. Bell's thesis that these industries were now the pivot of innovation and policy making. In Bell's view, a new intellectual technology, based on computers, was being created.

The phrase "post-industrial society" soon became a trendy part of the language. The subject was given wide publicity in books by such popular writers as Alvin Toffler and John Naisbitt.

In other quarters, however, there was skepticism about the whole idea. These challenges were in the tradition of Lewis Mumford, perhaps the most perceptive critic of 20th-century industrial society. Fifty years ago, Mumford had projected the growth of a humane, technology-based civilization in the United States. By the seventies he had drawn back, predicting instead a massive information-based, military-industrial establishment run by an expanding, oppressive bureaucracy.[3] In his critique of post-industrial optimism, socialist Michael Harrington has warned against the assumption that powerful, resistant social structures can be readily modified to meet new conditions.[4] All theory is gray, as Goethe reminds us, and most of what Dr. Bell and his academic defenders and detractors have told us is theory. Nevertheless, they were all addressing the fact that significant changes, based on the new importance of information-based activities, were taking place in American society.

The post-industrial thesis was given a strong boost in the late seventies with the publication of a massive U. S. government research study that attempted to define these changes. Entitled *The Information Economy*, the nine-volume report was sponsored by the Department of Commerce. Basically it confirmed the Machlup thesis that the dominant trend in the American economy involved expansion of information-related activities in the services sector. The Commerce report used more sophisticated research criteria than was employed in the Machlup study to project a view of the economy in which almost half of the gross national product is tied to information production and distribution, while nearly half of the labor force is engaged in these service-sector activities. Overall, the study seemed to confirm a major shift in the American economy, and by extension the whole society.[5]

By the middle eighties, revisionist views about the post-industrial thesis had gained wide currency. One of the most telling critiques was contained in research intended to update Fritz Machlup's 20-year-old study of the "knowledge industries." Written by two of his associates, Mary Huber and Michael Rubin, the study indicated that, contrary to Machlup's predictions, there has been a steady slowing of growth in the information sector. The pattern, according to Huber and Rubin, is an uneven one. There are more managers and sales workers, they discovered, but fewer clerks and technical workers. Why the displacement of clerks and technical workers? The answers, in part, may involve a development that Fritz Machlup had not anticipated back in the sixties — the mass introduction of computers and other highly automated equipment, resulting in the laying off of workers in offices and on production lines.[6]

Other recent research has challenged the general post-industrial thesis that an information-based service economy is the natural successor to an industrial-based economy. This viewpoint was articulated forcefully in a 1987 study by Stephen Cohen and John Zysman of the Berkeley Roundtable in International Economy at the University of California. While conceding the importance of the new information-dependent economy, they argued that the choice is not between reducing the traditional manufacturing base in favor of information-dependent services. The two sectors, they suggest, are inextricably linked:

> If the United States wants to stay on top — or even high up — we can't just shift out of manufacturing and into services...Insisting that a shift to services or high technology is "natural" is irresponsible analysis and perverse policy. The competitiveness of the U. S. econ-

omy — the ability to maintain high and rising wages — is not likely to
be enhanced by abandoning production to others. Instead of ceding
production, public policy should actively aim to convert low-product-
ivity, low-wage, low-skill production processes into high-technology,
high-skill, high-wage activities — whether they are included in the
manufacturing unit itself or counted largely as service firms."[7]

Other researchers have pointed out more recently that the post-
industrial trend is not all that new. Dr. James Beniger of the University
of Southern California traces the key role of information technology
and services in an industrial economy back 150 years or more. He cites
the importance of the telegraph (1838), the telephone (1876), the
modern typewriter (1873), and even carbon paper (1872) and pencils
with erasers (1858), in laying the groundwork for the information age,
or what he calls "the Control Revolution." "Just as the Industrial
Revolution marked an historical discontinuity in the ability to harness
energy, the Control Revolution marks a similarly dramatic leap in our
ability to exploit information."[8]

The debate about the form and direction of the evolving information age will continue for a long time. Meanwhile, beyond the
academic forums and lecture halls, massive changes in the information
environment are affecting the shape of American society in very concrete ways. This development has all the characteristics of a permanent
shift, and it is one whose longer-term impact is difficult to grasp. Some
of the implications of these changes were defined in broad terms by the
theologian-paleontologist Teilhard de Chardin when he described:

> the increasing degree in which present-day thought and activity are
> influenced by the passion for discovery; the progressive replacement
> of the workshop by the laboratory; of production by research; of the
> desire for well-being by the desire for more being....Research,
> which only yesterday was a luxury pursuit, is in the process of be-
> coming a major, indeed the principle, function of humanity. As in the
> case of all organisms preceding it, but on an immense scale, humanity
> is in the process of "cerebralizing" itself.[9]

De Chardin's vision still seems utopian. Nevertheless, it is an early
warning of the cultural changes implicit in the evolution to a new kind
of information-rich society. Given the momentum with which we are
moving into this environment, we need to get our bearings now in order
to develop strategies for managing it.

What scenario can we project for this shift to the information age?
The research and theories developed by academics in recent years can
provide insights, but no firm answers. The closest historical precedent is

the introduction of printing in the 15th century, an event the reaction to which was spread out over centuries.

Unlike Gutenberg's printing press, however, today's technologies have an almost instantaneous impact. The computer pioneer, John von Neumann, pointed out that modern technology increases the rate of change not so much by shortening the time involved as by expanding the areas — political, economic, and cultural — that are affected. In the communications and information fields, new technologies no longer develop in a linear fashion, separated by decades, with enough time in between for their implications to be sorted out and phased into active use. Now we are dealing with a wide range of converging technologies, forcing us to make immediate choices and allowing considerably less margin for error.

Forecasting change under these conditions is a risky business, particularly when it involves, as in this country, an already complex information and communications structure. Nevertheless, a general pattern is emerging. It can be seen roughly as a three-stage progression, beginning with changes in the basic information production and distribution industries, leading to a greater range of services available for other industries and for government, and resulting in a vastly expanded range of information facilities at the consumer level. It will be useful to take a summary look at this progression.

The first stage of transformation is already well underway. It is concentrated in what the Department of Commerce's 1977 study called the "primary information sector." This sector is dominated by a relatively small group of large corporations that are the builders and operators of the basic information and communications infrastructure. Their size and influence are awesome. The largest of them, the American Telephone and Telegraph Company, had a gross income greater than the individual gross national products of 118 foreign countries before the 1982 decision to split up the company. The industry is dominated by acronymic giants — IBM, GTE, MCI, DEC, CBS, and so on. Clustered around them are groups of smaller firms with little-known names such as Digitech, Valtec, Transnet, and Micom. These minor players are no match for the giants in terms of economic power, but they represent an important trend. Many of them compete successfully against the established leaders by introducing innovative ideas and techniques with a flexibility and flair often lacking in the old-line companies. The result is a newly competitive tone in what has heretofore been a cautious, conservative sector of the economy. But whether with established firms or feisty new challengers, the industry is building the high-technology infrastructure that will form the basic pattern for the information economy. A large part of the structure is already in place. Much of the rest of it is on the drawing boards, ready to be built and completed well before the end of the century.

Meanwhile, the next stage of the new information economy is emerging. It involves the industries and organizations, both private and public, that will be the primary users of the new high-technology network. Their dependence on the services of the new technology is already extensive, and it is increasing exponentially. The banking industry, for instance, is moving toward a universal electronic funds-transfer system that will gradually replace most of its paper transactions, including the more than 45 billion checks written every year in the United States. The national health-delivery system will be supported increasingly by automated, computer-based data systems whose functions range from storage of medical records to long-distance monitoring of patients. The education industry, with its $350 billion annual budget, will move more rapidly into electronic learning systems. Hopefully, this industry will benefit from lessons learned in the sixties, when it attempted to automate instruction for the wrong reason, that is, to save money rather than to improve the learning process. Computer-assisted instruction, already used by millions of students, is becoming commonplace. Computer literacy is increasingly regarded as a basic skill. The driving force for this will be the increasingly ubiquitous personal computer. Over forty million of them have been installed in American offices and homes.

Some of the most extensive changes will take place in business offices. The trend toward automated office operations is already running strong in large organizations. In the nineties, it will encompass even the smallest firms, making them essentially computer-based communications centers. It took the telephone 75 years to reach the level of penetration in offices that the small computer has attained in 10. The automation of office procedures will probably account for the largest dollar-volume share of the expanded information sector in the next few years.

Meanwhile, the vast public sector bureaucracy is adapting to the new technologies. The United States Government is now the world's largest repository and dispenser of information, from cookbooks printed by the Government Printing Office to maps of Mars produced by the Space Administration. One small federal agency, the National Technical Information Service, is the largest publisher of books and reports in the world, using a computer-based system that has almost nothing to do with conventional printing presses.

The third and most far-reaching stage of the information age will accelerate during the coming decade. This is the mass consumerization of high-technology information services. Communications and information resources in the United States are more complex than in any other society. They are relatively primitive, however, considering the prospects created by the application of available technology to a new kind of mass information network. As inventor Peter Goldmark put it, our communications are still in the "tom-tom stage." The changes are coming fast, however. Advanced information and communications resources, once limited largely to use by big business and big government, are being extended to homes and small organizations, providing a wide range of computer-based information resources that is well beyond anything previously available. Over half of all American homes are already linked to cable or direct-broadcast satellite systems.

This trend conjures up visions of whirring, blinking computers in the living room and other Sunday-supplement dreams. The reality is somewhat different — and more reassuring. Most of the new services will be made available through two devices already present in most American homes — the telephone and the television set. These familiar instruments can be the links to a new kind of information richness.

In Britain, an information network with the unassuming name of Prestel already supplies thousands of homes and offices with a full range of computerized information services. The system is based on the telephone, the television set, and a "black box" attachment that costs less than $200. The service is linked to hundreds of data bases, providing hundreds of thousands of "pages" of information that can be ordered up on the television screen by dialing the appropriate computer through the telephone system. The data ranges from the frivolous to the practical to the profound: *What is my horoscope for today? Who won the fifth race at Ascot this afternoon? Which library provides the best bibliographic information on the combinatorial mathematics of scheduling?* Prestel tells all, for a fee that is added to one's telephone bill at the end of the month.

Similar videotext information systems are being developed in other European countries. The French have taken the lead with a system called Minitel, involving a simple computerized video screen attached to telephones in homes and offices. Minitel was originally designed as an electronic replacement for bulky printed telephone directories. The project's managers quickly realized that Minitel could provide a range of other information services. By 1989 over three million Minitels had been installed, with 3,000 information services, ranging from airline schedules to lonely-hearts clubs, available to users. A major reason for Minitel's success has been the offering of messaging services, permitting on-line dialogue between users, without any restrictions on content. Similar services have been slower to develop in the United States, although the next decade should see the rapid expansion of national videotext networks.

Prestel and other projects that plug millions of people into a vastly expanded system of information services are Model T versions of what may be a taken-for-granted part of daily life by the end of the century. The present systems are designed primarily to connect their subscribers to relatively large central computer banks. The next step, well within the capacity of present technology, has subscribers developing their own data banks. This information can be sent to central data banks, passed on to other subscribers directly as a public service or for a fee, or stored for future reference. Here we have a new kind of First Amendment democracy — every person his own data collector and publisher, unmediated by any authority, public or private, as long as he pays the telephone-computer service bill at the end of the month.

The full possibilities of this technology will be felt only in those democracies — a discouraging minority of the world's nations — that are committed to open inquiry and the ambiguity of conflicting challenges to authorized, conventional wisdom. The United States and like-minded societies have had only limited experience with such an environment until now because of technical and economic constraints on universal information access. But, we are beginning to grapple with the implications of the changeover. It will, for instance, affect the way in which we learn, not only in school but in the long years afterwards. For all our commitment to mass education, we are still living in a time of educational incapacity. Formal learning for adults is generally cut off in the late teens or the early twenties, leaving most of us diminished in an environment that requires lifelong retraining. With the new technology, continued learning will be more than a question of refresher courses and other "adult education." It will involve, rather, an environment that adds a stunning dimension to information seeking and creative thinking. Norman Macrae, an editor of the *Economist*, has projected what could happen when the new technologies are applied in ways that remove the present limitations on lifetime access to information.

The prospect is, after all, that we are going to enter an age when any duffer sitting at a computer terminal in his laboratory or office or public library or home can delve through unimaginable increased mountains of information in mass-assembly data banks with mechanical powers of concentration and calculation that will be greater by a factor of tens of thousands than was ever available to the human brain of even an Einstein. From the 99 percent perspiration and one percent inspiration that was Edison's definition of inventive genius before he died in 1931, we have in the four decades since his death already provided the machines that can reduce the main part of that perspiration much more than 99 times over. Because this will eventually make research a task that can be undertaken more effectively (even part-time) by many more people, this must surely increase the prospect by unearthing more people with Edison's or Einstein's divine afflatus. I do not believe that heretofore more than a small fraction of mankind's potential geniuses have ever had a chance to indulge in research work if they wanted to.[10]

The prospect of crowds of Einsteins and Edisons is enough to give us pause. More immediately, a full-scale information network will break the old constraining bonds of limited access to information resources. Computer scientists have a phrase that fits the new situation, "distributed intelligence." Until a few years ago, Norman Macrae's future geniuses were limited to large, centralized data bases. The new technologies — mini-computers and high-speed data networks — are changing this, making possible a new kind of flexibility and creative individualism. Geographically dispersed data terminals, each with its own information storage and computing capability, can operate independently, be linked to each other, or be linked to large central data sources. The focus in computer development has moved from the relatively simple management of central data bases to new patterns of "distributed intelligence" — a phrase that defines much of the creative promise of the coming information age.

The image of the genius working at a computer terminal in a small room appeals to our pride of technological prowess as well as to our democratic faith in individualism. What is difficult to imagine is its replication tens of thousands or even millions of times. This calls for a quantum leap of both imagination and of faith in the promise of a new information environment. Our understanding of freedom, creativity, and democracy will take on different dimensions in the new era.

British communications scholar, Anthony Smith, predicts a seismic effect of these changes on the notion of authorship as an individual process and the protection of information property rights as a result of the new technologies. He points out that, whereas in the age of Gutenberg print, the author became supreme and the machinery of information was under the control of the author, the computer age is beginning in many ways to unwind this concept of information. More and more, Smith notes, research and authorship are being recognized as collective acts, not individual ones. Moreover, he adds, the information age is a transnational age. Information systems that were national, *uni*lingual and *uni*confessional are giving way to systems that are *multi*national. Inevitably, governments and societies will act to preserve national voices and channels, particularly in reaction to societies like the United States that export vast amounts of information in many forms.

The promise of the information society is intangible and elusive. We are not going to vote on it one day any more than our 18th century ancestors voted on the industrial age. There is no specific critical moment when we can decide how we want to handle the new environment. The issues are spread out in time and place, across a fragmented array of institutional decisions. As we shall see, this makes development of a broad strategy for the new age problematic. We have, in any event, moved beyond easy notions that we can fill our information needs simply by plugging in bigger and better machines. To be sure, the technology for such machines is available. The challenge is in applying them with a clear perception of social needs and in giving emotional texture to the new environment they will create. As Jacques Maritain once noted wryly, "The telephone and the radio do not prevent man from having two arms, two legs, two lungs, falling in love and searching for happiness."[11]

The technocratic visions of the thirties and forties, in which communications were a mechanistic linear process, collapsed under their shaky assumptions about human behavior. Many of the subtleties of the communications process still elude us and probably always will. However, its human dimensions are better understood now as a result of the increased attention given them by researchers in all disciplines from animal biology to mathematics. One of the most fruitful research areas has been the study of how animals, from dolphins to chimpanzees, communicate in elaborate patterns. Another has been the study of nonverbal human communications, the use of body gestures and other signals that, according to anthropologist Edward Hall, make up 70 percent of our communication patterns. The result, as Harold Lasswell noted, has been to reduce the parochialism of the larynx in our understanding of communications.

If it has not come up with final answers, the new research has emphasized the complexity of the communications process. Human beings are not information processors, but code crafters. They don't think straight, if "straight" is taken to mean adhering to standards of right-thinking predetermined by some higher authority. This ambiguity is the most subtle and useful quality we bring to the task of fashioning a truly creative information environment. In this work, we are heirs to the great tradition of men and women who, through the ages, have sought to organize knowledge for civilizing purposes.

Success in our generation will depend on the degree to which we shape the new information technologies in accordance with human values. For most of this century, futurists and planners have imagined human progress in terms of a technological society, a chromium wilderness in which emotional richness has been overtaken by programmed happiness. H. G. Wells, among others, described this solemnly in his works. Aldous Huxley added the saving grace of satire in *Brave New World*. We have moved away from these monstrous models toward more humanistic ones, in which machines are a subordinate rather than a controlling factor. The cold metaphor of the impersonal, technocratic machine is being replaced. The new metaphor is a blooming, buzzing garden in which each of us — including those new Einsteins and their computers — can cultivate a personal plot. This involves combinations of order and disorder, as well as the surprises that spring from the widened boundaries of creative imagination.

Programmed utopia or blooming, buzzing garden — these are, in simplified form, the alternative ways in which we can begin to understand our choices in the emerging information environment. It is a familiar problem for Americans. The tensions between democratic, humanistic ideals and technocratic imperatives thread through our history. However, the new information machines add an insistent, even urgent, dimension to this conflict. They do this by amplifying intelligence dramatically in much the same way that the machines of the Industrial Revolution amplified physical strength. Computers and other information machines are the new motor power, pulling us toward a transformed society faster than we can understand where we are going. The machines can help to orient us in these ambiguous passages, but they are not panaceas. Their mechanical innards do not contain certain formulas for surviving and thriving.

Neither will we find the answers at the Delphic shrines of the technocrats and their systems analysis dogmas. As Herbert Stein has pointed out:

> The dream of thinking everything out before we act, of making certain we have all the facts and know all the consequences, is a sick Hamlet's dream. It is the dream of someone with no appreciation of the seamless web of causation, the limits of human thinking, or the scarcity of human attention. The world outside is itself the greatest storehouse of knowledge. Human reason, drawing upon the pattern and redundancy of nature, can predict some of the consequences of human action. But the world will always remain the largest laboratory, the largest information store, from which we will learn the outcomes, good and bad, of what we have done. Of course, it is costly to learn from experience, but it is also costly, and frequently much less reliable, to try through research and analysis to anticipate experience.[12]

Who sets the social directions and policies in this complex new environment? Government is only one of the major actors in the process. Industry, labor, the financial community, and universities all play critical roles. Given the sensitivity of the subject, the process demands a new kind of awareness of the relationship between technology, economics, and social needs. Decisions on the future pattern of communications and information resources differ from those dealing with, for example, medical care or housing. Communications and information policies involve basic questions of personal identity and values. The overriding concern should not be specific programs or techniques but rather the pattern by which influence is exerted and information becomes effective in a pluralistic society. Strategic decisions will depend on how we see ourselves and project our own interests as we face an uncertain future. A large democracy thrives only when its citizens share enough information, beliefs, and assumptions to function together in a rough consensus. This consensus becomes more important as the pace of change accelerates, upsetting present assumptions and clouding future expectations. We need to collectivize our intelligence, not in centralized, authoritarian fashion, but by encouraging dialogue based on shared information and leading toward agreement on strategies for surviving and thriving as individuals and as a society.

This imperative for both personal and communal awareness is underscored by political scientist, Karl Deutsch.[13] He suggests that we are coming closer to the boundaries within which our intellectual equipment is able to cope with present complexities. He calls for greater emphasis on "intelligence amplification," using information technologies to increase human understanding. Part of the problem with this is our ignorance about the capabilities of the new machines. We tend to see them primarily as improved means for storing and distributing information. Their greatest value, however, may be as satellites of consciousness, monitoring and identifying social needs in much the same way as a remote-sensing satellite in space monitors earth's environmental conditions. This calls for a new kind of information and communications pattern well beyond our present limited system, one that is universal, interactive, and accessible to everyone.

One advantage we have is in not being bound by the easy assumptions of earlier generations about the value of technical progress; we see more clearly the contradictions involved in this process. The French sociologist, Jacques Ellul, has developed a sobering catalogue of these paradoxes. He points out that

- All technical progress exacts a price; that is, while it adds something on the one hand, it subtracts something on the other.
- All technical progress raises more problems than it solves, tempts us to see the consequent problems as technical in nature, and prods us to seek technical solutions to them.
- The negative effects of technological innovation are inseparable from the positive. It is naive to say that technology is neutral, that it may be used for good or bad ends; the good and bad effects are, in fact, simultaneous and inseparable.
- All technological innovations have unforeseeable effects.[14]

These strictures apply with particular sensitivity to the spread of communications and information technologies. For all our willingness to assume that the new networks are a good thing, there are warning signals to the contrary. Consider, for example, Citizen's Band (CB) radio, a form of electronic populism that has given over 30 million Americans their own two-way broadcasting capabilities. Advertisers of CB sets stress safety and convenience as benefits of their products. There may be such advantages, but they mask the deeper reasons for the CB craze. The less advertised factor is CB's appeal to more personal needs. Communications researcher, Bert Cowlan, sees the CB phenomenon as:

> a desire to overcome alienation and to have the opportunity to manage one's own communication system, coordinate one's own resources to survive in what many perceive as an increasingly hostile, bureaucratic, and depersonalized, costly, inefficient and high-risk environment.[15]

The CB user may broadcast in an urgent megavoice, but he or she often displays a penchant for anonymity with a glamorized pseudonym. Tom, Dick, Harry, and Mary Jones turn into Crusader Rabbit, Super Stud, the Ace of Spades, and Crazy Mama. As one of the characters in the perceptive 1977 film, *Citizen's Band*, says about CB's influence in a small town: "Everyone in this town is somebody they're not supposed to be."

The telephone has also become an electronic shield, allowing individuals to be in contact with others anonymously without the pains and pleasures of face-to-face contact. This is reflected in the astonishing growth in what the telephone companies euphemistically call "group bridging" services, with names like Phone-A-Friend, Dateline, and Sportsline. In over 50 American cities, callers can dial advertised numbers and join in or listen to a conversation with as many as 10 people. In the year after such service was introduced in 1987 in eastern Massachusetts, the New England Telephone Co. handled over 12 million such calls.[16]

The tendency to hide one's identity behind an electronic shield can be found in another well-known phenomenon — the unlisted phone number. Once the preserve of a self-conscious minority, the unlisted number is now common. Almost a million phone numbers in New York City are not listed.[17] The private number is a symbol, albeit an absent one, of the dark side of our assumptions about the importance of being in touch, of being part of the network. It is a reminder that, for many people, the openness promised by new communications technologies is a threat, not a promise.

These examples are not aberrations, but merely some of the doubts, fears, and other human frailties we bring with us to the expanded information environment. The promising aspect of the new technologies is that they may expand democratic humanistic options, allowing more sharing of responsibilities and rewards. They can, obversely, have less rewarding effects, propping up outmoded institutions and narrow interests. Such rigid use of technology leads to political alienation and social unrest, resulting in the kind of bloody-minded Ludditism that characterizes so much of the popular attitude toward impersonal technologies and the managers who control them. In the short run — the next decade or two — the first attempts to apply the information machines effectively will compound this problem. This process will call not only for technical efficiency but also for a new kind of democratic equity, a person-centered perspective that assumes neither men nor machines need to be changed radically before human progress can take place.

We are moving into a new ecology of information, defined in large part by the computer's ability to amplify intelligence. This liberating potential of the information machines is still only partially understood. In these first decades of computer technology, the machines have been regarded primarily as useful, somewhat exotic storage bins and calculating devices. Their misuse and underuse is characteristic of our technological and social illiteracy. The problem is computer literacy, a subject commanding more and more attention from researchers and educators.

British critic, George Steiner, has observed that computer language may be a more logical common tongue than English or any other so-called world language. Probably, a new polyglot will develop from computer-oriented English and ideograms. A sort of universal Pidgin may emerge, similar to the special patois that airline pilots use as they take off and land in a multilingual range of cultures.

Developing a comprehensible, comprehensive language is only part of the problem of computer literacy. Equally important is developing a level of literacy that will stimulate creative use of the machines as intelligence amplifiers by nontechnical users. As computer scientist, Alan Kay, puts it: "Simple tasks must be simple and complex ones must be possible."[18] In the late 1970s, Kay and his colleagues at the Xerox research center in Palo Alto began studying ways in which to expand creative application of personal computing systems. Significantly, they turned to the inventiveness of young children for their insights. The project, known as SMALLTALK, involved hundreds of children, ranging in age from 6 to 15, who were given wide latitude to program computers. Along the way, the Xerox researchers learned a lot about learning, particularly about the fragile balance between free exploration and structured curricula. Similar research at M.I.T.'s Artificial Intelligence

Laboratory confirms the computer's simulating value in expanding the prospects for imaginative learning.[19]

Children have taught the SMALLTALK researchers to program more imaginative uses of the simulating property of computers. Most adults use computer simulation as a crutch to confirm their versions of reality. Children have far fewer inhibitions. They use the computer to create what Kay calls "splendid nonsense," simulations that stretch the limits of human imagination beyond conventional ideas. This may be the greatest force unleashed by the new high-capacity information machines, with games played by children pointing to a new kind of expanded human creativity. The computer programs created by children in the Xerox lab are the modern equivalent of the "splendid nonsense" with which the movers and shakers of civilization have always challenged conventional thinking.

Alan Kay's experiments with children are part of his vision of computer power that goes beyond limited economic and technical uses to its true potential as an extension of the human mind. This vision is encapsulated in what he calls the Dynabook — a powerful computer as small as a notebook. In addition to its own encyclopaedic store of information, Dynabook could be plugged readily into networks containing the sum of human knowledge. Kay would equip Dynabook with artificially intelligent "agents" — small computer programs that will link these networks in ways that assure access to information, without the need for technical expertise, for everyone from preschool children on up. The computer would become a universal, liberating resource. As Kay explains it:

> I realized that the computer was like paper, except with extensions into time and into other dimensions. Paper can hold the same kinds of marks that computers can. But it's hard to have a piece of paper that can look at the marks and do what they say. All the newness of the computer comes from its dynamic quality — that's why I call it the Dynabook. The computer is a new kind of medium. Gutenberg has come and we haven't recognized him yet.[20]

The Dynabook concept is still a distance from practical reality, but its evolution toward everyday applications is a matter of years, not decades.

The stumbling blocks to realizing this mind-extending potential lay not in those who exaggerate the computer's capability, but in those who fear it. There is a disturbing tendency to retreat from the implications of the new machines, to deny the possibility of a viable technology-powered democratic society. These antitechnology forces, the new Luddites, seek solace in astrology, artificial Waldens, and bad poetry. Most of us still accept, if with some reservations, the traditionally American secular faith in technology and its benefits. We recognize that technology is not an all-purpose solution. In a divided world, it exerts a powerful influence in keeping us divided. Nevertheless, as Harold Lasswell has noted, an effective information and communications system, at home and abroad, is needed to sustain the powerful trends pushing us toward a new form of world order — the shaping and sharing of basic values and the introduction of specific procedures for more stable social and economic development.[21]

Whether such a pattern can be realized will depend not only on our own efforts but ultimately on decisions made in hundreds of highly diverse societies beyond our borders. Each of them must deal, in its own cultural context, with the new information machines and with the need for difficult institutional changes at the political, economic, and social levels. American experience has a powerful attraction for other societies searching for their own versions of a new Eden. The difference now is the renewed strength and universality of the search. There is, as Janet Flanner said, a strong wind blowing for all men of different colors on different parts of the globe with a steady, unending velocity, unlike the limited cyclonic gusts of the past. Americans have had practical experience with this liberating spirit for more than two centuries; for others, it is a traumatic new experiment.

In its "export" overseas, the American example has taken on a wider identity. It is the gospel of modernization. Since modernization describes much of the psychic environment in which the global information age is developing, it is an important part of our story. Modernization is the doctrine of organized universal betterment. As a worldwide civil religion, it is more influential than nationalism or such limited movements as democracy, fascism, or communism. It shows itself as a psychic mass migration toward a better life. Once this idea makes contact with a society, it diffuses in ways that irrevocably affect traditional institutions and values. It becomes the universal social catalyst, changing everyone it touches.

The gospel of modernization has had to undergo adjustment to some persistent realities since it was first proclaimed in the 1950s. The tone then was one of unalloyed missionary zeal, involving the transformation of the world's underdeveloped areas into local versions of middle-class American suburbs. Reluctantly, its proponents have had to scale down this vision considerably in recent years. Modernization now tends to be described in such uninspiring terms as the New International Economic Order. The emphasis is on sober subjects such as technology transfer, export subsidies, protection prices for raw materials, and the like. Nevertheless, behind the facade of this new sobriety, faith in modernization remains strong. It is a gospel that speaks to the common desires of human beings, as the British critic, Malcolm Muggeridge, once stated:

> What they all want...is what the Americans have got — six lanes of large motor cars streaming powerfully into and out of gleaming cities; neon lights flashing, and juke boxes sounding and skyscrapers rising, story upon story into the sky. Driving at night into the town of Athens, Ohio (pop. 3,450), four bright colored signs stood out in the darkness — "Gas," "Drugs," "Beauty," "Food." Here, I thought, is the ultimate, the *logos* of our time, presented in sublime simplicity. It was like a vision in which suddenly all the complexity of life is reduced to one single inescapable proposition. These could have shone forth as clearly in Athens, Greece as in Athens, Ohio. They belonged as aptly to Turkestan or Sind or Kamchatka....There are, properly speaking, no Communists, no capitalists, no Catholics, no Protestants, no black men, no Asians, no Europeans, no Right, no Left and no Center....There is only a vast and omnipresent longing for Gas, for Beauty, for Drugs and for Food.[22]

Western democratic capitalism has undoubtedly fostered and diffused the modernization idea faster than any other system. However, it would be wrong to equate modernization exclusively with America's own political and economic experience. Many of our mistakes in dealing with the Third World are based on this kind of misperception. Nevertheless, the American example stands as a major force, despite the apparent erosion of our political and economic influence abroad in recent years. "America is a gigantic theater," wrote Ceasare Pavese, "where, with greater candor than elsewhere, is being played out the drama of us all." The drama others are observing now is an America moving beyond the conventional modernization process into an advanced evolutionary phase in which information rather than material production is the focus.

This is usually demonstrated in economic terms, but the American contribution goes further in defining its social dynamics. We add the hitherto startling notion that we expect to live through two or more sets of futures in one lifetime. This is reflected in an educational system that, at its best, prepares for a future that is unpredictable, different, and — still the American hope — qualitatively better. This is a long psychic jump, not without peril, from the assumptions of most other societies with their still-powerful legacies of hierarchal immobility. Such traditions are being eroded everywhere as the gospel of modernization spreads.

Americans proselytize most effectively when they do so least consciously. In his masterful work on propaganda systems, Jacques Ellul emphasizes that unstructured "social propaganda" as expressed in Hollywood films or the *Reader's Digest* has far more impact than the highly organized propaganda attempts of the Nazis, communists, or even our own government's programs of official political persuasion aimed at overseas audiences through the Voice of America. The impact of unintended American social influence — from Levis jeans to IBM computers — is a potent part of the dynamics of modernization.

The coming of the information age complicates the modernization process. Even the limited communications channels available over the past four decades served as powerful diffusers of the new gospel. The new communications and information machines will speed this diffusion dramatically. The developing high-technology networks around the world are predominantly American in style, as is the tone of most of the modernization messages flowing through them.

A new map of the globe is being drawn. It is an information map, comparable to a weather map in that it indicates environmental conditions rather than linear directions. The map shows a dense mass of organized information over North America, with smaller masses over Europe, Japan, and the Soviet Union. Elsewhere the density of information shade off into thinness. The new technologies can change this map radically by helping create a global knowledge grid. How much of the grid can be in place by the end of the century? By the year 2010? To what extent will political, economic, and ideological factors cause delays?

The answers will depend on the strategies and actions we choose during the coming decade, both within our domestic framework and in our relations with other societies. Americans have tended to see the modernization process in terms of the political and economic power it may confer on us. This view is shortsighted. The end benefit, to us and to every other society, will be a stunning global dimension to learning and knowledge. This new dimension can convert our fixation on modernization into a powerful civilizing force.

We are heirs to a great tradition of men and women who saw the organization of available information as a basic condition of human progress. It is the tradition of Ptolemy I Soter (350–283 B.C.), who founded the great library of Alexandria, the first attempt to gather all the world's books in one place and catalogue them scientifically. Its collection of perhaps 700,000 volumes was not matched again until the past century. The destruction of the library in 391 A.D. was a major disaster for Western civilization, reducing the stock of organized knowledge to a few hundred manuscripts. Fortunately, the tradition was kept alive by small groups of Benedictines and other monks, who copied and preserved the few works that survived. The next great step, following the invention of printing and cheap paper, was the work of the French Encyclopedists and their equally enlightened Scottish counterparts, the creators of the *Encyclopaedia Britannica*. Both attempted to summarize the world's knowledge in one set of books. Theirs was an astonishing effort, with (in the case of the French) direct revolutionary implications. The concepts spread to the development of the modern Alexandrine counterparts — the Library of Congress, the British Museum library, and other great library centers.

In the early part of this century, H. G. Wells proposed the development of a World Brain, a project for gathering and storing all information in one place, using the latest technologies. His World Brain was dismissed as fantasy at the time, but the concept is realizable today in the computer, whose capabilities go well beyond those he proposed. The contents of the Library of Congress, over 30 million volumes, could now be stored microelectronically in a relatively small room. Reduced to digital computerized form, the Library's total holdings could eventually be transmitted in a few minutes over high-capacity networks. These may not be practical possibilities, but the growth of massive data banks, linked to users throughout the world by high-speed circuits, already constitute a new civilizing force in the great modern library centers.

Here is a challenge to match the promise of our democratic society as we move toward a new century. In little more than a generation, the technology to meet this challenge has moved from the laboratories into everyday use. Our applications have been primitive compared to the potential of the new machines. The United States has expanded its information production to the point that it is now the repository of the largest share of the world's organized knowledge. Greater benefits may come, however, not from the knowledge we give or sell to other societies, but from what we receive over the new electronic circuits from them. We need these outside resources not simply as accretions to our own knowledge inventory but for the health of our society. They are needed, as the veteran diplomat George Kennan once said:

> just as rain is by the desert and needed...for our sakes alone, for our development as individuals and as a nation, lest we fall into complacency, sterility and emotional decay; lest we lose our sense of the capabilities of the human spirit, and with it much of our sensitivity to the possible meaning and wonder of life itself.[23]

The American influence on a global knowledge network will depend primarily on decisions we make about our own national future. The issue is the development and application of technologies vital to the future of our democratic society and its place in the world. A strategy will emerge either by design or default; for the present, we have not decided which it will be. Given our reluctance to turn over the decision and control functions in this area to government, we have relied largely on haphazard, unstructured decision making, driven primarily by economic forces that have given us the most advanced communications and information structures in the world. The question is whether we can continue on the same course in the same manner or whether we have arrived at a moment when a different national strategy is needed.

How does a society shape strategies for its survival? There is no formula to guide us into an uncertain future with its combination of enhanced intelligence capabilities and greater social ambiguities. Our greatest resource in meeting the challenge is a three-pound electrochemical device, slightly alkaline, which runs on the power of glucose at 25 watts. It is the human brain. It has one striking advantage which even the most sophisticated computer will eternally lack — the power of divine afflatus, imagination, or even just common sense.

NOTES

1. Daniel Bell, *The Coming of Post-Industrial Society* (New York: Basic Books, 1973), p. 212–14.
2. Fritz Machlup, *The Production and Distribution of Knowledge in the United States* (Princeton, NJ: Princeton University Press, 1962).
3. Lewis Mumford, *The Pentagon of Power* (New York: Harcourt Brace, 1970), pp. 293–99.
4. Michael Harrington, "Post-Industrial Society and the Welfare State," in *Libraries in Post-Industrial Society*, Leigh Estabrook, ed. (Phoenix: Oryx Press, 1977), pp. 19–29.
5. U. S. Department of Commerce, *The Information Economy* (9 vols.), (Washington, DC: Government Printing Office, 1977).
6. Michael R. Rubin and Mary T. Huber, *The Knowledge Industry in the United States: 1960–1980* (Princeton, NJ: Princeton University Press, 1986).
7. Stephen S. Cohen and John Zysman, "The Myth of the Post-Industrial Economy," *Technology Review*, February-March 1987, p. 62. The Cohen-Zysman thesis is outlined in detail in their book, *Manufacturing Matters: The Myth of the Post-Industrial Economy*, (New York: Basic Books, 1987).
8 James Beniger, *The Control Revolution*, (Cambridge, Harvard University Press, 1986).
9. Pierre Teilhard de Chardin, *The Future of Man* (New York: Harper & Row, 1969), pp. 166 and 173.
10. Norman Macrae, "Multinational Business," *The Economist* (London) (January 22, 1972), p. 10.
11. Julie Kernan, *Our Friend, Jacques Maritain* (New York: Doubleday, 1975), p. 177.

12. Herbert Stein, "Designing Organizations for an Information-Rich World," in *Computers, Communications and the Public Interest*, ed. Martin Greenberger (Baltimore: Johns Hopkins University Press, 1971), p. 47.

13. Karl W. Deutsch, *The Nerves of Government* (New York: The Free Press of Glencoe, 1963).

14. Jacques Ellul, "The Technological Order," *Technology and Culture,* 3 (Fall 1962): 394.

15. Bert Cowlan, "Communications for the Individual and Extension of choice" (Paper presented before the annual conference of the International Institute of Communications, Washington, DC, September 1977), p. 4. See also Jon T. Powell and Donald Ary, "Communications Without Commitment," *Journal of Communication,* 27, no. 3 (Summer 1977): pp. 118–21.

16. "If a Stranger Calls, Many Are Waiting." *New York Times,* 6 December 1987, p. B-1.

17. "The Unlisted Numbers List is Growing." *New York Times,* 17 December 1977, p. 35.

18. Alan C. Kay, "Microelectronics and the Personal Computer," *Scientific American* (September 1977): p. 231.

19. See Seymour Papert, *Mindstorms: Children, Computers and Powerful Ideas* (New York: Basic Books, 1980) for a description of pioneering research on computers as learning tools conducted at the MIT Artificial Intelligence Laboratory.

20. Frank Rose, "Pied Piper of the Computer," *New York Times Magazine,* 8 November 1987, p. 56.

21. Harold G. Lasswell, "Communications in a Divided World" (1977 Louis G. Cowen Lecture, sponsored by the International Broadcast Institute, London, 1977).

22. Malcolm Muggeridge, *Things Past* (London: Collins, 1978), p. 125.

23. Quoted in Wilson Dizard, *The Strategy of Truth* (Washington, DC: Public Affairs Press, 1961), p. 172.

CHAPTER 2

The American Stake

In considering strategies for the information age, we must be aware of the psychic forces that have created the new environment. The most important of these is the American technological myth, the search for a new Eden through the melding of nature and the machine. This machine-in-the-garden is a persistent vision from the beginnings of American thought. At once utopian and pragmatic, millenial and immediate, it is a view of society as a progression toward an earthly ideal, not, as in older civilizations, an acceptance of unchangeable conditions.

Benjamin Franklin, kite in hand, may be the best-known symbol of the search for an electrically powered paradise. Thomas Jefferson, the farmer-philosopher who distrusted the new industrialism, saw America as sufficiently removed from the evils of European society to be the model for fusing values with technology-based wealth. A half-century later, the quintessential national philosopher, Ralph Waldo Emerson, wrote, "Machinery and transcendentalism agree well.... Our civilization and these ideas are reducing earth to a brain. See how by the telegram and steam the earth is anthropologized." This is the rhetoric of the "technological sublime," in Leo Marx's phrase, and it runs like a golden thread through the national uplift literature.[1]

This American faith has been a powerful force propelling us toward new forms of post-industrialism. Its focus has changed somewhat as American society has become more complex, and particularly as it has expanded its global interests. However, even the recent lowering of expectations about the United States' role in world affairs has not seriously affected the myth. The lure of the Western frontier has been largely replaced by the lure of the equally elusive global village. This folksy creation of the late Marshall McLuhan appeals to our desire to reduce the wide world to familiar proportions. McLuhan is, significantly, one of the best-known of the present generation of believers in the transforming power of electricity. (Others of the faith have included biologist, Julian Huxley, theologian, Teilhard de Chardin, and engineer, Buckminster Fuller.) In a metaphysical flight, McLuhan once declared that the computer "promises by technology a Pentecostal condition of universal understanding and unity."[2]

Social salvation through better communications and information has been a steady promise within the American technological myth. The promise has, moreover, been translated into practice here on a scale never attempted by other societies. The statisical measures of growth toward a new kind of information society are awesome — in numbers of telephones, computers, and other devices. The newly proclaimed information age is, however, less an accretion of machines and techniques than a declaration of faith that electronic salvation may well be within our grasp. The proofs of the faith are found these days in the pea-size products of the microelectronics industry — the stunning range of technologies that began with the transistor in the 1950s and came of age with the integrated circuit, tiny semiconductor devices that are the building blocks of the post-industrial era.

With all its sophisticated capabilites, the new technological environment includes some stubborn problems. Its initial impact has been to raise the level of social complexity. We try to temper this, often by anthropomorphizing the new machines. Where but in America, to use the old lead-in, would a bank try to sell the services of its computerized teller machines by advertising a mechanical pal named "Tillie the Teller" — and succeed? "We promoted her personality," said an official of the First National Bank of Atlanta. "She a bubbly, giggly kind of character."[3]

Tillie the Teller aside, we will have to come to terms with some changing realities in our search for the electronic Eden, the machine-in-the-garden. And here the dark side of the technological myth has to be faced. Henry Adams was one of the early doubters. In *The Education of Henry Adams*, he saw the dynamo, the symbol of technology, as a threat and sought refuge in the virgin cult of the Middle Ages. Mark Twain expressed his skepticism by having Hank Morgan, the hero of *A Connecticut Yankee in King Arthur's Court*, become trapped by an electrical fence that he had intended to use as protection against the primitive Britons.

In more recent times, an incisive critic of the technological myth has been Lewis Mumford. In his early career. Mumford accepted the optimistic view of technological benefits espoused by his teacher, Patrick Geddes, the Scottish biologist and urban planner. In *Technics and Civilization* (1934), Mumford declared that electricity would be the great instrument of social balance in American civilization. But in his last great book, *The Pentagon of Power* (1970), he attacked easy optimism about the benefits of technology, including those associated with communications and information. Whatever its early promise, he declared, the new technologies were being used to magnify and vulgarize the dominant components of the power structure, making it easier for a small elite to dominate large populations.[4] His conclusions were anticipated some years before by a Canadian scholar, Harold Innis, who challenged the idea that communications would lead to a democratic diffusion of power. Innis saw what he termed the tragedy of modern culture here and in Europe as the influence of print and electronic media undermining space and time in the interests of commercial and political power.[5]

The warnings of Mumford, Innis, and other critics have continued in recent years. Victor Ferkiss of Georgetown University believes American society is at a critical juncture in its inability to understand adequately the political consequences of technological change.[6] At the popular level, Alvin Toffler sees the prospect of social breakdown as the result of uncontrolled information overload.[7] University of California researcher, Herbert Schiller, maintains that the manipulation of communications and information resources by a military-industrial establishment is undermining the prospects for democratic society in this country.[8] One of the most striking criticisms of the perils of microelectronic technology is found in a study sponsored by an organization with certified establishment credits — the New York-based Conference Board, a business research group. Its report, *Information Technology: Some Critical Implications for Decision Makers*, takes a somber view of our ability to cope with the choices opened up by computers and other information technologies.

> We may create and strengthen the power of management elites, circumscribe the freedom of man, and create a new kind of rich-poor gap between those, regardless of economic status, who know how to command information and those who do not.[9]

Although their approaches to the subject vary, these post-Mumfordian critics concur in their assessment of technology as a double-edged weapon that is being misused. Their pessimism is grounded in the dark perceptions of technological consequences outlined by French sociologist, Jacques Ellul, in the sobering precepts listed in Chapter 1. None of these critics has stated the case of unintended consequences more sharply than the distinguished American philosopher, Morris Raphael Cohen. He would propose a dilemma for his students: If there was an invention that would enormously increase individual freedom and mobility but demanded the sacrifice of 30 thousand human lives annually, would you take it? The invention was, of course, the automobile. No one in the early years of this century could have assessed its benefits and costs. The new information technologies will, if anything, have a greater impact — although perhaps not involving the direct loss of lives in quite the same way.

This unease spreads well beyond the problems posed by those few individuals who ponder the philosophical implications of change. It is reflected in the ambivalence ordinary men and women feel about the new environment. The extreme form of this ambivalence is the Ludditism and other types of defiance exhibited by countercultural critics of the system. But it is also present, less dramatically, in the general attitude or feeling that something is wrong, that a ubiquitous "they" is ganging up on the rest of us. This attitude breaks through in daily irritations about computerized credit card mix-ups, erroneous bank statements, wrong numbers on the telephone, transportation delays, and shoddy "quality controlled" products in the stores. These incidents feed into a vague sense that technologies have now crossed the threshold into uncontrolled power and consequences from which there may be no turning back. It is reinforced by the piling up of larger problems, such as diminishing energy resources and environmental pollution, where technology emerges as cause rather than cure. Taken together, these problems are seen not as minor obstacles but rather as the end result of a serious, persistent disequilibrium. As Victor Ferkiss has noted, this attitude highlights the difficulties of fashioning viable social institutions and processes to deal with a more complex, technology-driven structure.[10]

If Americans are being currently denied the sunny certainties of onward-and-upward technological progress, we have some sober compensations. These take the form of a greater, if still reluctant, readiness to face up to the situation. Under the pressure of events, there is somewhat less wandering in the meadows of easy assumption about the changed environment of post-industrial society. We have succeeded in shucking off some of the more romantic notions of the technological myth. Hopefully, we have begun to see more clearly the prospects of a free society in which technology can be applied more effectively on a mass scale to serve both material needs and those intangibles that enrich the quality of life. To deny this hope, or not to act on it, would be to erode — perhaps beyond repair — the social mystique holding us together as a civilization that has moved beyond the traditional cultural ties of race or place. The electronic Eden, the machine-in-the-garden, still has a powerful role to play, newly revised to suit conditions that our forebears could not imagine. The question is whether this new reality can be matched with old values in a way that strengthens our prospects for a humanistic democracy.

Here is where the new capabilities of communications and information become critical. They are not simply microelectronic add-ons to the economic structure. They are a controlling resource, the social brain and nervous system holding society together and keeping it in some sort of working equilibrium during a difficult transition. The Wright brothers' unstable flying machine is a useful analogy. It was designed with enough new information input to allow it to move through a turbulent three-dimensional environment under its own power. We have the same problem in our own turbulent times. Do we have sufficient information and adequate communication to navigate this perilous passage? To a considerable degree, the deciding factor will be the ways in which we understand the critical role of advanced information resources in a post-industrial democratic society.

Since the focus here is on the American stake in communications and information, we must take the somewhat risky step of separating developments in these fields from those in other technologies. The risk is in trying to factor out the implications of one set of technologies as if they were independent variables. They are not, of course. The cautions are particularly apt in the study of communications and information patterns. These patterns involve fundamental chemistries of change, infusing all other elements of our lives and altering them. Moreover, these patterns are themselves changed as they affect human attitudes, values, and actions, which then feed back into the entire process.

Such analytical pitfalls must be kept in mind in assessing the American stake in a new strategy for communications and information. The task requires triangulating economics, technology, and politics to arrive at an integrated view of the problem. This kind of overall assessment has, until recently, been curiously neglected. The volume of research in communications and information has risen steadily in recent years. It is still largely conducted, however, in tight clusters of academic disciplines — among the graph-riddled economists, the mouse-maze psychologists, the group-dynamic sociologists, and so forth.

One of the pioneers in modern communications research, Wilbur Schramm, reminded his colleagues many years ago that communications is the crossroads where all the disciplines meet. He was trying to tell them that, essentially, they were all talking about the same thing. They duly noted his maxim and turned back to their narrow projects. Fortunately, a hardy group of interdisciplinary souls heeded Schramm's advice and moved toward more integrative studies. They included Ithiel de Sola Pool at M.I.T., Anthony Oettinger at Harvard, George Gerbner at Pennsylvania, and Edwin Parker at Stanford. Their respective angles of vision on the subject were different, but they all accepted the complexities of a new environment where human communications — and therefore understanding — were increasingly mediated through high-technology machines. They shared a fascination for, and an increasing body of research and insights about, the implications of this change.

Meanwhile, real world events did not wait on the promise of better understanding. The new microelectronics-based grid is being assembled without the benefit of clear-cut projections of its many impacts. Even with the most careful studies, the breadth and depth of these impacts make any precision difficult. This should not excuse us from trying to identify where we are now and where we are going in this area. The stakes are too high to justify any Micawberish hopes that something will turn up. A century ago, the historian Jacob Burkhardt warned that the denial of complexity is the beginning of tyranny. The best approach, as proposed above, is to attempt an integrative look at this complexity in communications and information affairs by triangulating their economic, political, and technological aspects.

Microelectronic technology is, for the present, the driving force among these factors, with its active promise of a new era of abundant resources. Economics is next, as industry demonstrates its ability to transform technological capabilities into marketplace realities. The most critical side of the triangle is the political one. Here is where understanding and actions are weakest, threatening the chances that viable strategies for dealing with the new environment will emerge. The choice, in simplest terms, is whether resources adequate to meet our needs can be assured through a linear extension of past political and social practices or whether a new set of strategies is needed. The argument is a common one in discussions of post-industrial problems, but it has particularly sensitive relevance in the communications area.

The dispute runs across the political and social spectrum. At one end are those who would leave present policies and practices essentially alone, adjusting them in small ways as specific conditions change. There is some nostalgia for laissez-faire, muscular capitalism by proponents of this approach. Their more compelling arguments, however, involve the recurrent suspicion that, whatever the beneficent intentions of political and/or social actions in this area, such intervention is inevitably counter-productive and even dangerous. They point out that the American experiment in restraining public intervention in communications and information affairs has worked well so far. The duplications, confusion, and other inefficiencies of the system, they argue, are a small price to pay, now or in the future, compared to the costs of public actions based on doubtful premises of social efficiency and economic rationality.

At the other end of the spectrum is a small, persistent band of interventionists. Some of them draw their inspiration from various forms of socialism, native to America and otherwise. Another faction is the heirs of a 1930s type of technocratic thinking that believed that the only way through the current rough passage was to apply more rigorous social engineering, based on centrally directed technology.

The answer lies between these ideological extremes. In this society of compromise and deal-making, our real strategic options can be found toward the center of the spectrum. What is clear is that, for all their power, technological and economic forces themselves cannot make the overriding social decisions needed to assure a viable environment in which communications and information resources match our needs. The decisions involve factors well beyond technological advances or market-place economics. In the last analysis, the issues are strategic and political.

What are the policy choices for the new information environment? Finding out requires the kind of basic assessment that Americans are generally reluctant to make. For all our attachment to efficiency and planning, we are not moving in an orderly fashion into the new environment. We are backing in, with, at best, an over-the-shoulder view of things to come. And there are few junctures along the way that will permit us to get our critical bearings.

In assessing planning efforts in this area, a Harvard study group has declared:

> Decisions of vital importance — national, international, corporate and personal — are being fought out in dimly lit arenas under rules that are not clear even to the lawyers, engineers, economists and bureaucrats who devised them. Rosters and score cards are rare. Some of the players are unnumbered; others wear the wrong numbers.... There are many kinds of information technologies, but it is becoming clear that there is really only one information system, no matter how disconnected the parts may seem. Information is a basic resource, fully as important as materials or energy. While materials and energy have not lacked for public scrutiny and policy attention, information resources have developed willy-nilly, their potency overshadowed by their technical details, their pervasiveness so complete they are taken for granted, like the clean air we breathe.[11]

Communications and information policies are a thicket of laws, regulations administrative decisions, and encrusted practices carried out by hundreds of public entities at the federal, state, and local levels. The pattern is confused and often overlapping and contradictory in both purpose and application. Despite the faults of the system, it reflects — not always clearly — a rough consensus. This includes the agreement that there is a need to limit the growth of a central authority that could undermine First Amendment rights and the wide-ranging interpretation of these rights, both in law and tradition, which has been developed over two centuries.

As a result, no one is in charge, by design. Moreover there is no firm consensus on how to proceed in adjusting the system to new realities, or whether to do so at all. One striking example of this confusion can be seen in attempts to revise the only basic communications legislation ever approved by Congress, the Communications Act of 1934. Simple logic argued that a law, which was written over a half century ago to define telephone, telegraph, and radio broadcasting regulations, should be brought up to date in the age of computers, satellites, and other exotic technologies. Congressional hearings on such a revision began in 1976. They have involved millions of words of testimony by hundreds of experts. Long years and many rewrites later, the process fell apart with no prospect of a comprehensive solution yet in sight. Significantly, the debates have not involved disputes over the issue of First Amendment rights. No one has seriously proposed any widening of government controls over communications and information. The vast bulk of the proposals, in fact, suggested weakening the public role.[12]

There are many reasons for this policy immobility. In part, it involves a general lack of public discussion of the issues. In a hyped-up media environment that thrives on sensationalism, sober discussions of communications policy attract little attention. The more immediate reason for the impasse, however, usually has been the inability of the major vested interests to agree on a formula for compromise. If a solution is found, it will be primarily through the interplay of these economic and political forces.

And there probably will be something missing. The debate over the rewriting of the 1934 Communications Act has been long on economic arguments, but short on substantive discussion of overall national needs, beyond ritualistic incantations in support of a bigger, better communications system. To a considerable extent, this reflects a lack of firm social indicators that could give direction to a full public discussion of the issue. Such indicators would not be definitive or determining, but they could provide raw material for a more meaningful debate on policy options than has been the case up to now.

The idea of social indicators for communications and information is not new. The Japanese and Swedes, in particular, have been experimenting with such projects for some time. The results have enabled them to identify conditions on a national scale with some precision. The Japanese knew before they started that they had an annual 10 percent increase in the rate of information production. What they found out through their indicators project was that there was only a 3 percent annual increase in the use of this information. Thus, questions were raised: Did this mean that more than half of the information produced went to waste because people lacked the time to handle it? What was useful information and what wasn't? The Japanese had no easy answers to these and other issues raised in their indicators surveys, but they did have a new set of questions. In Sweden, there is a similar interest in the day-to-day pattern of information use, especially in the present and potential impact of computer communications on ordinary citizens.[13]

No country turns out more social research on communications and information than the United States. It piles up in mountains of monographs, books, computer tapes, and microfilms — some of it very good, some of it very ordinary, and most of it written in the special corkscrew prose through which social scientists attempt to communicate with one another. The problem lies not merely in its bulk or its uneven quality but in the fact that it is so fractionalized. There is every reason to encourage independent and even adversary research. The question is whether, or how, it can be made more useful and comprehensible in the public policy debates in this field.

Plans for some sort of comprehensive social-indicators system crop up perennially. Numerous proposals for funding such a project have been launched, most of them aimed at the Treasury Department in Washington. In the euphoric days of his "Great Society" program, Lyndon Johnson proposed a federally sponsored annual social-indicators index. The idea was promptly rejected by Congress, which did, however, permit the Census Bureau to issue occasional reports. Over and above charges of academic boondoggling, the idea of an annual assessment ran into entrenched suspicions about so-called social engineering.[14] In this area, most Americans have a vested interest in ambiguity. For all our professed devotion to facts and figures, we back away from official attempts to track and measure the conditions of social consensus. In the American version of participatory democracy, with its emphasis on special-interest negotiations, we do not want to be tied down to any plan that purports to codify, under the rubric of objectivity, the social alternatives open to us. As a result, communications and information policies and actions evolve generally without firm indicators of the social conditions involved or the full range of options available.

The lack of a firm consensus on communications and information needs does not excuse us from more precision in defining them. There is a tendency to identify with simple options, from a Pollyannaish everything-will-turn-out-fine attitude to the somber scenarios of Lewis Mumford and other pessimists. As noted earlier, Mumford saw American society moving toward a fascistic megamachine future because of the lack of adequate social controls over technology. (His analogy was that of a locomotive, with neither brakes nor engineer, inexorably gathering speed and heading toward a crash.) But he underestimated the role of the web of checks and balances in American society in preventing such an extreme course. This system has worked tolerably well up to now. However, there are legitimate questions about its ability to maintain its resiliency in coping with the information needs of a more complex technological society.

The political implications of this problem were identified over two decades ago by Karl Deutsch in *The Nerves of Government*.[15] Information is power, Deutsch noted, and — equally important — it is a multiplier of power. In a high technology society, he argued, control of access to information is more important than control of physical forces such as the police or the military. One of our democratic assumptions is that everyone has equal access to information. In reality, of course, access to information is highly uneven for many reasons. The problem is complicated, Deutsch noted, by an increasing flood of information, which pushes us toward the limit of human capacity to cope. The solution, Deutsch suggests, is a new approach to what he calls "intelligence amplification" through computers and other information technologies that can provide a greater sharing of access to the data that allows us to survive and thrive.

Intelligence amplification in the service of a democratic society is the goal of a strategy for the information age. It is a goal squarely within our national mythos. It identifies and illuminates the psychic bounds of a new kind of post-industrial society whose energies are moving away from the production of things toward the production and distribution of ideas. The objective, after all, is the construction of a national (and eventually global) interactive information grid, capable of connecting everyone on earth with everyone else and with a wide array of information resources. The microelectronic base for the network is essentially proven and available. If a strategy combining technology, economics, and politics can be worked out this high capacity grid can be in place in North America, Europe, and Japan well before the end of the century, and in most of the rest of the world in the early decades of the new century.

Any such strategy can benefit from lessons already learned in the building of a smaller mass communications grid during the past century — namely, the telephone system. The American phone network services 95 percent of the populace directly and most of the remaining 5 percent one step removed — that is, with pay phones. Over a billion voice calls are made through the system every working day. Only Canada, among major countries, matches the United States system in its coverage and use. The phone network offers, moreover, a wide array of communications services over and above what the engineers call POTS — Plain Old Telephone Service. Data communications and other services are providing a larger share of network revenues. What we now call the telephone system will be called something else because of its extended capacities (Infonet? Comnet? Or simply, the Network?). The point is that the telephone network exists as an almost universal grid, and it works very well. More significantly, it is pragmatic proof of the American commitment to the idea of a universal communications system. This commitment has been further tested since the 1984 breaking up of AT&T's near monopoly of telephone service. This development (discussed in Chapter 6) will test whether an integrated telecommunications system can be operated on a more competitive basis in ways that benefit us socially as well as economically. However, as the expanded network develops, it will have the many forms of the present telephone system to use as a reference — technologically, economically, politically, and socially. The new expansion involves upgrading and supplementing an already extensive grid, centered around the AT&T, its former local Bell companies, and hundreds of independent phone systems. There are also an increasing number of competing networks, some of them successors to the old telegraph systems and others newcomers either starting from scratch or as spin-offs from other industries. In Chapter 5, I will examine the complex relationship between these many elements, old and new, in the communications and information sectors. For now, however, it is useful simply to get an overview of how the expanded network will fit into the new information economy. Although the present network provides some guidelines, they are inexact when set against the size and complexity of the new grid. The cost of the expanded network will be staggering, measured in hundreds of billions of dollars before it is completed. It will involve technological options on a scale never before tried. Moreover, no one is sure how the system should be configured in terms of its potential use.

Inaccurate estimating of communications and information usage is nothing new. Alexander Graham Bell thought the telephone network would be primarily an entertainment instrument, transmitting concerts and operas to homes.[16] To his credit, he eventually saw the phone's advantages as a device for personal use rather than for mass broadcasting. The developers of the first modern computer in 1945 predicted that six of the machines would serve all foreseeable world needs. In 1980, 30 years after the fact, the IBM Corporation humbly admitted that in the early fifties it had estimated its market for computers would be limited to about 50 machines.[17] Underestimations of the demand for goods and services has been one of the consistent elements in the communications and information industries since World War II. In fact, these industries are the only areas of the economy that have expanded steadily in recent years, not following the zig-zag course of other economic trends.

One result of this has been to confuse economists. In Chapter 1 we looked briefly at research that has documented how information related activities now dominate the economy in terms of gross national product and work force. These studies highlight a fundamental, and still little understood, shift in the focus of American society away from the production of goods to the production and distribution of information. For all its thoroughness this research has left many details of this new economic environment unexplored.

By and large, economists are not comfortable with the intangibles of communications and information. They acknowledge the growing importance of information-related activities, but the subject does not fit neatly into their formulas the way more measurable resources, such as industrial products or energy do. How do you put a price tag on a fact or an idea? How is information productivity measured when it involves a scholar ruminating in a library or a scientific researcher manipulating computer data? It is probably true that half of the information produced in this country is underutilized, used only a few times or not at all. Does this mean that too much information is being produced, or only too little of the right kind in the right place at the right time? Who decides what is "the right kind" of information? One question leads to another. How will the information economy change living patterns? What kinds of jobs will be available? If so, where will they be?

These are practical questions that go well beyond the difficulties economists may have in providing answers. They involve everyday problems of jobs, family, and community. Deeper down are psychic questions, the doubts of ordinary men and women about the so-called benefits of technology. Here Pollyannaish optimism gives way to concerns about the impact of computers and other information-communications machines on prospects for jobs and professional advancement and on personal status in a society where one is identified by what one does from 9 to 5. These elements have always been present in technological shifts. But they are taking on new force as the United States moves into a period of exponential technological acceleration, particularly in the information and communications fields.

This cycle is just beginning. The fears that computers and other information machines will create hardcore unemployment or downgrade job opportunities are still largely muted. Information machines have generally created new jobs in roughly the same proportion as they have eliminated older ones. But workers are not economic statistics whose lives can be measured in balanced-out equations. Machines both eliminate and create jobs, but the shift is never smooth for the men and women involved.

Nevertheless, even in this early stage of microelectronics the shift is being felt. It is particularly striking in those industries and services that have the financial resources and planning skills to take advantage of the new technologies. A good, close-at-hand example is the telephone system. After the federal government, the telephone companies constitute the largest private user of computers and other information machines in the country. Between 1972 and 1977, there was an 18 percent increase in AT&T telephone calls, but the system's labor force dropped from just over 1,000,000 employees to 940,000. Equally significant was the change in the system's mix of employees in the same period. The number of managers, clerical employees, and semi-skilled workers dropped, while the number of professional specialists increased by 17 percent and the number of technicians by 50 percent. Similar changes in the size and employment patterns at AT&T took place in the late eighties, following the breakup of the original company.

The telephone system is an outsized example of what happens when high technology becomes an integral part of an industry. Its experience is being replicated, in varying degrees, across the range of United States industrial and service enterprises. The banking business is a typical case. Why have a labor-intensive bank branch, usually in an expensive location, when a customer can go to a machine and use the magnetic tape on the back of his bank card to make withdrawals and deposits directly? This system requires fewer tellers, less paper work, and gives better service. Another increasingly familiar example is the computerized check-out counters in supermarkets that add up purchases, monitor inventories, and order new stock in one operation — again, requiring less personnel and giving more efficiency and better service. These are not futuristic fantasies. They are rapidly becoming commonplace. Their advantages are those that have always accrued over the long run when goods and services can be made available to more people with less physical labor. The new information machines will accelerate this process, and the impact on peoples' lives will be more direct than ever before.

Such changes are usually seen as American success stories, modern legacies of the technological myth. The shift to microelectronics can mean more efficient production, lower costs, better products, and a work force with greater professional responsibilities. But there is another side to the story, one that is beginning to be seen more clearly in the light of the economic difficulties plaguing the United States economy. Of the nostrums offered to counter economic sluggishness, none has more crowd pleasing appeal than the idea of "reindustrialization," generally interpreted as the shifting of industrial activity toward more efficient high technology activities. The fact that this has been happening steadily over many years has not restrained its enthusiasts from proclaiming the doctrine as new and revolutionary. Communications and information rank high on the reindustrialization agenda, since these sectors of the electronics industry were the leading growth area during the eighties. Reindustrialization is, in fact, a short-term cliché for the longer range push to adjust the economy to the needs of an information-based, post-industrial society.

Whatever the trend is called, there is growing agreement within the Western industrial nations that microelectronics is a critical area in their economic projections. "The next century's underdeveloped nations," the authoritative London *Economist* says, "will be those industrial societies which fail to harness the explosion of microelectronics technology to all that they make and to the factories that make it."[18] This borders on editorial hyperbole, justified perhaps by the newspaper's discovery of a report that indicated that only 5 percent of British firms were using high technology electronics. The report was useful in pushing the British government into more effective support for microelectronic research and development — a step taken earlier by the United States, Japan, France, and other industrial powers. Their motivation was basically the same: the hope that microelectronics could overcome some of the constraints on productivity growth that have hurt their economies. A secondary motivation has been the assurance of their shares of the multibillion-dollar world market for these technologies. Microelectronics research and development have boomed at a rate unmatched by any other technology. A new generation of microelectronic circuits has been developed every 12 to 18 months in this country during the past decade.

American technological innovation in microelectronics would seem to add another chapter to our national success story. However, there are other considerations, involving some negative side effects. As Colin Norman has noted,

> The nostalgic hope seems to be that microelectronics, along with other high technology industries, will lead the way back to the golden days of the postwar era, when the world economy expanded at a rate that provided high demand that in turn created millions of new jobs. Such a development is at best unlikely...The development and application of microelectronics and other technologies will help to stimulate growth, but it will do little to remove the underlying causes of sluggish economic growth.[19]

Norman and other researchers see the need for more effective public strategies to deal with these dislocations. They cite, in particular, the problem of "jobless growth" in industries where production is being automated and workers face layoffs. But the issues are not confined to economics; they will be increasingly political and social as the United States moves more deeply into the new high technology environment.

There are, in short, some disturbing flaws in the vision of information-based high technology sectors strengthening the prospects of social and economic progress. Richard McGahey of New York University's Urban Research Center points out that services and high-tech jobs generally pay less and offer less mobility than older manufacturing jobs: "Dazzling high-tech factories are designed by highly-paid professionals but staffed by low-skilled, low-paid workers." He notes that, in California's Silicon Valley, computer assemblers earn about 70 percent of the hourly wage of auto workers. Moreover, jobs in high technology industries are not likely to grow as rapidly as they did in recent decades. The low-skilled nature of many new jobs makes them vulnerable to technological displacement and foreign competition.

How will the high capacity information network evolve? As noted above, it will be, to a considerable degree, an extension of the present grid — the basic telephone network and the smaller specialized networks that have emerged in recent years. These facilities will be upgraded, widened, and in many cases interconnected over the next decade, primarily in response to specific economic needs. The speed with which this is happening has led economists and others to identify the phenomenon as a distinct new structure defining a network pattern in post-industrial America. They see the evolving grid as radically transforming older, slower economic activities by channeling them through high speed circuits linking buyers and sellers in a vastly expanded electronic market. The concept has been given several name tags, but the one that may stick was developed by a team of University of Southern California researchers led by Herbert Dordick: the "network marketplace." Dordick and his colleagues took a look at the aggregate effect of the many electronics-based information networks being developed or planned and concluded that:

> an important industry is rapidly emerging from the marriage of computers and telecommunications. This industry permits users to interact directly with one or more computers, associated data files and problem solving algorithms from remote terminals. It may include access to distributed information systems within and between organizations, remote transaction recording, data base inquiry and computer conferencing....All the usual services of a marketplace can be offered within a large information network. Products and

services can be advertised and sellers can be located; ordering, billing and deliveries can be facilitated; and all manner of transactions can be consummated, including wholesale, retail, brokering, and mass distribution. Indeed the entire range of such products and services for business, industry, the consumer and government can be perceived as a marketplace — a marketplace on a communications network or the network marketplace.[20]

This concept of marketplace will be a critical element in the forming of the expanded information infrastructure of American post-industrial society. It will not be the product of a master design, however theoretically efficient such an approach might be. It will develop from a pattern of many decisions, large and small, tied to different (and often conflicting) projections of marketplace needs. This is the reality behind the high flying predictions of a universal information grid that have become part of the standard scenario of futurists in recent years. Their vision of a plug-in future, of computers in the living room, of global teleconferences, of robotics factories controlled by telepresence techniques, and of a new quality of life based on access to vast information resources is, nevertheless, too close to possible realization to be dismissed any longer as sci-fi fantasy.

The new network may, however, fail to match these prospects. Its capabilities may be limited largely to providing more efficient communications services to the higher reaches of American business, on the other hand, it can also become a truly universal service grid with a strong economic base, servicing a full range of economic and social needs of both consumers and businesses. This choice will be critical in the definition of American strategies in the new information age. It is useful, therefore, to look at the factors that will determine how and for what purpose the new grid will be assembled.

The choice of a mass or elite network can go either way. The grid is now only in the very early stages of development. Its present development is comparable to that of the telephone system after World War I. Like the phone system of that era, it is a collection of separate networks, large and small. In fact, it was not until the thirties that all the separate — and often competing — telephone systems in this country were interconnected to permit universal subscriber service. Will this serve as a precedent for a new integrated grid of high capacity communications and information services? There are similarities between the two systems, but many of the details are different. It took a half-century to sort out the economic, legal, and social aspects of a relatively simple integrated phone system. These factors are immensely more complex in the new network, with its expanded capability for voice, visual, and data services. Moreover, in these early years of the grid's development, public policy and pressure from industry strongly favor a competitive system of network diversity.

The United States grid, in short, will not be built following any centralized master strategy. It will be the outcome of many competing plans. Consequently, the first integrated national grids will probably be built in Europe and Japan. Although these countries are currently trailing the United States in high capacity networking, their practice of government control over telecommunications development gives authorities greater leeway in laying out a national strategy for an integrated system. They are generally not tied down by the cat's cradle of legal, economic, and social restraints we have imposed on ourselves, beginning with First Amendment inhibitions about government involvement.

The rapid growth of wide service networking has already demonstrated American industry's ability to meet the difficult, usually economically based needs of large government and business bureaucracies. Industry's ability to meet the needs of smaller organizations and individual consumers of information is less clear. Herbert Dordick and his colleagues have noted that this can pose a serious problem for a democratic society. As mentioned earlier, we may be moving toward a new and hazardous form of information inequality, well beyond the traditional gap separating those who have the economic and social means to gain access to information resources and those who do not.[21]

Most of the options favoring a full-access grid are still open. For the present, the network is being designed to meet a variety of limited purposes. Will all these purposes add up to a full range of communications and information services needed by a healthy post-industrial environment? Or should we begin to develop some new kind of national strategy that will assure such a range of services by applying social resources to marketplace economics? For the present, Dordick and his associates point out, "There is not now or in the wings a network policy for the United States."[22]

Right now, there is little prospect for an all-inclusive national policy in this area, but a network construction boom is in progress, in part as a result of federal government decisions to open the industry to greater competition. These decisions exposed a cautious, hidebound industry to new forces — forces that triggered a dramatic expansion of networks and related services in the seventies, which have grown even more rapidly throughout the eighties. Experience to date has confirmed that doing business in the network marketplace can be cost effective, particularly with the rising cost of labor. There are other factors — better overall management control, reductions in energy costs, more effective quality controls over goods and services, plus the intangibles of convenience. However, the ultimate economic prize is the expanded marketplace access gained by buyers and sellers on the network. This will not come automatically; there are still many questions to be resolved as the networks expand. These include pricing of services, public regulatory controls, technical compatability between networks, and capital formation. A number of promising network ventures have already foundered in the midst of such hard realities. A classic case in the mid-seventies was that of the Datran Corporation, a self-styled David that took on the Goliath-like telephone company and, contrary to Biblical form, lost. The additional competitive forces released by the breakup of AT&T in January 1984 have added to the prospects for change.

For the present, the new networks are designed primarily to serve the needs of the United States business and government structure — a major step toward a post-industrial economy. The process, however, will be incomplete if the networks fail to serve efficiently the wider field of mass consumer services as the telephone network succeeded in doing forty years ago.

Universal telephone service resulted from a national strategy decision embedded in the Communications Act of 1934. It came about after a hard-fought struggle between industry and government, in which the two sides traded economic concessions for social gains — a process that has been maintained, with some adjustments, ever since. But the conditions required for replicating such a scenario in the future will not be the same. Nevertheless, there are sufficient similarities to suggest that definitive policy decisions extending high technology, full-service networking to mass consumer levels are needed.

This will involve the integration of economics, technological, and policy factors in new and innovative patterns. Two familiar technologies — those of the telephone and television — are already available in most American homes, schools, and other institutions, providing the physical means for consumer access to the network. The high capacity circuitry to deliver full service is already installed in over one half of these sites via cable television. This percentage will expand in the 1990s, with increased use of thin fiber optic wires in place of expensive copper cables. Other technologies, such as direct broadcasting from satellites and terrestrial multipoint distribution services, are competing with cable systems for the consumer market. This expansion is currently being fueled by the demand for pay-television films. Increasingly, cable home-delivery systems will provide other specialized entertainment and information services, many of them retrieved from computer data banks.

These "wired nation" strategies have been puffed up for years, only to be deflated by the difficulties of fitting the technological, economic, and political pieces together. The difficulties are still there, but the outlook for overcoming them is more favorable now than ever before. Driven by economic forces, the new networks are expanding beyond business and government services into the consumer sector. But the long-term pattern of expansion remains to be seen. Will it be an elite service, aimed primarily at those in the upper income levels, whose information needs are more readily identifiable and marketable? Will it merely reap easy profits from lightweight entertainment services, replicating patterns of commercial television? Will it provide expanded services to the full range of the population, including people who live in such neighborhoods as Watts in Los Angeles, Liberty in Miami, or East Harlem and Bedford-Stuyvesant in New York City?

In their study of the network marketplace, Herbert Dordick and his colleagues suggest that this problem of neighborhood "local loop" services will be the critical one in determining whether mass consumer-oriented services will be available. The economics of high density business networking is already clearly favorable. The problem will be in so-called "thin route" networking down to homes and smaller institutions, not only in middle-class communities but in inner cities and rural villages. Dordick suggests a 1990s scenario in which Congress is asked to declare a Universal Network Access principle in much the same way as an earlier Congress laid down a similar principle for the telephone system in the 1934 legislation.

The distance between that possibility and where we are now is considerable. There are too many intangibles, ambiguities, and other surprises involved to predict any firm kind of pattern. Nevertheless, America has too important a stake in the outcome to leave the subject stranded in the belief that everything will turn out all right. It is too easy to project a flawed strategy in which we may move, in Lewis Mumford's phrase, toward a "megamachine society" in which a self-serving elite uses information and communications resources to control the levers of power. The old confidence, tied to our technological mythos, that it cannot happen here is no longer as steady as it once seemed. Social erosion, what Alvin Toffler calls "demassification," is taking place; traditional groups are breaking up, leaving their former members drifting and alienated. Communications and information resources as such cannot stem this erosion. They can, in fact, hasten it. However, they can also supply new linkages between the pluralities of American society in ways that can reinforce communal trust and creativity.

The question is: How can we keep our essential freedoms while developing new information patterns to meet the problems of a more complex post-industrial society? The answer lies somewhere between authoritarian control and laissez-faire drift. It is here that the conflicting pressures of technology and economics must serve the needs of social equity.

Whether successful strategies are designed and followed will depend only in part on technical or economic decisions. The primary decisions are political. They depend on our willingness to adapt basic social institutions to the opportunities of the new information age. How much readjustment must be made and whether we have the collective ability to make it in time, are open questions for the present. Before examining these policy questions, we will look at the technologies that will shape a large part of the decision process.

NOTES

1. Leo Marx, *The Machine in the Garden* (New York: Oxford University Press, 1964), pp. 232–34.
2. The quotation is cited in James W. Carey and John J. Quirk, "The Mythos of the Electronic Revolution," *The American Scholar* (Summer 1970): p. 402.
3. "Banks Promoting a Mechanical Pal," *New York Times,* 8 August 1977, p. 37.
4. Lewis Mumford, *The Pentagon of Power* (New York: Harcourt Brace, 1970). p. 293.
5. Harold A. Innis, *Empire and Communications* (Toronto: University of Toronto Press, 1950). pp. 166–70.
6. Victor Ferkiss, "Technology: The Hidden Variable," *The Review of Politics,* 42, no. 3 (July 1980): pp. 349–55.
7. Alvin Toffler, *Future Shock* (New York: Bantam Books, 1971), pp. 350–54.
8. Schiller has elaborated his theories in a series of works including *Mass Communications and American Empire* (Boston: Beacon Press, 1971), *The Mind Managers* (Boston: Beacon Press, 1973), and *Information and the Crisis Economy* (New York; Oxford University Press, 1986).
9. The Conference Board, *Information Technology: Some Critical Implications for Decision Makers,* report no. 537 (New York: The Conference Board, 1972), p. v.
10. Ferkiss, "Technology," p. 386.
11. *Information Resources Policy: Arenas, Players and Stakes* (Annual Report of the Program on Information Resources Policy, 1975–76, Harvard University, 1976), p. 4.
12. The hearings on the "rewrite" of the Communications Act of 1934 have taken place in the Senate Banking Committee's communications subcommittee and in a similar subcommittee of the House Committee on Interstate and Foreign Commerce. An excellent introduction to the issues debated in both committees can be found in U. S. Congress, House, Committee on Interstate and Foreign Commerce, *Option Papers: Committee Print 95–13,*

95th Cong., 1st sess. (Washington, DC: Government Printing Office, May 1977).

13. The excellent Japanese research on this subject is not available in English in most cases. For a useful summary of Japanese views (and American reactions), see Alex S. Edelstein and Sheldon M. Harsel, eds., *Information Societies: Comparing the Japanese and American Experiences* (Seattle: University of Washington International Communications Center, 1978). For a useful summary of Swedish views, see *New Views: Computers and New Media.* (Report by the Commission on New Information Technology, Stockholm, 1979).

14. "People Satisfied, Says U. S. Survey," *Boston Globe*, 19 January 1981, p. 10.

15. Karl W. Deutsch, *The Nerves of Government* (New York: The Free Press of Glencoe, 1963).

16. For a summary of Bell's early perceptions of telephone use, see "Bell's Electrical Toy: What's the Use?," in *The Social Impact of the Telephone*, ed. Ithiel de Sola Pool (Cambridge, MA: MIT Press, 1977), pp. 19–22.

17. "One of the Great Miscalculations in IBM History." Advertisement in *New York Times Magazine,* 4 May 1980, p. 127.

18. *The Economist* (London), 23 September 1978, p. 91.

19. Colin Norman, "The Menace of Microelectronics," *New York Times,* 5 October 1980, p. G–5.

20. Herbert Dordick, *The Network Marketplace* (Norwood, NJ: Ablex Publishing Co., 1981), p. ix.

21. *Ibid.*, 235.

22. *Ibid.*, 242.

CHAPTER 3
The Technological Framework
Communications Networks

In his masterful study, *Empire and Communications*, the Canadian scholar, Harold Innis, demonstrates how all societies, from Babylon to the present, have been shaped by the production and distribution of information.[1] His emphasis is on the unsettling effects of new technologies. Innis's perceptions apply to our current transition to a new kind of information society. Here we will take a broad look at the technologies involved in this shift and their impact on our future.

Consider a fable about some fifteenth-century citizens faced with evaluating a new technology. In the city of Mainz, Master Johann Gutenberg has just developed a machine that can reproduce manuscript-like pages in many copies. News of his work has reached the local ruler, the Elector of the Rhineland Palatinate. In the spirit of Renaissance inquiry, the Elector asks a group of scholars and businessmen to assess the machine's impact on the local economy and culture. Since bureaucracy is just beginning to assert itself as an organizational force, the group is designated the Select Committee to Evaluate Multiple Manuscript Production.

The committee visits Gutenberg's workshop, where the proud inventor demonstrates his machine. The committee is impressed, but skeptical. After considerable debate, the group submits its report to the Elector. The machine is undoubtedly a technological advance, the report concludes, but it has only limited application to Palatinate needs. The committee recommends that the government not invest research and development funds in the project. Its reasons are direct and cogent: (1) a large work force of monks copying manuscripts would lose their jobs if the Gutenberg machine were encouraged; (2) there is no heavy demand for multiple copies of manuscripts; and (3) the long-term market for printed books is doubtful due to the low literacy rate.[2]

It is easy to feel superior to the Elector's select committee and its lack of foresight, but it is wrong to do so. The same errors have consistently been made in our own supposedly enlightened times. One example of such an error is the initial reaction to the wireless radio early in this century. The United States Navy installed radio transmitters on ships of the Great White Fleet for its round-the-world voyage and then discarded them in favor of carrier pigeons. In the 1890s, a British publication, *The Electrician*, saw the telephone as a positive menace:

> It seems to us that we are getting perilously near the ideal of the modern Utopian whose life is to consist of sitting in armchairs and pressing a button. It is not a desirable prospect: we shall have no wants, no money, no ambition, no youth, no desires, no individuality, no names and nothing wise about us.[3]

In our own time, equally wrong predictions about the influence of computers, satellites, and other technologies have been commonplace.

We cannot, in any event, take refuge in the conventional wisdom that "technology is not the problem." In fact, technology is more at the core of the problem than ever before. Until recently, major communications advances could be dealt with on a linear basis. Since they were phased in gradually, there was time to make the political and economic adjustments needed to integrate them into the existing structure. The inventions of the telegraph and the telephone were separated by 40 years, another three decades passed before wireless radio came on the scene, and it was still another 30 years before the advent of computers. The time line has been drastically compressed in recent years, with a full range of technologies converging over the entire spectrum of the production, storage, and distribution of information.

The wild-and-wooly situation in microelectronics technology known as large-scale integration (LSI) is typical. Despite its name, LSI involves the miniaturization of electronic circuits. Using LSI techniques, a silicon chip the size of a fingernail can contain the equivalent of hundreds of thousands of circuits. Properly configured, a chip can have all the attributes of a computer; it is a microprocessor with the computational power of a 1950s wall-size machine. Microprocessor technology came out of the laboratories 20 years ago; since then it has gone through at least five technological generations, each involving major advances in capacity and efficiency.

The pace will step up in the coming decades, with the introduction of a wide array of innovations. Among them are:

- Superconducting materials, which lose all resistance to electricity at very low temperatures. This enables them to handle computations in trillionths of a second, a hundred times faster than existing computer circuits.
- Optical fiber communications channels, carrying the equivalent of a quarter-million telephone circuits on a light beam shot down hair-thin cables.
- Computerized storage systems, now under development, that will house as much information as in the entire book collection of the Library of Congress in a small room.
- Massive space platforms, structures assembled thousands of miles above the equator, from which will be hung communications satellites capable of beaming signals into pocket-size portable receivers.

Our understanding of the benefits and costs of these technologies is limited by our still primitive experience. But we can now see the possibilities of having a high capacity, mass access information network much earlier than anyone would have considered realistic even a few years ago. The costs — beyond the enormous economic investment required — are the dangers of building this network haphazardly without fully considering a strategy for long-term needs. Technologists can identify the physical potential of their innovations with impressive accuracy. The political, social, and economic implications are much more elusive. This uncertainty has the effect of intimidating policy makers, both public and private. As an M.I.T. study put it several years ago: "Communications technology is flooding policymakers with options they do not understand, among which they must choose, and which will have profound effects on society." The statement underlines the importance of looking at the new technologies not simply in terms of their capabilities but also in the context of a viable social strategy for their use. This calls for some understanding of the modern evolution of the science of communications and information. In this chapter, we will look at the development of communications network technology; in the next chapter, the information machines that plug into these networks will be examined.

The so-called communications revolution is, in reality, a succession of three overlapping technological stages that have taken place during the past 150 years. The first of these was the *Wire Age* (1844–1900), the second was the *Wireless Age* (1900–1970), and the third is the one we are now entering — the *Integrated Grid Age,* in which wire and wireless technologies are brought together in powerful combinations. These linkings will form the structure of the future global information utility. The technological advances that occurred between the beginning of the Wire Age and the present are awesome.[4] The early Western Union telegraph machines that opened the Wire Age could relay about 40 words a minute. Western Union's first domestic communications satellite, the successor to the old telegraph line, was placed in orbit in 1975 with a capability of transmitting eight million words a *second*. Both machines — the telegraph transmitter and the satellite — nevertheless contributed to the cumulative impact of technology on how we communicate. It is useful to take a brief look at the three evolutionary stages that brought us to where we are today.

The Wire Age was largely the creation of a group of crusty, pragmatic American inventors, beginning with Samuel F. B. Morse and his single wire, which transmitted electrical impulses in code from Washington to Baltimore in 1844. The Morse telegraph was a major technical breakthrough, but it also involved two other innovations crucial in American communications development. The first was the federal government's decision to contribute research and development funds for the Morse invention. It involved modest sums, but set a significant precedent for the hundreds of millions of public research dollars now being invested annually in communications technology. The second innovative decision was that the telegraph system would be developed and controlled by private companies, not by the central government. This pattern distinguishes the American communications structure from that of almost every other nation, whose governments own or strictly control local communications systems. As a result, commercial revenues fueled the rapid expansion of the Morse telegraph system as well as the other major innovation of the Wire Age — the Bell telephone.

A century ago, it seemed inevitable that mass communications networking would be based on wire circuits. Nineteenth-century futurists, looking at the growth of telegraph and telephone systems, would have been safe in predicting that one day all mankind would be linked by wires. They would have forecast, correctly, that wire technology would be improved in ways that would eliminate such problems as fading, unreliable switching equipment, and high costs.

The wire networks were put to many imaginative uses in the late nineteenth century. The telephone was seen as a mass medium for the distribution of services we now associate with broadcasting — news, music, entertainment, and public affairs programming. Within a year after his first successful telephone experiments, Alexander Graham Bell transmitted musical programs by wire in Ontario. Stereophonic music transmitted over the telephone was demonstrated five years later at the 1881 Paris Electrical Exposition. The results encouraged a number of

European opera houses to install telephone outlets to transmit live performances to other locations.[5]

The most extensive experiment with mass-media telephone service took place in Budapest. Beginning in 1884, the local telephone system carried a daily program of news bulletins, town happenings, sermons, music, and theater performances through a network that eventually extended 168 miles. The system operated until the late 1920s. Similar experiments on a smaller scale were carried out in other European and American cities. Service was efficient and cheap: a Budapest phone subscriber paid the equivalent of two cents each time he used the news and entertainment network.

The telephone system was not, however, destined to become the all-purpose wired network envisioned by Bell and others. This potential was undercut by another politically and economically powerful technological development — wireless communications or the transmission of radiant energy in the form of invisible waves moving through the air. The possibility of transmitting without wires had increasingly intrigued inventors during the last half of the nineteenth century: the United States Patent Office registered a number of patents for "aerial conduction" of electric signals in the 1870s. But the significant breakthrough was made by Guglielmo Marconi, who began work on the problem as a precocious teenager in the early 1890s. He had the good luck to have a mother, a well-to-do Englishwoman, who took it upon herself to convince the British Post Office that they should pay attention to her son's experiments. Marconi proceeded to demonstrate his ideas in 1896 to a group of British officials, who were intrigued but skeptical. The group may have included some of the same officials who some years earlier had dismissed the idea of large-scale use of the telephone in Britain on the grounds that there were enough little boys available to deliver messages.

More astute Britons grasped the potential benefits of wireless communications, both for business and for political links with the nation's overseas empire. They encouraged Marconi to market his invention and to lease transmitters and receiving sets on ships as a monopoly. Other governments, including the United States, quickly recognized the political dangers of such monopolistic control of communications. They convened a conference of the International Telegraph Union in 1903 that approved regulations prohibiting any nation from claiming exclusive control over wireless communications. Meanwhile, Britain and other major European powers equipped their naval ships and military installations with the new technology.

Their experience in World War I convinced governments that the wireless should be harnessed to strategic national purposes. Its value had been greatly enhanced when voice capability was added to transmission previously limited to dot-and-dash Morse code signals. The result was radio broadcasting and radio telephony. European governments moved quickly to nationalize both techniques, as they had done earlier with telephone and other wired networks. No leader at the time was more perceptive about the potential of radio broadcasting than Lenin. He recognized that radio broadcasting — what he called the "newspaper without walls" — could be a powerful instrument of political and social control. He ordered rapid development of radio stations in the Soviet Union before he died in 1924.

The American response was somewhat different. Given the well-entrenched position of the commercial communications companies, there was no doubt that wireless communications would be part of the private sector. At one point, the federal government encouraged the setting up of a "chosen instrument" company, the Radio Corporation of America, to assure a strong United States presence in the field, particularly in manufacturing the new equipment. On the domestic broadcasting front, the American Telephone and Telegraph Company tried to add radio broadcasting to its near-monopoly in telephone services. The attempt failed, and radio networking was eventually divided among a number of companies.[6]

American radio broadcasting was not brought under effective regulatory control until the Communications Act of 1934, the legislation that still defines much of national policy for both wire and wireless services. The law confirmed that both services were to remain in private hands, with regulatory controls administered by a new agency, the Federal Communications Commission. The 1934 legislation legitimized what had become, through commercial pressures, a close relationship between wire and wireless technology. As in Europe, wire services were confined by law to individual point-to-point messages — telephone calls, telegrams, telexes and the like. Wireless was also used for point-to-point messages, but its greater significance was its capability for centrally directed radio — and, later, television — broadcasting.

Wireless broadcasting was to become, in the words of British communications scholar Anthony Smith:

> the supreme cultural instrument of the nation-state...a vast socializing instrument by which all the members of a society could be contacted simultaneously. With the wireless would automatically arrive the possibility of defining cultural policy as deliberately as economic policy; it created national markets for cultural production, national arbitrage for artistic reputation and a new constituency for politics.[7]

The early advocates of controls over wireless broadcasting were sufficiently aware that *wire* transmission could be competitive and therefore had to be restricted as a mass medium. Wire is the carrier of decentralized culture, unmediated by public authorities or commercial firms. Thus, it was a threat to the centralized content control that characterized over-the-air broadcasting. This was the motivation behind the controls foreign governments imposed on broadcasting, from the relatively light-handed approaches of the state-chartered British Broadcasting Corporation to the more direct controls imposed by other governments. The United States was an exception to this general pattern. The motivation for broadcasting regulation here was essentially economic and technical, although there has always been a political factor, implicit or explicit, in the process. In any event, the wire–wireless pattern that has shaped communications practices, and a good share of our culture, for the past half-century was set by these policies and reinforced by the enormous profitability of both broadcasting and other services.[8]

This pattern is changing. This decision to separate the functions of wire and wireless technology 50 years ago was based on perceptions of how the technology of that time could be used for political and economic ends. Similar perceptions obtain as we move into a new technological era. A watershed has been reached where the capabilities of wire and wireless are coming together to form a radically different communications pattern. Despite the efforts of vested economic interests to keep them separated on the old two-track system, the distinctions between wire and wireless are being eroded. This melding of capabilities forms the base of a new information environment — the Age of the Integrated Grid — in which messages can move in any form (voice, visual, or print) through an integrated, linked network of wire or wireless channels. Wire and wireless are becoming interchangeable parts of a unitary information utility, the nervous system of post-industrial America. The political, economic, and social impact of the new utility can be understood only in terms of the way wire and wireless technologies are converging after a century of separate development.

First, the wires. Early advances in wire technology generally involved wrapping more wires in bigger cables. There was a limit to this because of the sheer bulk of the cables. In the 1940s, Bell Laboratories developed the coaxial cable, a relatively thin configuration of sheathings and wires with greatly expanded circuit capacity. The new cable could provide a large number of circuits for narrow band use, such as in telephone, telex, and so on, or a smaller number of broadband circuits for such services as television and high speed data transmissions. Coaxial cable became an important part of the AT&T long-lines network for telephone, television, and other sevices in the 1950s. Later, such cables provided the technical base for the cable television industry.

The new cables also made possible high-capacity international communications, particularly in the North Atlantic region where telephone traffic was heavy. Although there had been oceanic cables for almost a century, they were restricted to simple telegraph message services. Coaxial cable technology expanded this capacity to telephone and other services that had been limited previously to unreliable wireless circuits. The first transatlantic coaxial cable began operations in 1956, with a capacity of 36 telephone circuits.[9] Since that time, eight more cables have been strung across the Atlantic, each more technically advanced than its predecessor. The latest cables have capacities equivalent to 40,000 phone circuits. Defining cable capacity in terms of phone calls makes the subject somewhat more comprehensible to laymen. However, these new cables can handle any form of high-speed electronic communication — voice, visual, or print — in any combination simultaneously.

This capability is shared and immensely magnified by the newest type of cable technology — fiber optics. In fiber optics communication, information is transmitted in optical form (that is, in light waves) along glass fiber whose thickness is comparable to that of a human hair. The fibers have many useful attributes, the most striking of which is their information-carrying potential. Theoretically, for a given diameter of cable, optical transmission on a single wavelength can carry 30 times more traffic than a coaxial cable.

The idea of using light waves for communications had been understood for a long time. Alexander Graham Bell experimented with what he called a "photophone," a device for sending messages by sunlight reflected from mirrors. It did not work well: sunbeams are scattered by air and rain, and, in any event, the sun does not always shine. Two research breakthroughs were required before optical communications would be practical. The first was the development of a light source that could provide the concentrated, narrow band of frequencies useful for communications applications. That came in the late 1950s with the first demonstrations of the laser, a device that gives off a concentrated beam of light at a single frequency. The second major breakthrough was the development of a suitable optical transmission medium — the channel down which the laser beam travels. As Alexander Graham Bell found out, transmission of light beams through the atmosphere is severely limited. However, wires, or "lightguides," made of pure glass can trap light waves and carry them for miles with little loss in signal intensity. The technical problems of developing a glass fiber with few impurities to impede the beam have been reduced in the past decade by scientists at ITT, Corning Glass, Bell Labs, and other research groups. Today's fibers are so transparent that light loses more intensity passing through an ordinary windowpane than it does in thousands of feet of glass fiber. If seawater were as transparent, one could easily see to the bottom of the deepest ocean.[10]

The information-carrying capacities fiber of optic wires are awesome. A pair of copper wires is needed for a single telephone call, but a pair of hair-thin optical fibers can carry nearly 2,000 calls simultaneously. Another advantage of the fibers is their potential low cost. The basic material out of which they are made is silicon, which is universally available and cheap. Only five cubic centimeters of silicon is needed to make a fiber a kilometer long. The costs are in the refining of impurities out of the silicon. As this technology has improved and as volume production of the fibers has increased, the price of optical fibers has dropped dramatically.

Meanwhile, the fibers have many other advantages. They can be installed in tight spaces — a major factor in the new microelectronic devices. They also have high reliability. An optical fiber by itself is a fragile thing, but considerable research has gone into coatings to improve the fiber's durability. Plastic jackets, developed by Du Pont and other firms, allow the fibers to be twisted, turned, and tied in knots. The fibers are unaffected by water, varying temperatures, or corrosion. Their light source, the lasers, may be no larger than a grain of salt and may emit light continuously for a hundred years.

Fiber optic applications have been limited until recently by the short distances a signal can be efficiently transmitted. In the first practical uses, this distance was limited to a few feet inside the human body. Since the late fifties, fiber optic medical probes, known as endoscopes, have been used like tiny flashlights to examine parts of the body previously accessible only through exploratory surgery. The next step was to use optical wires as substitutes for copper wires in electronic equipment such as computers and telephone switching installations. Now, as their long distance capabilities are improved, fibers are being used more extensively as high-capacity communications circuits.

In 1983, AT&T completed a long-distance fiber optics line between Washington and Boston as the first leg of what will eventually be its national fiber network. A few years later, seven regional telecommunications firms formed a fiber-optic consortium to develop National Communications Network, which competes with AT&T, MCI, and GTE Sprint in the lucrative long-distance market. By 1988, over 20,000 miles of optical cables had been installed across the country by AT&T and others.[11] Similar fiber optic expansion is taking place abroad: British Telecom, the major telecommunications company in the United Kingdom, plans to have over half of its long-distance lines converted to fiber optics in the early nineties. In Japan, Nippon Telephone & Telegraph (NTT) has completed a high-capacity fiber network throughout the country.

A new era in international cable operations opened in 1988 with the inauguration of the first trans-Atlantic fiber optic cable, known as TAT-8. With its 40,000-circuit capacity, TAT-8 more than double the capabilities of the seven previous North Atlantic coaxial cables. As with earlier oceanic cables, AT&T was a partner with European telecommunications agencies (usually government-controlled) in the project. TAT-8 cost $335 million to build, and runs 4,500 miles from New Jersey to Widemouth in England and Penmarch in France. It will be an important resource in meeting the expected increase in transatlantic telephone and other requirements from 19,500 circuits in the mid-eighties to 98,000 circuits in 1995.[12]

AT&T is also a partner in a similar Pacific Ocean fiber cable linking California with Hawaii, Guam, Japan, and the Philippines. In both the Atlantic and Pacific, AT&T and its traditional overseas cable partners face competition for the first time in the form of cable systems financed as entrepreneurial ventures by other firms.[13]

Technology is pushing these prospects at a faster pace than even the most enthusiastic fiber boosters had imagined a few years ago. Achieving greater purity in the optical fibers is a major thrust of current research. The Japanese have taken the lead in techniques for removing such impurities as hydrogen and oxygen atoms, which impede the passage of light down an optical cable.[14] Other research efforts focus on the replacement of the current generation of electronic switching components at either end of fiber optic circuits with thin-filmed optical equivalents of these switches. For the present, electronic switches are incapable of handling the full capacities of most fiber optic cables. The new optical switches could be combined on a single microelectronic chip to form a completely integrated optical circuit with vastly higher capacity.[15]

These circuits will be connected to computers that use laser beams to make an optical switch flip on and off at the rate of one trillionth of a second. Such a computer would calculate a thousand times faster than the fastest electronic machines now in service. Researchers in America and Europe have also been experimenting with optical devices analagous to a transistor. Potentially, the device could switch from one transmission state to another in about a picosecond, or a thousandth of a billionth of a second.[16]

Despite optical technology capabilities, present and potential, it would be unwise to predict the displacement of metallic cables by fiber optics. As noted above, a number of technological restraints remain. Although production costs of optical cables have dropped dramatically in recent years, the shift to fiber networks is still an expensive process. One deterrent is the economic loss involved in writing off billions of dollars now invested in metal cables. In the late eighties, AT&T still had 800 *million* miles of installed copper wires in its inventory. Nevertheless, fiber optics technology has a bright future. Arthur C. Clarke, the science writer, confidently predicts that prospecting for cast-off copper wires will be a latter-day version of the old-time gold rush. The rewards could be significant. In 1986, the New York Telephone Co. began a 10-year project to replace copper cable under New York City streets with fiber optics; the company estimated that 33,000 tons of cable worth $11 million would eventually be removed.[17]

Another major technological change is taking place in the machines that switch messages through the telephone network and other communications grids. Until recently, these switches transferred messages through mechanical relays in a step-by-step process. There have been steady improvements in this method over the years, primarily through the introduction of semi-electronic devices. Nevertheless, mechanical switching is a relatively slow and cumbersome process.

Switching methods are now being revolutionized by the first completely new technology since telephone networks were introduced almost a century ago. The technology is the *digital switch,* which replaces mechanical and semi-electronic connections with computers. Instead of noisy racks of switching gears, silent microchips convert messages from telephones and other devices into digits, the binary codes that computers can understand and manipulate. The efficiencies that result are such that a race is on to digitalize the world's communications networks. The new digital machines account for a large part of the estimated 1989 global expenditure of $89 billion on telecommunications equipment, nearly twice the amount of only five years before.

Despite the high cost of replacing older systems with the new machines, digitalization will become the world network standard in the coming years. Digital exchanges require less space, are more easily maintained, and provide more message capacity and clearer lines. They make possible additional capabilities such as automatic transfer of calls, paging, electronic mail, and other facilities that the telephone companies call "value-added services."[18]

By bringing the power of the computer to communications traffic, digital switching will hasten the day when all the world's networks are connected in ways that allow transmittal of any kind of electronic message — voice, video, or data. This is not possible now because of the proliferation of incompatible standards between networks. The computerization of the switches (and the equipment they serve) permits a vast array of functions and services on a single "digital highway." This requires global agreement on standards to eliminate current technical barriers between networks.

This standard setting is taking place in international negotiations to develop an *Integrated Services Digital Network* (ISDN), designed to integrate voice, data, and other services on the same circuit. The focus of the negotiations is an obscure technical committee at the Geneva headquarters of the International Telecommunications Union (ITU), the United Nations agency that coordinates communications standards. The group's technical experts have been working on ISDN standard setting for a decade, and may need another 10 years to finish their work. Meanwhile, initial installation of ISDN-compatible equipment has begun in the United States, Europe and Japan.[19]

These services will be in big demand initially by large business organizations. Lacking the kind of integrated facilities ISDN will make possible, these firms use separate networks for telephony, data, facsimile transfers, and the like. ISDN promises to provide them with a single "information pipe," serving multiple functions. In its initial stages, ISDN's benefits will be limited primarily to large institutions that need the kinds of expanded capacities the new standard will provide. Eventually, however, ISDN capabilities will reach down to homes, supplying a wide array of "electronic cottage" information services.

The rapid advances in cable technology, noted above, will benefit from the new capabilities made possible by ISDN standards. Equally affected will be improvements in *wireless* technology. This effort has focused on more effective use of the radio spectrum, the invisible physical resource that makes possible the vast network of wireless circuits. The spectrum is a figurative thing: it does not exist until it is used. Until recently, it has been regarded as an esoteric subject for engineers only. The radio spectrum, is, however, no longer an avoidable technical concern. Its efficient use is now a significant element in defining networking prospects in the information age. These prospects will be influenced as much by political, economic, and social factors as by the work of technologists. These nontechnical considerations were relatively benign only a short time ago. The spectrum was little used, and it was treated as a kind of electrical Wild West frontier with few restrictions.

Today the spectrum, like many other natural resources, is in danger of becoming degraded through overexploitation. This is so despite the fact that the spectrum is not a depletable resource. It is finite, but it is always there. The problem is to use it efficiently. At one level, users themselves create interference through their own electronic activities. Noise pollution — the familiar phenomenon of static — is a by-product of the greater general use of electrical power. (Much of this interference comes from automobile ignition systems.) The problem is compounded as more powerful transmitters are designed to punch through the noise, resulting in more noise, particularly if the transmitters are not perfectly adjusted. Most of the other difficulties with the spectrum have to do with the steadily rising number of users and types of uses, all trying to crowd into a finite physical resource. Two decades ago, probably 90 percent of spectrum use took place in a relatively narrow band across the Northern Hemisphere, from Tokyo east to Berlin. The heaviest users are still found within this band, but they must now consider the needs of a hundred or more developing countries, all of whom are expanding their use of the spectrum.

The spectrum is, therefore, a major political and economic concern, not only domestically but internationally. Since the early part of this century, it has been subject to treaty restrictions, under the supervision of the International Telecommunications Union (ITU), which is now a United Nations specialized agency. The ITU was, until a short time ago, an old boy's club composed of the Western industrial powers, the Soviet Union, and Japan. These powers gathered periodically to decide how they would allocate and manage the spectrum for their own uses. This arrangement is now finished; the rest of the world has joined the club.[20]

Under the ITU's one-vote-per-country rules, the newcomers from the Third World have considerable influence on the future patterns of spectrum use. Particular attention has been focused on their needs and demands in a series of international conferences convened for the purpose of reviewing and revising world spectrum regulations to meet changing needs. The largest of these meetings, the 1979 World Administrative Radio Conference, approved major shifts in spectrum use that will affect all communications users throughout the rest of the century. Smaller follow-up conferences have taken place since then to discuss specific spectrum problems not resolved at the 1979 meeting. In the process it is becoming clear that the radio spectrum is no longer the exclusive province of the technical experts. Given its role as the most important natural resource of the information age, it now attracts the attention of a wide range of political, economic, and social interests.[21]

It is useful, therefore, to take a closer look at the spectrum, noting some of the policy questions involved in each of its major segments. These questions will be cropping up again as we examine the political and economic issues of the information age in later chapters.

The raw material of the radio spectrum is *electromagnetic radiation* — radiant energy in the form of invisible waves moving through space and matter. This phenomenon was identified in theory in 1864 by James Clerk Maxwell, director of the Cavendish Laboratories at Cambridge

University. His theories were confirmed in 1888 when a German physicist, Heinrich Hertz, produced the first man-made electromagnetic radiation by sending a strong electric charge across a spark gap and thereby causing a smaller spark — evidence of the presence of an electric field — to jump across a second gap some distance away. The history of wireless communication has been a progressive enhancement of our ability to devise equipment for generating and receiving electromagnetic radiation in the radio frequency range and to use such waves for telecommunications.

The usable part of the spectrum extends from 10 kilohertz (KHz) — roughly the lower limit of human hearing — to 275 gigahertz (GHz), a frequency that begins to approach that of light waves. A *hertz*, our permanent tribute to the redoubtable Heinrich, indicates the number of radiated "waves" that pass a given point in a second. One GHz is a thousand million cycles per second. The companion measurement is the *length* of each wave; the wavelengths for the usable spectrum run from 3,000 meters — almost two miles — down to one millimeter. The spectrum is divided into eight bands, ranging from very low frequency (VLF) to extra high frequency (EHF). Each band covers a "decade" of frequencies or wavelengths. Thus the high frequency band goes from three megahertz (MHz) to 30 MHz, or 100 meters down to 10 meters.

Spectrum use has been tied to the development of increasingly sophisticated transmitters and receivers designed to exploit this resource. The progression has generally moved from the low frequencies to the higher ones, with one interesting exception. The United States Navy is developing uses for the very bottom (and currently unusable) end of the spectrum — below 10 KHz, which is so low it is not included in the ITU's spectrum responsibilities. The Navy is interested in the ability of these frequencies to penetrate many fathoms of ocean water and to remain relatively unaffected by upper atmosphere nuclear bursts that can blank out higher frequency communications. These attributes have important implications for communications with nuclear-missile-bearing submarines whose effectiveness depends largely on their ability to avoid detection while submerged. Very low frequency communications with the subs cannot be monitored by a potential enemy. The Navy's plan to install such a system has, however, raised difficult political problems. The system's "transmitter" involves thousands of miles of wires crisscrossing hundreds of square miles of earth. The transmitter site has to have specific geologic characteristics which, in this country, are found in the northern reaches of Minnesota and Michigan. For years, citizen groups blocked the transmitter, despite a public relations campaign by the Navy stressing the national security benefits of what was dubbed, perhaps too coyly, Project Sanguine. After considerable negotiation and compromises, the plan was approved, with completion of the full system scheduled by the early nineties.

Just above the low frequencies are the *medium frequencies*, best known for their use in radio broadcasting. The medium wave band has many uses beyond broadcasting, such as long-range navigation devices for ships and aircraft. This part of the spectrum now serves a hodgepodge of uses. It could be better utilized for purposes other than radio broadcasting if there were not such a heavy world investment in radio transmitters and consumer receivers adapted for these frequencies.

The next step up the spectrum is the *high frequency* band (HF). This band has been described as the jewel of the spectrum because of its special capabilities, but it is beginning to look a bit antique. Unlike medium wave, whose transmitting capabilities are very limited geographically, high frequency can have a global reach. When used for this purpose, its frequencies are refracted downwards by charged layers in the ionosphere in a hopscotch pattern, bouncing between earth and sky around the world. Exploiting this capability is a neat trick, but it does not always work. HF's effectiveness varies from hour to hour, day to day, year to year. It is also affected by geography and the sunspot cycle. The whole band can be crammed down to a very narrow usable section during high points in the 11-year sunspot cycle.

Despite these limitations, HF channels are in high demand. Before the advent of satellites and large submarine cables, they were used for international telephone service. They are still useful for radio "hams," aircraft, and maritime communications, and radar tracking. Another well-known application is shortwave broadcasting. The United States, with its Voice of America network, is only one of over 70 nations operating in this highly competitive field. The Voice of America's transmitters have a total of over 20 million watts of power — the equivalent of 400 large domestic stations. Despite this, the United States lags behind the Soviet Union, the People's Republic of China, and other countries in total transmitting hours per day.

Some of the pressure in the HF band comes from a flamboyant upstart in spectrum use — Citizen's Band (CB) radio. CB is electronic populism with its own peculiar customs, language, and folklore. In 1973, there were less than a million CB receivers in operation in this country. A conservative estimate of current operating sets would be over 30 million. CB's 40 channels are grouped in a betwixt-and-between area of the HF spectrum — a point at which receivers can be extremely cheap but where the incidence of interference is high. CB receivers interfere with television and with police radio; CBs get interference from industrial machines, medical equipment, and even washing machines. Interference is increased by certain weather conditions as well as by the practice of many CB users of installing illegal amplifiers to get greater transmitting range. This electronic free-for-all makes the job of policing this part of the spectrum very difficult; the Federal Communications Commission has long since given up any serious monitoring of CB use. The FCC's reluctance is influenced in part by the fact that CB owners represent a very large voter block who have come to regard the maintenance and expansion of their spectrum space as a natural right.

The next steps up the spectrum are the *very high frequency* (VHF) and *ultra high frequency* (UHF) bands, best known as the locations of FM radio and television channels. These bands are also the spectrum home for many so-called mobile services — police, taxi, military, and public service radio, as well as automobile telephones. Over 1.5 million two-way mobile stations are authorized by the FCC, not counting CB installations. With expanded frequencies allocated by the 1979 World Administrative Radio Conference, mobile radio will be a major area of communications expansion in the coming years. The most dramatic expansion is taking place in a new kind of mobile telephone service known as cellular radio. Using sophisticated computerized switching techniques, the service picks up portable telephone calls within small geographical "cells" and transfers them to other portable phones or to any other phone in the world. The service is generally available in all major United States metropolitan areas and in many smaller towns. Other types of mobile services are being developed. In 1977, NASA demonstrated a mobile radio transmitting and receiving device that fit into a small briefcase. The equipment, powered by batteries, sent and received signals from a remote area of Georgia to a Baltimore hospital via a NASA satellite in an experiment designed to test its use for emergency situations.[22] In 1983, NASA announced plans for a joint United States-Canadian mobile satellite for more advanced experiments.

As a result of this and other experiments, a national satellite system capable of providing mobile voice communications to automobiles, trucks, ships, and planes will be operational in the early nineties. An international mobile satellite service known as Inmarsat has been operational since the late seventies. A consortium owned by 47 countries, Inmarsat has offered communications services primarily to ships on the high seas. In the late eighties, the consortium expanded its satellite facilities internationally to include aircraft.

A related service, now being implemented in the United States and abroad, goes by the formidable name of radiodetermination satellite service (RDSS). Simply put, RDSS is a satellite-based network that lets you know where you are. It is useful if you are an airplane pilot, a truck driver on an unfamiliar stretch of highway, or a hiker lost in the woods. RDSS technology was born out of tragedy. In 1978, a mid-air collision between a Pacific Southwest Boeing 727 and a private plane in clear skies over San Francisco resulted in the loss of 147 lives. The accident prompted Gerald K. O'Neill, a Princeton University physicist and a pilot, to plan a satellite-based system for accurately determining the position of a moving object on earth. His initial aim was to provide airplane pilots and ground controllers with precise positioning navigational information and collision warning. It was clear, however, that the system would also work with trucks, cars, ships, and people.

The system uses two satellites to get a fix on a map point in response to an electronic signal from that location. The signal, sent from a small transmitter, is beamed to both satellites and passed back to earth to a central processing computer. Because the two satellites are at different points in space, the signals arrive at the processing center at slightly different times. Using a digital terrain map, the difference is enough to pinpoint the location by triangulation. The information is then sent back by satellite to the requester. The entire process can usually be completed in a second or two.[23]

At the top end of the usable spectrum are the *super high frequency* (SHF) and the *extremely high frequency* (EHF) bands. Here is where the microwaves operate, and where the most controversial advances in spectrum use have taken place. The microwave frequencies lay below the infrared region of the spectrum, with wavelength ranges from about a hundred centimeters, or 40 inches, down to a millimeter or 1/125th of an inch. (By contrast, the wavelength distance at the low-frequency end of the spectrum is almost two miles.)

The microwaves are the heavy-duty workhorses of the spectrum. They were harnessed in the 1930s when equipment was developed that could generate higher and higher frequency radio waves with proportionately greater message capacities. Microwave technology was a crucial factor in World War II, when it served as the basis for radar. Microwaves can be focused in directional beams and reflected back by such objects as airplanes. The first radar installations were limited and unreliable. As the military pressed for better definition and accuracy, technologists pushed further up the spectrum, developing equipment that allowed precision targeting by the end of the war.

The microwave revolution got underway in earnest in the late forties. A microwave system, using relay towers, was opened between Boston and New York in 1947; by 1951, a coast-to-coast network was in operation, using 107 towers. (Since microwave transmission is line-of-sight, the towers are placed on elevated points when possible.) Over a quarter of a million microwave relay towers have been built since then in this country for telephone, television, computer data, and other transmissions at increasingly high capacities. Microwaves also have non-communications uses, such as in surgical operations, in household and industrial ovens, and in agricultural experiments to kill weeds and insects. The "death ray" weapon, favorite of Sunday-supplement editors, remains mercifully elusive, although the military is experimenting with various uses of microwaves in the increasingly sophisticated field of electronic warfare.

If the death ray remains a theory, a more immediate threat from electromagnetic radiation is just beginning to be debated publicly. This involves the concern that microwave circuitry may be responsible for new forms of environmental pollution, a kind of electronic smog that can affect human and animal well-being. In December 1971, a White House task force summed up the possible threat in these words:

> The electro-magnetic radiations emanating from radar, television, communications systems, microwave ovens, industrial heat-treatment systems, medical diathermy units and many other sources permeate the modern environment, both civilian and military. . . . This type of man-made radiation exposure has no counterpart in man's evolutionary background. . . unless adequate monitoring and control based on a fundamental understanding of biological effects are instituted in the near future, in the decades ahead, man may enter an era of energy pollution comparable to the chemical pollution of today.[24]

Given political and economic stakes in microwave transmission, the general reaction to this and other warnings, until recently, has been to ignore or play down the problem. However, a number of events have directed greater public attention to the potential hazards of radiation pollution. The most publicized of these incidents occurred in the mid-seventies at the American Embassy in Moscow, where health problems among personnel were attributed to the Soviet practice of aiming electromagnetic beams at the building. Whether or not this was true, the incident focused attention on an aspect of our post-industrial communications structure that needs more careful monitoring.[25]

In the meantime, microwaves are the aerial pathways of a major space age development — the communications satellite. The satellites are basically microwave switching stations, the space equivalent of a ground relay tower. The difference is that a satellite gives the microwave path a line-of-sight capability that stretches across one-third of the earth. Floating 22,300 miles above the equator, the satellites effectively break the boundaries of the earth's horizon. At that height, they travel at the same speed as the earth's rotation and, therefore, appear to be stationary; they are, in the engineer's phrase, "geostationary." Since the mid-sixties, the satellites have provided high quality communications circuits to nations in Asia, Africa, and Latin America that would otherwise not have had them for many more years. By 1988, over 115 countries accounting for over 96 percent of all international traffic, belonged to Intelsat, the world satellite organization that runs the basic network.[26]

In less than 30 years, communications satellites have gone through seven technological generations. The first "birds" were weakly powered machines, capable of providing only limited services. Later generations, relying on microelectronic technology, have had progressively more sophisticated circuit capacity and transmitting power. The seventh generation Intelsat satellite can transmit a combinatioin of 120,000 telephone calls and three television channels simultaneously. (By contrast, the first Intelsat generation had a capacity of 250 telephone circuits or one television channel.) Moreover, the newer satellites have a greater capacity for handling digital data, permitting use of such techniques as data packet transmissions.

The greater capabilities of the newer satellites permits the expansion of services beyond such point-to-point transmissions as telephone calls. They open the way for radio or television broadcasting from space to small earth terminals. Direct broadcasting satellites (DBS) were first tested in the mid-seventies. A NASA experimental satellite, *ATS–6*, beamed educational and other public service broadcasts to remote earth terminals in Appalachia, the Rocky Mountains, and Alaska. *ATS–6* was shifted in 1975 halfway around the world to provide educational transmissions to over 2,000 remote villages in India.

DBS technology has advanced rapidly in recent years; a number of space broadcast services are operational in Europe and Japan. American adaptation of the service has been slower. In 1983, the Federal Communications Commission authorized eight firms to proceed with the construction of domestic DBS networks, designed primarily to provide a range of entertainment, news, and other services to homes. None of these projects were implemented at the time, primarily because of doubts about the marketability of the new service in the face of competition from cable systems, network television, home videocassette recorders, and the increasing number of "backyard dishes," the small earth terminals used in rural America to pick up entertainment programs being relayed to cable systems. In the late eighties, however, there was renewed interest in DBS projects by American firms for entertainment and other services.

Meanwhile, DBS has stirred lively controversy in the United Nations, where developing countries have pressed for limitations on broadcasting into their territories without their prior consent. Such broadcasting, they argued, would be "cultural imperialism" by American and other Western broadcasters.[27] In an ironic twist, these arguments have been undercut by the rush to install small earth terminals in

Third World countries, designed specifically to pick up entertainment-program signals from satellites. Such "dishes" are a common sight throughout Central America and the Carribean, with one Mexican city reportedly having 15,000 terminals pointed toward U. S. satellites.

Because they involve a familiar service — television — broadcast satellites are well publicized. However, the range of satellite uses, present and potential, is considerably wider. Two dozen countries now use satellites for domestic as well as international communications. A special satellite network, *Inmarsat*, provides communications services for ships at sea. Eventually, a similar network will link aircraft to ground traffic control stations. Military satellites are an integral part of the global communications networks of the Soviet and the United States defense systems. There is also an increasing number of so-called sensing satellites that monitor weather and earth resources, returning data to worldwide networks of earth terminals.

In the nineties, two technological developments will shape the role of communications satellites. The first involves a major change in satellite technology itself. The second, and related, change deals with the evolution toward smaller and smaller earth terminals — the pie-shaped "dishes" that transmit and receive satellite signals.

The mid-nineties will see a new generation of communications satellites with awesome technical capabilities. Until now, most such satellites have supplied an important but limited service — passively retransmitting a signal beamed from one earth terminal to another earth terminal. There have been steady improvements in the efficiency of this service since the first satellites of the early sixties, but not in the basic operating pattern. A technological breakthrough in this pattern is now becoming a reality with NASA's experimental Advanced Communications Technology Satellite (ACTS) project. The first ACTS experiment is to be tested in space in the early nineties with follow-on operational satellites later in the decade.

ACTS is a package of technologies designed to optimize message transmissions between earth stations. The package includes a *high-speed digital switchboard*, an outer-space version of a telephone company local exchange office, with capabilities well beyond those of present satellite switching equipment. Secondly, ACTS will have *multi-beam antennas*, which conserve the radio-frequency spectrum and expand communications capacity. This is done by automatically focusing the antenna beams only between those points on earth where messages are being received or transmitted, all within a fraction of a second. Finally, ACTS is being equipped with *laser-beam circuits* that will permit transmissions between satellites in space. This technique will eliminate the double-hop satellite transmissions that are now required when a message's destination is beyond one satellite's "footprint," the geographic area that its beam covers.

The other technology that is changing satellite communications is the small earth terminal. The weakly-powered satellites of the sixties and seventies required massive dishes, up to a hundred feet in diameter. With more powerful satellites, the terminals have become steadily smaller. Big terminals will continue to be useful for specialized tasks, but the future of satellite communications lies with the smaller dishes.

A familiar application of small terminals are the so-called "backyard dishes" that dot the American landscape, primarily to receive entertainment programs from satellites. By 1989, there were over 1.7 million of these terminals in American backyards. There will be more of them as more networks for direct satellite broadcasting to homes are developed. Moreover, in the coming years, the ungainly round dishes will be replaced by small flat-plate terminals that can be attached unobtrusively to houses or other structures.

Round or flat, the backyard dishes have their role to play in American communications. The wider significance of the new small dishes, however, lies in the commercial area. Here they are being used to provide a new kind of communications networking for business firms, government agencies, and other institutions. Technically, they are called VSATs, for *very small aperture terminals*. VSAT dishes by the tens of thousands are being used to form networks that bypass the telephone companies and other circuit providers. Cost is a critical factor in this development: VSAT equipment is becoming steadily cheaper as its usage increases. Another benefit is that the little dishes can be placed almost anywhere, including remote locations where other network facilities are unavailable.

A VSAT network has three parts: the central ground control station or hub, a satellite, and the small terminals. The hub transmits signals to the satellite, which relays them to the terminals. Throughout the eighties, most of these terminals functioned as receive-only facilities, i.e., one-way transmissions from hub to dish. Despite this limitation, over 40,000 VSAT terminals were installed throughout the United States. Increasingly, VSAT terminals are being installed with two-way capabilities, making them parts of a fully interactive network.

Corporations have been the largest sponsors of VSAT networks. One of the major VSAT users is the K-Mart department store chain, with a network that will eventually link all of its 2,000 stores. Another group of institutions that promise to be major users are colleges and universities. A 1987 survey of 2,000 colleges and universities by the American Association of Community and Junior Colleges found that two-thirds of the schools had access to satellite downlink systems, many of them involving small dishes. Market surveys indicate an expansion of the American VSAT market to over 200,000 units in the early nineties.

With so many satellites floating in a narrow corridor above the equator, a unique kind of traffic jam has been created. The choicest frequencies and orbital slots — where the satellites are "parked" — are filling up fast. Given a NASA estimate that there will be a massive increase in international demand for satellite circuits by the end of the century, the problem of crowded frequencies and orbital slots may soon be critical. At present, the congestion is concentrated in the high traffic areas over the Western Hemisphere and the North Atlantic region. The satellites are many miles apart in the immensity of space; adding a few more might seem to be as simple as introducing a few more cars on a lonely stretch of highway. However, unless satellites using the same frequency band are kept several degrees apart (about 250 miles), ground stations cannot discriminate between their separate signals.[28]

This has become an international issue in recent years as developing countries insist that the industrialized countries' current near-monopoly of satellite frequencies and orbital slots be ended in favor of a system assuring access to these resources for Third World countries. The issue came to a head in an ITU conference in 1988 to develop arrangements for more equitable distribution of space communications frequencies and orbital slots.

The solution lies in the efficient use of more complex satellites. The current thrust of satellite research and development is in this direction. Whether technological advances can keep ahead of the quickly rising global demands for more circuits is an open question. So far, this has been done by providing more transmitting power in the satellites themselves and by developing techniques for more sophisticated use of frequencies. By the mid-seventies, RCA had commercially demonstrated its *Satcom* satellite's ability to send two signals on the same frequency, thereby doubling circuit capacity. The eighties saw a new generation of hybrid satellites, capable of several different tasks. Among these is Western Union's *TDRSS* (Tracking and Data Relay Satellite System), which operates standard commercial services and also relays data to earth from other satellites operating at lower orbits as well as from NASA's space shuttle. Earth terminals can "see" the shuttle and these low-flying satellites only for a short time before they disappear over the horizon. *TDRSS* can literally look down on them from its position further out in space and track them more than 80 percent of the time. In the nineties, operational versions of NASA's Advanced Communications Technology Satellite (ACTS), described above, will add new capabilities to satellite services.

ACTS and other advanced satellite projects are designed around digital circuitry, capable of moving information in voice, video, or data form at much greater speeds. This is important for handling the increasing volume of transmissions between high speed computers. It takes several hours to transmit a reel of computer tape at the rate now generally available — 9,600 bits per second. At digital transmission speeds of up to 1.5 megabits per second, tansmittal time is reduced to three minutes.

Efficient use of orbital slots is complicated by the fact that most present satellites that preempt a slot have a limited purpose. The newer multipurpose satellites — the so-called hybrids — will ease this limitation somewhat, as each will be capable of doing the work of several of the older satellites. Other techniques for easing orbital and frequency congestions are being studied. One of these involves building large space platforms to orbit above the equator. Many satellites could be hung like Christmas tree ornaments from these structures, which might measure several acres in size. Moreover, the platforms would also support large solar cell arrays to supply power to all the equipment on the platform. The platforms would be assembled in space by work crews using parts delivered by the space shuttle and other transporters. Periodic maintenance checks of the platform and the satellites would be made by space-suited repairmen. The net effect would be to group a half-dozen or more satellites, each using different frequencies, in an orbital slot normally taken up by a single satellite. A prototype platform is being designed under a NASA research program for possible operational use by the mid-nineties.

A less dramatic but possibly more practical approach has been advanced by engineer Paul Visher of Hughes Aircraft. He proposes clusters of separate satellites in an orbital slot, each transmitting its signals through a nearby master satellite. (Satellite-to-satellite communications is quite feasible, thanks to recent research breakthroughs.) A wide range of signals for various purposes could be transmitted, utilizing only one orbital slot. The value of Visher's concept is that it can be realized with currently available satellite technology. Space platform research is still in the theoretical stages; moreover, the platforms will be very expensive pieces of hardware when and if the technology proves feasible.

Other intensive research in the expansion of satellite capabilities focuses on the radio spectrum itself. Here the effort is on techniques for making more microwave frequencies available. Theoretically, there is plenty of room in the spectrum for this since, despite the research breakthroughs of recent years, less than 10 percent of the spectrum is being utilized for communications and other purposes. To illustrate this point, let us assume that the total radio spectrum up to 300 GHz represents an area the size of the United States. On this scale, one MHz — roughly the medium wave frequencies — would represent a 60-foot strip of Atlantic beach. Thirty GHz — the outer limit of most present applications — would take us 300 miles inland. Everything beyond would be largely *terra incognita*, or what the spectrum engineers call EHF for extra high frequencies. The halt at 30 GHz is equivalent to westward migration across the United States that has stopped at the Appalachians.[29]

Any further "migration" in the spectrum is liable to be slow for technical reasons. The 1979 WARC conference allocated specific frequency uses up to 275 GHz. These allocations in the EHF bands are intended largely for specialized purposes such as radio astronomy. One such proposed use is for a radio telescope to be placed on the dark side of the moon, shielded from earthly radio interference. Another involves sending signals to civilizations beyond our solar system — a favorite project of astronomer Carl Sagan, and other enthusiasts of what is known as SETI, the search for extra-terrestrial intelligence.

Meanwhile the technological push is on to open higher reaches of the spectrum for more mundane needs such as television broadcasts and telephone calls. The most intensive research is in the 20 to 30 GHz bands — just above the present limits of most microwave transmissions. The potential rewards of breakthroughs in this area will be vast numbers of new higher capacity microwave channels for satellites and for terrestrial use. The difficulties are formidable; not the least of them are the adverse effects of heavy rainstorms and other weather conditions on transmissions in these higher bands. The very short microwaves at these frequencies can be wiped out by rain or snow drops. One way to overcome this is to establish satellite earth stations in pairs, sufficiently separated and positioned so that such interference will not occur at both stations simultaneously. NASA has a long-term research and development program to open up the 20–30 GHz bands for communications and other purposes.[30] If the tests are successful, overcrowding in the lower parts of the microwave frequency spectrum could be eased considerably. The Europeans, Japanese, and Soviets are also working on the problem, and all of them are as aware as the United States of the economic and political rewards of opening these bands to practical uses.

It is clear that communications satellite usage will continue to expand during the coming decade. This expansion will be tempered by increased competition from fiber optic cable networks, both domestically and internationally. As noted above, optical cables have vastly greater circuit capabilities than their technological predecessors, the coaxial cables. In regions where there are high-traffic communications needs (e.g., the Boston-New York-Washington corridor), fiber optic networks will dominate. Internationally, there will be intense competition between satellite and fiber optic networks for the lucrative traffic between

Europe and the United States in the North Atlantic region. By the early nineties there will be two, and possibly three, transatlantic fiber cables competing with satellites.

The result, at least temporarily, will be a circuit glut. In the price competition that will take place between satellite and cable firms, the satellites will lose some of their present market share. They should not be counted out, however, for two reasons. The first is the improved ability of efficient new satellites to compete directly with fiber optic networks. The second is the fact that satellites can provide direct links between any two points, an advantage that fiber optic lines will not be able to match for a very long time.

In summary, the past 20 years have seen enormous parallel expansion in the range and capacities of both wire and wireless technology. Each mode has its distinctive capabilities. What they share is a greatly enhanced ability to handle most communication tasks interchangeably, carrying voice, visual, or data messages. Sophisticated integrated switching equipment no longer distinguishes between the type of circuitry it serves. Both wire and wireless circuitry will make up the new universal grid, providing a wide variety of high capacity channels.

Wireless communications — and microwave circuits in particular — were the fastest growth area in telecommunications during the past three decades. However, there will be greater competition in the coming years from sophisticated wire technologies. The present work horse of high capacity wire technology is the coaxial cable, the familiar phone-company cable that runs under city streets. However, the future lies with fiber optic cables and with millimeter waveguides that can send 15 billion bits of information a second down a metal pipe — strange kinds of wires indeed. These developments represent a long technological leap from Samuel F. B. Morse's experiment in transmitting a few coded words a minute over a flimsy telegraph line 150 years ago. The Wire Age started by Morse, now technologically compatible with the Wireless Age, has come full circle in the Age of the Integrated Grid.

NOTES

1. Harold A. Innis, *Empire and Communications* (Toronto: University of Toronto Press, 1972), pp. 1–11. The work was originally published in 1950.
2. The fable of the evaluation committee for the printing press was proposed by the distinguished American communications scholar, Harold Lasswell. For a comprehensive review of the initial impact of the Renaissance printing press, see Elizabeth Eisenstein, *The Printing Press as an Agent of Change* (New York: Cambridge University Press, 1980).
3. Asa Briggs, "The Pleasure Telephone: A Chapter in the Pre-history of the

Media," in *The Social Impact of the Telephone*, ed. Ithiel de Sola Pool (Cambridge, MA: MIT Press, 1977), pp. 40–59.

4. Anthony Smith, "The Wire and the Wavelength — An Historical Study," in *Cable: An Investigation of the Social and Political Implications of Cable Television*, a report published by the Standing Conference on Broadcasting (London, 1974), p. 29.

5. *Ibid.*, pp. 31–32.

6. Erik Barnouw, *The Sponsor* (New York: Oxford University Press, 1978), pp. 24–25.

7. Smith, "Wire and Wavelength," pp. 36–37.

8. Anthony Smith, *Shadows on the Cave* (Urbana, IL: University of Illinois Press, 1973), p. 351.

9. For a useful summary of international cable developments, see Arthur C. Clarke, *Voices across the Sea* (London: Luscombe Publishers, 1974).

10. Morris Edwards, "Fiber Optic Links Forge Paths for the Expected Information Explosion," *Communications News*, February 1978, p. 30.

11. "Spinning webs of fiber optics across the U. S.," *Washington Post*, 13 September 1987, *Washington Business* supplement, p. 1. See also "Fiber optics: the national network race is on," *Communications Week*, 8 September 1986, p. 16.

12. The figures represent projections made by American and European telecommunications carriers, and are taken from an AT & T Long Lines study, "North Atlantic Planning Process Technological Alternatives Update," 7 November 1983.

13. "Optical fibers straddle the globe," *The Economist* (London), 22 March 1986, p. 84.

14. "Pure is best," *The Economist* (London), 4 October 1980, p. 93.

15. Ammon Yariv, "Guided Wave Optics," *Scientific American*, April 1980, pp. 64–72.

16. Eitan, Abraham, Colin T. Seaton, and S. Desmond Smith, "The Optical Computer," *Scientific American*, February 1983, pp. 85–93.

17. "New York Tel's going fiber under sidewalks of New York," *Communications Week*, 14 December 1987, p. 22.

18. "New lines for old — a survey of telecommunications," *The Economist* (London), 17 October 1987, p. 21.

19. "ISDN — new trials under way," *Financial Times* (London), 19 October 1987. Special supplement on telecommunications, p. xxvii.

20. For a useful description of ITU history and current activities, see Codding, George and Anthony Rutkowski, *The International Telecommunications Union in a Changing World*. (Dedham, MA: Artech House, 1982).

21. The most extensive survey of the political and economic implications of ITU decisions can be found in ten articles on the 1979 World Administrative Radio Conference in *Journal of Communications*, Vol. 29, no. 1 (Winter 1979), pp. 143–207. For a description of the technical problems facing the ITU, see Charles Lee Jackson, "The Allocation of the Radio Spectrum," *Scientific American*, February 1980, pp. 34–39.

22. "Small radio could bring aid in a disaster," *New York Times*, 13 November 1977, p. 61.

23. For a detailed description on RDSS, see Stephen Chesten, "Radiodetermination Satellite Service: a New Path for Global Cooperation," *Telecommunications Policy*, June 1987, pp. 135–39.

24. U. S. Office of Telecommunications Policy, Executive Office of the President, *Program for Control of Electromagnetic Pollution of the Environment*, Electromagnetic Radiation Management Advisory Council, December 1971, p. 12.

25. A critical view of radiation pollution is given in Paul Brodeur, *The Zapping of America* (New York: W. W. Norton & Co., 1977). For an industry-oriented response to Brodeur's criticism, see "The Conning of America," *Microwave Journal*, October 1978, pp. 18–19.

26. For further background, see Joseph N. Pelton, *Global Talk*. (Rockville, MD: Sijthoff and Noordhoff, 1981).

27. For a summary of the broadcast satellite controversy, see Wilson Dizard, "Direct Broadcast Satellites: the U. S. Position" in *The Cable/Broadband Communications Handbook*, Vol. 2, 1980–81 (Washington, DC: Communications Press, 1980), pp., 73–86.

28. "A traffic jam in outer space," *New York Times*, 26 March 1980, p. D–3.

29. The Rand Corporation, "Radio's Last Frontier," *Rand Research Review*, Vol. 2, no. 1 (Spring 1978), p. 1.

30. Cutbacks in Reagan administration space budgets threatened this and other NASA advanced research projects, although the communications satellite effort was protected annually through strong congressional support. See "Government Role in Advanced Satellites Continues Despite Reagan's Opposition," *Aviation Week and Space Technology*, 7 July 1986, pp. 108–9.

CHAPTER 4

The Technological Framework
Information Machines

Having looked at the technologies forming the new networks, we now turn to the information machines that plug into the grid. These are the computers, terminals, telex printers, and other devices that are the nodal points where human thoughts are transferred into electronic impulses and fed into the system. Their capabilities need to be understood as we try to measure their impact on strategies for a new information age.

We have seen how a convergence of research breakthroughs has revolutionized wire and wireless networks. This pattern of new technology is, if anything, more complex when we take into account the machines that are served by these networks. There are many technological paths leading up to this convergence and many possible outcomes. There are also significant elements shared by the machines and the networks. The most important of these is their common reliance on microelectronic technology, which provides each of them with new levels of reliability and capacity and new operational functions. Microelectronic products, many of them no bigger than a fingernail, are a key resource in powering the second industrial revolution. Here I will, somewhat parochially, limit my concerns to one part of this process — the postindustrial information structure, a complicated pattern of machines linked to a growing communications grid, all made possible by the commonality of microelectronic devices.

A letter sent across the country by conventional means may involve a typewriter, a postal truck, canceling and sorting machines, an airplane, a pushcart, more trucks and sorting equipment, and finally a mailman walking his route. This is, with luck, a three-day process. A single machine — actually two terminals at either end of a satellite circuit — can deliver the contents of the letter in less than a minute. The technological advantage of this is clear. There are, however, economic, political, and social considerations where the advantages are considerably less obvious. The postal system is more than an institution potentially capable of one-minute mail delivery. It is the friendly mail carrier, Christmas cards, junk mail, and stamp collecting, all of which have to be fitted into, or discarded from, this new one-minute system. The question is relevant to any future information strategies we may devise: To what degree are we willing to modify or even dismantle comfortable ways of thinking and acting in order to accommodate the new technologies?

This accommodation is a tall order for any society. The United States is being pressed to make decisions well ahead of any other country because of its long lead in developing a mass communications system. Competitive economic pressures, in particular, will force decisions either by design or default. We will look more closely at this decision process in later chapters. Here we will survey the present state and future expectations of the new information machines.

The survey begins with microelectronics — the technological common denominator in the new integrated information grid. Its products have, of course, uses beyond communications and information equipment. However, it is probable that one-half or more of the industry's basic product, semiconductor chips, goes into such equipment. Computers alone accounted for 40 percent of the use of world semiconductor output by 1980. Communications and information applications have set the pace in what has come to be called "the microelectronics revolution." As in most self-proclaimed revolutions, the semantics are imprecise. A more exact, if somewhat less stirring, description would be "speeded-up evolution," with a footnote that the process has not been, nor will it be, a smooth one.[1]

Smooth or not, the evolution is impressive. The primitive era was a scant 40 years ago. At that time, interconnected radio vacuum tubes were the only device for transmitting a current of electrons between electrodes in communications and information equipment. The tubes worked, but they were bulky and fragile. In the early fifties, the process of replacing them began with *transistors*, developed by the Bell Laboratories. In a transistor, the current connecting electrodes flows through solid materials, usually silicon, known as *semiconductors*. The next step, which took place around 1960, was the development of *integrated circuits*, or many interconnected transistors on a single piece of silicon, popularly known as a *chip*. Research has since centered on the progressive sophistication of integrated circuits with larger capacities and expanded functions. The first integrated circuits had 10 transistors on a chip. This capacity has been pushed up to several hundred thousand components per chip in recent years. A million-transistor chip is being tested experimentally. By the end of the century, a billion-component chip should be available.[2]

Improvements in circuit capacity have opened the way for the chips to take on new functions. The most striking change has been the incorporation of the *microprocessor*, a complex type of integrated circuit that can function as a computer. A single chip can contain the equivalent of the central processor of a small computer, which performs arithmetical and logical functions, plus some memory. It works in conjunction with *memory chips*, which store information, and with *input* and *output chips*, which are used to get information into and out of the central processor. The technological distance between the old vacuum radio tube and the present-day integrated chip is formidable. The pioneering ENIAC computer, developed during World War II, weighed 30 tons, filled a large room, and had 17,000 radio tubes, which required round-the-clock replacement maintenance.[3] A present-day chip incorporating a microprocessor the size of a thumbtack can have more computational power than ENIAC. Microprocessors are still a small, specialized part of integrated circuit production, accounting for only about 10 percent of such production. However, this percentage is expected to double within a few years.

In Chapter 5 we will take a closer look at the industry than churns out these products. The semiconductor companies were the most dynamic industrial sector of the 1970s, expanding from $1 billion in annual sales at the beginning of the decade to $10 billion by the end. By the late eighties, the industry was producing at the rate of $30 billion annually.[4] This growth is all the more phenomenal considering the average price of a transistor component in a chip is now less than a penny, compared to $10 twenty years ago.

Advanced chips wiii be, in the words of one developer, the jelly beans of the electronic age — plentiful and cheap. They are adapted so quickly to so many uses, from toys to telephones, that they have often been in chronic short supply. At one point in the early eighties, United States firms were caught up in delivery delays of up to 10 months. Thanks to the competitiveness of the industry — and particulary the growing threat of Japanese competition — these shortages were made up. Another longer term problem is not so readily solved by production speed-ups. This is the inability of many chip users to get the software they need for the tiny devices. There are still too few trained *software programmers*, the technicians who write the instructions. Moreover, program writing is an expensive operation and is becoming even more so. A decade ago, two-thirds of the cost of integrated circuitry was in hardware, the rest in software. This ratio has since been reversed.

As computer hardware becomes more sophisticated, software becomes even more important. A generation ago, computers were simpler, and operated largely by technicians and others who understood them. Today's machines are infinitely more complex, and used by millions of people who will never need to understand how computers work. The trick is, in the well-known phrase, to design user-friendly machines. As computer theorist Alan Kay has noted, simple tasks must be made simple, and complex tasks made possible.

This requirement became an imperative in the eighties with the introduction of personal computers. In the new diffusion of computer power, software increasingly defines what kind of information people get and what they do with it. It is the reason that software is a $30 billion annual market worldwide, and growing at about 20 percent a year. It is also a volatile market, with a constant turnover of winners and losers among software firms. New products supersede older ones overnight. The range of available programs is daunting. American software companies were offering over 60,000 products in the late eighties.[5]

With this new emphasis on software's importance has come a change in its role. Previously, most software programs were designed for limited tasks to be carried out by a specific computer produced by one company. This benefited the companies (most notably IBM) for the simple reason that a customer was locked into their software standards. Transferring data from one set of computer products to another had to be done by hand, a time-consuming, expensive process that canceled out a lot of computer efficiency. With the mass applications of computers, software patterns are changing rapidly. Software design is now focused on the need to allow all kinds of computers to "talk" to one another. This kind of integration calls for common technical standards, similar to the Integrated Digital Services Network (ISDN) software plan for telecommunications networks described in Chapter 3.

But computer standardization is a somewhat more complex problem. There is already a proliferation of "standard" computer programs. Moreover, the demands people make on computers are amazingly varied and subject to continual change. Not all programs need to talk to each other, or to say the same thing. Finally, the new attempts at integrating software will continue to be plagued by error-prone programs — the "bugs" that infest even the best systems. Computer development in the next decade will focus increasingly on the complexities of a new generation of integrated software. As we shall see in Chapter 6, the results will have a strong impact on the economic fortunes of computer firms, including the once-invulnerable IBM.

These problems will not seriously delay the shift to microelectronics, particularly in communications and information. Chips are a basic construction module in the upgrading of networks and the machines linked to them. These pea-size devices are already being used to overhaul the network most familiar to us — the telephone system. The end result will be a phone network that will eventually be called something else, since conventional voice service will be only one part of its function.

The transformation of the phone network is well under way, mostly behind the scenes in exchanges and other system installations. Beginning in the mid-seventies, telephone companies have been replacing their old electromechanical switching gear with electronic equipment. One of the last pieces of equipment to be affected by this modernization program has been the telephone instrument itself. Telephones may be shaped like Mickey Mouse or a plastic doughnut, but the equipment inside most of them is basically the same. Most telephones are still based on 40-year-old technology; apart from push-botton dialing, the design and performance of the standard set has been unchanged since the 1950s. This is changing with the introduction of an all-electronic telephone, complete with chips. In one model, about 180 parts of the standard push-button telephone are replaced by 3 integrated circuits.[6]

The result will be not only a more efficient voice telephone as such but also an instrument better adapted, through microprocessor technology, to plug into other communications and information services, including computers. The days of the phone network's focus on POTS — Plain Old Telephone Service — are ending.

This shift is part of a larger pattern — the restructuring of the American communications and information industries. There are complex political and economic reasons for the change, as we shall see in subsequent chapters. However, the determining factor has been microelectronics technology. Given the capabilities of the new devices, it makes less sense to have a single monopoly network dedicated primarily to POTS. It was this technological imperative, more than any other single factor, that has led to the current massive transformation of the United States communications structure. The central event of this change was the 1982 decision to end AT&T's near-total monopoly over local telephone service, at the same time permitting the firm to operate competitively in the data communications market for the first time.

AT&T's reorganization removed major constraints on the application of advanced communications and information technologies in this country. For a decade before the government's decision to permit the breakup of AT&T, the company's dominant position had been eroding slowly. This was largely the result of a series of legal and administrative rulings permitting greater competition in telephone equipment and services. These limited decisions did not, however, seriously affect AT&T's dominance over the telephone network — the basic infrastructure of the information age. The 1982 decision to divest the local Bell companies from AT&T changed this. In the process, it opened the prospect of an era of technologically driven competition across the entire spectrum of American communications. Whether this prospect will be realized or not will be reviewed in Chapter 7, which deals with the economic and social implications of the changes. Meanwhile, many barriers to innovative application of advanced technology have been breached, from telephones to computers.

Computers are at the center of this post-industrial shift. Like the working group faced with Master Gutenberg's invention in our Renaissance fable, we have trouble getting the computer's measure. The developers of the first electronic computer in the 1940s thought that four computers, more or less, would satisfy the world's needs.[7] Given the state of computer technology at the time, their estimate seemed reasonable. But the fact is that there are now literally tens of millions of machines that can be classified under the broad heading of "computers." After three decades of specialized use in business and government, computers have become a mass consumer product. The next 10 years will bring almost universal use of personal home computers with their own data storage capabilities as well as links to outside data sources.

At many levels, computers are integral parts of the universal information grid. They would be important even if they were only able to store vast amounts of information, like highly efficient filing cabinets, or to serve as high speed calculating machines. Their great liberating use, however, is their power to extend knowledge, particularly by simulating reality (or even simulating what seems to be unreality) in ways the human brain finds difficult to do or is incapable of doing.

Modern computers and communications circuitry both have their origins in the work of a small group of scientists working on the East Coast and in Britain during the 1940s and 1950s. The mention of their names — Claude Shannon, Norbert Wiener, John von Neumann, Alan Turing, and others — causes few knowing nods, even among reasonably well-informed people today. It would be difficult, however, to exaggerate the contribution of these scientists to post-industrial America and, by extension, to the rest of the world. Working in the esoteric area known as "information theory," they understood that they had to define information and its characteristics accurately if their ideas about a more rational organization of information resources were to be realized. Their pursuit of this purpose in seminar rooms and laboratories and in faculty club discussions has had results that put an indelible mark on American society.

The basic orientation of the group was mathematics, and particularly the idea, advanced by Bertrand Russell and Alfred North Whitehead, that logic is the foundation of all mathematics. Russell's and Whitehead's 1910 work, *Principia Mathematica,* developed the calculus of propositions or the solving of problems in terms of statements that are either true or false. As a young M.I.T. graduate student in the late thirties, Claude Shannon demonstrated the practical applications of this calculus in improving the design of electrical circuits. Shannon's initial search, which became his master's thesis, showed that programming an electronic digital computer would be a problem not of arithmetic, but of logic. Later, at the Bell Laboratories, Shannon and his fellow researcher, Warren Weaver, expanded on these insights to propose a design for a general communications system.[8] They treated information input as a problem in statistics, permitting precise measurement of the amount of information delivered and the efficiency of the devices that handle it. Like computers, the theory deals with information rather than meaning. For the first time, communications and computer scientists had a definitive measure of their commodity — information.

That measure is called a *bit,* a contraction of "binary digit." The bit is the module for the input to most advanced electronic information and communications devices. It can be defined as the lowest common denominator of information, a unit resolving uncertainty or choice between two exclusive alternatives, for example, between yes and no, heads and tails, on and off, one and zero. It is the choice we exercise in choosing left or right when there are no other options, that is, when there is equal probability for each. In choosing, we resolve doubt. By putting many bits together in a computer or communications circuit, symbols (words, pictures, numbers) that transmit information take shape. Whatever form it takes, the information is transmitted onto electrical circuits digitally, that is, it is represented by two digits — 0 or 1 — in patterns that define the information. The letter A in a six-bit binary code can be 11001, the letter P can be 100111, and so on. The pattern 110001 100111 100111 100011 110101 010010 110001 010100 110011 110101 stored in a computer moves through the circuits and comes out as "applesauce." Trillions and trillions of symbolic 1s and 0s move through communications systems, each a coded part of a message that may be teenager's telephone call, a credit card transaction, a television soap opera, or a weather report from the Viking space station on Mars.

Shannon also demonstrated how to measure the capacity of a communications channel in terms of *bits per second* (BPS). The channel capacity for a telephone wire used for speech purposes is 60,000 BPS; for broadcast television, 90 million BPS, and on upward to the 15 billion BPS capacity for a millimeter wave-guide system. Shannon's contributions were only part of a convergence of concepts that made possible the new communications and information machines. Britain's Alan Turing had provided remarkable insights into the problem of digital computers in a paper written in 1937 when he was only 25 years old.[9] Another contributor was Norbert Wiener, an M.I.T. mathematics professor and an authentic genius who earned a Harvard Ph.D. in mathematical logic at the age of 19. Wiener explored the concept of self-regulating mechanisms akin to the human brain's feedback capabilities. Early work in computers spurred speculation about "thinking" machines and automation. Wiener coined a name for this field of computer control — "cybernetics" — in a book by the same name exploring the uses of such automata.[10] Meanwhile, mathematician John von Neumann, at Princeton was developing the *stored-program* concept, the idea that a machine could control its calculating sequences by modifying its own instructions. Taken together, these concepts moved computer technology beyond storage and calculating functions to electronic, digital stored-program machines, expanding dramatically their creative capabilities as intelligence extenders.

In identifying the logical parameters of information and communications machines, von Neumann and other information theorists laid much of the base for the high technology advances that have occurred in the last 40 years. Matching their own remarkable insights was the speed with which their ideas were put to practical use. In part it was the result of close collaboration between research and development organizations, both public and private, and American industry. The Department of Defense, pressing for quick military applications of these new technologies, was an important factor in this process. There was intense pressure within the industrial sector to exploit the potentially lucrative opportunities opened up by the new electronics. A production infrastructure developed quickly, with Remington Rand producing the first production-line computer, UNIVAC I, in 1951. By the end of 1953, 13 companies were manufacturing computers, including IBM, which soon became the giant of the new industry.[11]

The first electronic computers were large, free-standing information storage and calculating boxes, with no outside links. Later, computers with stored-program capabilities were developed and connected to remote terminals. These were, however, "slave" terminals, dependent on data and instructions from the main computer. By the mid-sixties, more sophisticated computer and remote terminal patterns, involving interactive networking, came on the market. These terminals could modify main computer instructions and data. More recently, they have been equipped with their own computer memory to handle "local" requirements independent of the main computer. This kind of flexibility has resulted in an explosive growth in computer-based data networks: in

1965 there were 50,000 installed computer terminals in this country; by 1975, this number had increased to over a million; over 30 million terminals are projected for the early nineties.

A Harvard researcher, Anthony Oettinger, has suggested that the computer communications phenomenon deserves a new name — "compunications." His elision of the words "computer" and "communications" is more than a semantic trick; the computer and its communications-circuit links to other computers or to terminals constitute an integral information machine. The fact that this "machine" may stretch across continents and oceans is more or less irrelevant. "Compunications" may not make the dictionary, but it describes a reality that has long-range political, economic, and social implications for the information age.

Meanwhile, computer engineers are putting more information power into smaller spaces. Many of the low capability, room-size computers of the forties and fifties are literally museum pieces. (A number of them are on display at the Smithsonian Institution's Museum of American History in Washington.) Large mainframe computers are not yet passé; they are just shrinking. At the same time, the economies of the big machines have been rapidly improving. In the early seventies, it cost $25 a month to store a million bits of information in an advanced IBM direct-access storage system. Now, twenty years later, the cost has dropped to pennies.

Big computing jobs require a special breed of machine — the supercomputers, or "number crunchers" as they are known in the trade. The best known of the early supercomputers was the United States Defense Department's ILLIAC installation in California, developed originally in the 1970s. Like most number crunchers, ILLIAC was designed for unique tasks. One of its jobs was to track Soviet submarines, which it did by processing data from sensing devices on the ocean floor designed to identify the subs by their acoustic "signature." ILLIAC reportedly could handle 300 million instructions per second and had a potential for expansion to handle over a billion.[12]

Supercomputer technology has advanced rapidly in recent years to the point where a new word has been coined to describe the machines' capabilities. The word is *flop*, defined as the ability to do a complex operation on two items of data in one second. A *gigaflop* is a billion flops. In 1988, Cray Research Co., a leading supercomputer builder, introduced a new model with a capability of up to four billion calculations per second — the four gigaflop machine. The supercomputer business is a highly competitive one, especially since the introduction of Japanese products in the past decade. During the coming decade, the competitive focus may shift to new types of *mini-supercomputers*, desktop models less powerful than the bigger machines but also far less expensive.[13]

The supercomputers will continue to do big special jobs, but the general technological focus has shifted to smaller machines. The trend began in the sixties with the so-called "minicomputers" — a description that has become almost obsolete in recent years with the debut of even smaller microcomputers and microprocessors. But whatever their names, minicomputers have staked out a significant middle ground between the big number-crunching mainframes and small machines. In addition to performing specialized tasks on their own, they have become the workhorses of the fast-moving distributed data processing field. This involves linking low-cost minicomputers and terminals into communications networks instead of putting everything in a big mainframe. Today's minicomputers have computational powers well beyond the big computers of the seventies. Equally important, their price tag makes them attractive to smaller business firms and other organizations. This adaptability to mid-level tasks is reflected in the growth of the minicomputer market. By the eighties worldwide sales were increasing at better than a 35 percent annual rate, as against a 15 percent growth for the larger mainframe machines.

With recent advances in microelectronic circuitry, minicomputers and their terminals are beginning to talk and to listen. They can understand spoken instructions and reply with synthetic speech. They can also store speech. One active prospect is voice mail — the storage of voice messages in digital form for delivery at a later time, either as reconstituted speech or as hard copy.

Eventually, voice mail will be part of an integrated electronic mail system involving telephones, computer terminals, facsimile machines, and communicating word processors. However, it is probable that talking and listening computers will operate alone for the time being. IBM research scientists have used a computer to transcribe speech, composed of sentences drawn from a thousand-word vocabulary and read at a normal speaking pace into a printed form, with 91 percent accuracy. The Orator talking terminal, developed by ARTS Computer Products, can be interfaced with a computer to produce synthesized speech with a full-word capability for use by the blind.

The fastest growth in the computer market during the past decade involves smaller machines known as *microcomputers*. These are the so-called personal computers, used widely in homes and schools. Aside from generating and storing information on their own, these machines can be linked to a wide array of data bases over telephone lines or other circuits. An increasing number of such services are already available to owners of small computers. Two of the best known, The Source and Comp-U-Serve, have been offering access to a wide range of computerized information resources to computer owners since the early eighties.

The chips that led the way to smaller, more efficient computers are themselves going through another change. They were originally identified as LSI (*Large Scale Integration*) technology. The new phrase is VLSI (*Very Large Scale Integration*). VLSI takes the chips up to what many scientists think may be the physical limits of miniaturization. The progression toward these limits has been swift. The problem, in simple terms, is to etch tinier and tinier circuit lines on a silicon chip. Every tenfold decrease in the width of the lines leads to a hundredfold increase in the number of circuits that can be put on the chip. Line widths have already been narrowed down to an average 2½ to 3 *microns* — a micron being a millionth of a meter. The goal is to narrow the gap to under one micron. This would be close to what, for the present, is considered the physical limit of tiny circuit patterns — lines one-third of a micron wide. If this limit is achieved, it will be the equivalent of packing 150 lines within the width of a human hair.[14] The chip designers achieved these initial successes with silicon-based semiconductors. In their search for more efficient chips, the designers have been looking at other approaches for building integrated circuits. A long-term prospect, described above, is optical switching, using laser-generated lightwaves. An even longer term possibility is the use of bacteria, genetically engineered to produce computer switching components, in the same way that bacteria are now being engineered to turn out insulin and other chemicals.[15]

Another prospect involves the use of *superconducting materials* in computers. Their advantage is that they lose all resistance to electricity at extremely low temperatures, thus eliminating problems caused by heat generated in present computers. IBM was a pioneer in superconductivity research a decade ago, working with materials that required temperatures at absolute zero, which is minus 273 degrees Celsius. The idea was to replace the standard semiconductor transistor with a superconducting version called the Josephson junction, named after its inventor, Brian Josephson of Cambridge University. The outstanding advantage of the new technology is that, having resolved the heat problem, the semiconductor chip could store 100 million bits of memory per square inch. Theoretically, large calculations could be performed in a billionth of a second.

The problem was how to do all this at such extremely low temperatures. The difficulties were such that IBM gave up its Josephson-junction project in 1983. The research effort was redirected toward finding superconducting materials that would be effective at less daunting temperatures. This goal was realized in 1987 with a series of break-throughs involving ceramic compounds that had superconducting capabilities at a comparably warm 98 degrees Celsius above absolute zero, four times higher than most scientists thought possible. This "high temperature superconductivity" research is still very much in the laboratory stage. Superconducting wiring on a semiconductor chip is, for instance, only a few billionths of a meter across. The problem of getting the wires to operate in a foolproof manner is still a formidable one.[16]

A more immediate solution has been the use of gallium arsenide as a substitute for a silicon base. Gallium is a bluish-white element obtained as a by-product of aluminum and copper smelting. Chemically, like silicon, it is neither fish nor fowl. It occupies the middle ground between conductivity and resistance that makes it a semiconductor — the raw material of integrated circuits. Gallium arsenide is more difficult to deal with in producing chips, but the rewards are worth the difficulty. Chips based on gallium arsenide technology offer circuit speeds two to five times greater than silicon. Moreover, these chips do not overheat and self-destruct at high speed, as silicon-based chips are apt to do. Gallium arsenide chips and related technological developments are bringing us closer to the most dramatic development in the computer's evolution since ENIAC, the first modern computer, was created back in the mid-forties. It involves the race to develop a totally new kind of computer in the coming decade.

These machines will be similar to the present supercomputers only in that they require extremely fast calculations. Beyond that, the similarities end. The new computers will be machines that "think." With this limited intelligence capability, they will be able to understand spoken and written languages, recognize objects, and reason as an expert in specific disciplines such as medicine or engineering. In the high-tech computer buff's phrase, it is the shift from ordinary DP (data processing) to KIPS (knowledge information processing systems).

The shorthand description for this undertaking is the fifth generation computer. The first four generations were largely the result of IBM research and production. The fifth generation will probably not be a uniquely IBM achievement — nor even an American one. The first nation off the mark in sponsoring a full-scale fifth generation effort was Japan in 1982. Supported in part by government research funds, Japanese manufacturers are spending half a billion dollars to develop artificial intelligence software and hardware technology for the new machines.

The fifth generation project is based on the technology of parallel processing — the manipulation of data by many different processors in the computer at the same time. The goal is to move more deeply into the new field of *artificial intelligence* (AI), replicating in a primitive way the heuristic ways the human brain works. Creating computers with many processors is relatively easy. Designing the machines for AI tasks requires processors that can work on a single problem in close co-ordination. The fifth generation goal of developing hardware and soft-ware to allow processors to work simultaneously on a *wide* range of problems is an even more awesome task.

There is no question that parallel processing will become standard in many advanced computers in the coming decade. They will be used for "expert systems," understanding and analyzing written information in any field and providing "advice" comparable to that which human experts can offer. They will teach basic skills, and translate language more efficiently than present "machine translation" efforts.

The Japanese have made significant progress in matching, and occasionally surpassing, comparable American "expert system" efforts leading up to a new generation of advanced computers. It is apparent, nevertheless, that the original timetable for significant R&D break-throughs in fifth generation computers has had to be pushed back, given the research complexities involved in the project.[17]

The Japanese "computer challenge" was at least part of the reason for a stepped-up effort in advanced computer development by the United States government and by private industry in recent years. In 1983, the Defense Department's Advanced Research Projects Agency (ARPA) inaugurated an artificial intelligence project with a modest $50 million budget. More significantly, a group of leading United States computer and semiconductor makers (with the significant exception of IBM) agreed, for the first time, to pool some of their research resources to develop technologies needed for the fifth generation effort. Their limited-venture partnership, known as the Microelectronics and Com-puter Technology Corporation, began operations at a new research facility in Austin, Texas, in 1984. Meanwhile, IBM, the prime mover behind the first four generations of computers, can be counted on to make significant technical contributions to the so-called fifth generation race in the coming decade.

In the late eighties, over 50 U. S. research and development con-sortiums were formed to pool high-technology resources. Their efforts are heavily concentrated in microelectronics-based products, from bio-technology to automobiles. The direct impetus for this resource sharing was 1984 congressional legislation, the National Cooperative Research Act. The act eases antitrust restrictions on cooperative research, which had been a major inhibiting factor to joint research by competing American firms.

The larger reason for the new cooperative program is the changing world economy. The focus of competition has shifted steadily from company against company to nation against nation. The example cited most often in the debate on the 1984 legislation is the close relationship between government and industry in Japan (largely through a Ministry of International Trade and Development) in developing high-technology products for world markets. American practice, with its emphasis on individual corporate R&D, is being modified to match the challenge posed by national policies and practices abroad.

The most dramatic of these challenges comes in semiconductor development. In Europe and Japan, governments have allocated hundreds of millions of dollars to high-tech research in this sector. One result is that the American share of the world computer chip market dropped from 60 to 40 percent during the eighties, with the Japanese share rising from 25 to 40 percent. Moreover, there were increasing indications by the end of the decade that the Japanese were beginning to widen their lead in semiconductor R&D.

In response, demands for a national semiconductor research effort in the United States arose. It was a major turnaround from previous practice since U. S. chip firms have been highly competitive in their R&D programs. After several years of debate, the result was the formation of Sematech, a research cooperative of 13 major companies, in 1987. The threat posed by the military and economic implications of the American semiconductor slump prompted Congress to appropriate $100 million to support Sematech — almost half the new venture's annual budget.

Sematech's research efforts will be shared among its member firms, which will decide how the technology is to be used. In a precedent-shattering move, both IBM and AT&T — normally the most secretive firms in R&D matters — agreed in 1988 to make some of their most advanced semiconductor research available to Sematech. With this advantage, Sematech has the prospect of becoming an important factor in expanding the U. S. role in the world chip market, which is expected to reach $150 billion annually by the end of the century.[18]

European computer manufacturers have been slower to enter the race. There are indications, however, that they will make a stronger showing in the coming years, supported in part by research and development funds from the European Economic Community. The results of this international effort should be computers that, in the 1990s, will make the present machines look archaic.

Whether or not this goal is reached, the new generation of chips is already having its impact on computers. The computing power of the new microprocessor chips equals that of a standard minicomputer. These so-called *high-end microprocessors* are faster and easier to program than their predecessors. They completely outclass the standard small computers in price and can be produced at a fraction of the cost of the minicomputer. The implication is that the microprocessors will replace the minis. However, there is room for a full range of computers in the new information environment. What will happen is that the bigger computers will increasingly consist of arrays of microprocessors and other chips. But they will shrink even further in size as they increase in computational power.

In the process, a new pattern of computer hardware is emerging, particular for business uses. Over the past decade, there were three levels of computer machines — the mainframes for big processing tasks, the minicomputer at the department level, and the personal desktop computer (PC). These distinctions were the basis for the global computer industry's steady expansion during the eighties. This pattern is being rudely shaken by newer technology. Specifically, the distinctions between minicomputers and PCs are being smudged by an advanced computer design, the *multi-microprocessor system*, capable of doing everything from spread-sheets to word processing and electronic mail. As a result, it is the minicomputer that will be phased out in many offices in the coming years. PCs will continue to flourish as a mass consumer product for homes and school classrooms.

Meanwhile, the multiprocessor "workstations" will bring a new level of inexpensive high-performance capabilities to offices. Their efficiency is measured in MIPS — millions of instructions processed per second. In the late eighties, an IBM mainframe might run at more than 80 MIPS and cost about $140,000 per MIPS. A Digital Equipment Corp. minicomputer could offer 20 more MIPS at $60,000 a MIPS. The new breed of microprocessor-based workstations were bringing these costs down to about $5,000 per MIPS. The prospect of such a dramatic lowering of computing costs has led to a shake-up in the computer industry, a subject whose economic consequences are discussed in Chapter 6.

These new machines will be linked in high-speed networks, increasingly centered around fiber optic technology. The potential capacities of these networks are nothing short of staggering. In 1988, the GTE Laboratories demonstrated a communications laser that pulses at a rate of 22 *billion* times a second. Linked to fiber optic circuits, the tiny semiconductor laser generates light pulses carrying digitized voice, video, or data. The GTE laser can transmit the print contents of 10 sets of the *Encyclopaedia Britannica* every second.[20]

Computers are the glamor machines of the information age. They are not, however, unique solutions for storing and distributing large amounts of information. There are other methods, many of which rely on the computer and its operations. The old-fashioned book is going through a technological revolution of its own, a sort of Gutenberg revisited. Production of standard books is becoming almost completely automated, expanding production capabilities to thousands of volumes an hour. The next technical step will be direct electronic publishing, a strange new world of paperless books. The first moves in this direction were made a decade ago with improvements in microfiche readers. Existing print books and other publications have been reproduced in microfilm rolls for a long time, primarily for preservation purposes. The problem, as any one who has dealt with microfilm knows, is to eliminate the awkwardness of searching for material through the long rolls. In the early eighties, Kodak announced a plan for melding computers and microfilm in ways that will reduce search time to a few seconds. The trick is in coding each microfilm "page" and entering the code in a data bank. When a page is sought, its location can be readily identified and the information put onto a microfilm reader. Such devices will probably not be used for standard books but for retrieval of archival materials and for reference publications.

Microfiche — the grouping of many pages on a plastic card — offers greater prospects for direct publishing. In the early seventies, the University of Toronto Press was one of the first publishers to offer all its output in both printed and microfiche form. Some scholarly magazines and publications with small circulations are now being produced only in microfiche form in an effort to cut costs. Another prospect for more efficient data storage is the *videodisc*, which looks like an LP record. Best known originally in its consumer version as a home entertainment device, the videodisc is also a storage bin for print and audiovisual information. One such version, developed by MCA Discovision, provides 54,000 separate "pages" of information on a single disc — the equivalent of the contents of the *Encyclopaedia Britannica*.

The next step is the "book" in a computer. In 15th-century Europe, Johann Gutenberg began the print revolution by printing Bibles and other religious works. In twentieth-century California, a computer expert, Bill Bates, may have set off the new print revolution with a cookbook. In 1980, Bates published *The Computer Cookbook*, a work of computer data. The contents were transmitted electronically from Bates's distributor in Ohio to customer terminals without benefit of paper, printing, binding, or other traditional publishing devices. Customers "signed on" through their terminals and browsed through the recipes on their cathode-ray screens at an hourly rate. They could also buy the entire text and have it transferred to a computer disk or even to an old-fashioned hard-copy printout.

Bill Bates, the electronic Gutenberg, saw his project as part of a logical progression toward a new information environment:

Today we can see that every cost associated with traditional publishing — distribution, labor, silver, film, gas, freight, cloth — is going up, whereas every single cost involved in the electronics industry — home computers, word processors, telephone and satellite transmissions, silicon chips — is going down and will continue to go down. At some point, where these two paths cross, electronic publishing is going to become very attractive.[21]

A variation on Bill Bates's book-in-the-computer is *desktop publishing*. This technology, readily adaptable to personal computers, allows people to design and produce documents that have the professional appearance of a traditional typeset product. In addition to a small computer, it requires a laser printer and the software for word processing, charts or drawings if desired, and publishing applications such as layout. The result is to create a new breed of publisher, most of them operating on shoestring budgets. In California, Tom Hamilton, a hot-air ballooning enthusiast, publishes *Balloon Life*, a monthly magazine (circulation 2,500), virtually single-handed. Jonathan Seybold, publisher of a newsletter on desktop publishing, estimates that over 300,000 desktop-publishing programs were sold in 1987, up from 60,000 the previous year.[22]

Somewhat further down the technological road is the large-scale use of *holography* — an electronically squeezed-in information storage process that can fit the equivalent of large libraries of data into the space of a table top. Holography uses lasers to record and retrieve information. Its ability to compress prodigious amounts of data into small spaces makes it particularly useful for major archival tasks, from recording birth certificates to logging the massive data output of scientific satellites circling the earth.

These developments may seem strange and even threatening in a literate society that relies on the traditional book for information and for cultural continuity. We are still very much the heirs of Gutenberg's movable-type revolution, despite Marshall McLuhan's unilateral declarations of the end of the age of print in the 1960s. McLuhan hailed the new electronic media as liberators, freeing us from the linear, left-to-right constraints print imposed on our thoughts and culture. He reportedly characterized cultural laggards who relied on books as POBs — print-oriented bastards. McLuhan's prophecies were quickly — perhaps too quickly — rejected by the POBs who read his books. Cultural considerations aside, there is a case for looking to electronic means for moderating the continually rising tide of paper we deal with in this country.

For all our electronic progress, paper is still a formidable factor in American information culture. Four out of every 10 tons of pulp and paper in the world are produced, and mostly consumed, here. Not all of this paper is used for information, of course, but that is the major use. Between 1981 and 1984 alone, it is estimated that American business use of paper grew from 850 billion to 1.4 billion pages annually. Per capita annual paper consumption in this country in the late seventies was 600 pounds. In the Soviet Union it was 75 pounds; in India, five pounds. This "paper gap" is one of the little-noticed factors in the information imbalance between this country and most of the rest of the world, particularly the developing countries.[23]

The differences cannot be measured only in pounds of wood pulp. Americans have their own distinct patterns of printed information. There is some truth to the European mandarins' charge that Americans are not serious book readers. Textbooks aside, the United States book industry, which produced 930 million books in 1987, is geared largely to lightweight recreational or how-to-do-it material. How different from the sober uncut-page products that fill European bookstores or the enormous per capita production of solemn books in the Soviet Union. American scholars can, of course, match their Old World counterparts footnote for footnote; they are also disproportionate contributors to the 60,000 scientific and technical journals published throughout the world.[24]

But the fact is that long-lasting encapsulation of wisdom is not our national style, for better or for worse. Printed information is, to a considerable degree, a throw-away item. It is the product of a new kind of printing press — the photocopier and the laser printer. The output of these machines far outweighs that of other publications or even the more than one hundred billion pieces of mail that move through the postal system each year. The paper flow in this country is so pervasive that it cannot be measured with accuracy. In 1975, a Stanford Research Institute study tried to pin down the volume of formal notices and forms used in business, government, and other organizations. The survey concluded that the total may be as high as 800 billion pieces of paper annually — well over 3,000 items for every man, woman, and child in this paper-choked republic.[25]

Such statistics are often viewed with dismay, which is probably a mistake. The figures suggest an uncontrollable paper glut with much waste and duplication. This is certainly a factor. On the other hand, there is a great deal to be said for a society the makes it easier for everyone to have his say through readily available paper resources and reproduction equipment. Even Marshall McLuhan, the scourge of print culture, paid his respects to photocopiers for their role in making every person his or her own publisher. This capability is being enhanced with the introduction of so-called *intelligent copiers*. Not surprisingly a strong lead in this area has been taken by the Xerox Corporation. Its new high technology copiers are actually electronic printing machines that can handle inputs from many sources, such as computers and word processors, store up to a thousand pages of material, arrange it in an appropriate layout, and then print it out electronically, employing up to 50 typefaces. Incidentally, it can also reproduce documents like any traditional photocopier.

Computers and associated equipment will vastly expand this populist possibility of giving everyone an updated version of the printing press. Whether this will reduce the present massive flow of paper is problematical. What is clear is that the potential exists for making a vastly expanded range of information available to more people. The computer will be the critical link; even in its present primitive stage of application, computer technology is changing work patterns and social expectations by doing the drudgery and routine tasks nobody wants to do. These jobs engage the computer at its simplest level. The more important prospect, however, is the information society's ability to exploit the coming generation of intelligent computers. As futurist Arthur C. Clarke notes:

> It's perfectly obvious that the development of such computers would restructure society completely.... And they are already doing this in many ways because our society now would collapse instantly if the computers that run it were taken away. And these are very simple, low-grade computers. This raises tremendous social and philosophical problems, not just the question of displaced people. What will the people that were only capable of low-grade computer-type work do in the future? There is the more profound question of what is the purpose of life? What do we want to live for? And that is the question which the intelligent computer will force us to pay attention to.[26]

This leads to subjects dear to science fiction writers: the possibilities of artificial intelligence beyond the limited prospects proposed in the so-called fifth generation computers. These ideas remain firmly in the realm of science fiction for the present. Dr. John McCarthy who helped create Stanford's artificial intelligence laboratory begins his discussion of the subject with the observation that he never met a computer that was smarter than the dumbest person he knows. Nevertheless, he is careful not to dismiss the prospect of some form of machine intelligence: "One way of putting it is to say that it takes 1.7 Einsteins and .3 of a

Manhattan Project, and it is important to have the Einstein first and the Manhattan Project second." Even this estimate is challenged by other experts in the field, notably M.I.T.'s Joseph Weizenbaum, who dismisses such projections as "simply and utterly ridiculous."

Arthur C. Clarke, in one of his science fiction stories, puts the issue in human perspective. He tells of the computer failure in a space ship that takes the craft into a disastrous orbit. A Japanese crewman teaches the rest of the crew to make abacuses out of wire and beads that are then used to calculate a course that saves ship and crew. The expectations offered by computers are extraordinary enough without delving too deeply into fantasy. One type of computer use, however, does skirt the edges of artificial intelligence and promises to be a major area of research and application during the coming decade.

This involves robots — or, more accurately, programmable automation. The idea of machines doing human work has fascinated and frustrated engineers for ages. In the eighteenth century the royal courts of Europe were entertained by the Green Lady, a mannequin with hidden machinery under her fancy costume, though all she could do was draw a single picture. Robot research took on new dimensions after World War I with the emphasis on production-line automation. The result was the servomechanism, which could perform relatively simple automation tasks. Today's work with programmable automation is spurred by the possibilities opened by microprocessors. NASA is stepping up its robotics research, for instance, in hopes of lowering the costs of deep-space probes. Its managers think that automated decision-making technology can reduce the need for already scarce trained people to program future missions. The Voyager mission to Jupiter in 1979 required 200 people over an 18-month period to provide its pointing, navigation, power, and experiment control sequences. NASA engineers believe they can cut back on personnel for such tasks by a factor of 10, freeing these employees for work on other space missions.

The big automation push is not, however, in space, but on factory production lines. Here the advantages are more immediate and profitable. Every major industrial country is subsidizing research in this area with the aim of upgrading industrial productivity. The Japanese are the leaders: half of the industrial robots operating in the eighties were in Japan, a quarter in this country, and the rest in Europe. Most of these robots still do simple mechanical tasks. The next step will be to develop robots programmed to follow optimum paths and assemble complicated products. Beyond that are the prospects for sophisticated remote-control tools, manipulated from across a room or a continent. Simple remote devices have been around for a long time; mechanical arms for handling nuclear materials are one example. However, the new remote-control devices, called *telepresence devices*, would have more humanlike sensory channels involving touch, pressure, textures, and vibration. The prospect has been imaginatively described by Dr. Marvin Minsky of M.I.T.'s artificial intelligence laboratory, a telepresence enthusiast.

> You don a comfortable jacket lined with sensors and musclelike motors. Each motion of your arm, hand, and fingers is reproduced in another place by mobile, mechanical hands. Light, dextrous, and strong, these hands have their own sensors through which you can see and feel what is happening. Using this instrument, you can "work" in another room, in another city, in another country, or on another planet. Your remote presence possesses the strength of a giant or the delicacy of a surgeon. Heat or pain is translated into information but tolerable sensations. Your dangerous job becomes safe and pleasant.[27]

Given the economic rewards it promises, programmable automation will be a major research and development area in the coming years. It is, perhaps, a paradox that the most sophisticated use of the technology to date has not been in factories but in the telepresence control of robots on the moon and on Mars.

Robots represent only one of the almost infinite ways computers and other information-related technologies can be combined. The remainder of this book will concentrate on the social dynamics involved in bringing these possibilities to full working reality. Politics and economics are critical parts of this process. The balancing factors, however, will be the deeper trends of our cultural patterns and, in particular, our continuing commitment to the American electronic myth.

The myth is still remarkably resilient. As the century comes to a close, Americans are expressing many doubts about their collective future. Among other concerns, they are uneasy about the effects of helter-skelter technological development. These attitudes are interpreted by editorial-page pundits as signs of a new national maturity or, conversely, as the ending of the optimistic American dream.

Communications and information are remarkably immune from these popular doubts. We may decide not to build an SST transport or to cut back on nuclear plants. However, no one has argued for fewer computers, telephones, or newspapers, or more restrictions on the rest of the apparatus of the information environment. This could reflect at least an instinctive belief that this environment is, by and large, exempt from the law of entropy that governs other physical resources, inflexibly causing energy to be degraded or, more exactly, made unavailable. Despite our recent experiences with oil and other depletable resources, we see communications and information in a hopeful light. In these areas, more is better; they seem to be immune to many of our usual doubts about the benefits of technology.

Thus, in the final analysis, technology is shaped by cultural values. In communications and information, these values are based on an equal combination of pragmatism and mythology. The reality is the concrete achievement of democratic freedoms in this society, based in large part on an open information system. The mythology involves transforming United States society through technology, moving toward the machine-in-the-garden, the technology-powered Eden. We turn now to the day-to-day realities involved in shaping the strategy of a new kind of information-rich society, beginning with a look at the economic prospects. The stakes involved in this area are critical. They were aptly summarized in a 1979 OECD report: "The electronics complex during the next quarter century will be the pole around which the productive structure of advanced industrial societies will be organized."[28]

NOTES

1. For a useful overview of microelectronic developments in nontechnical language, see T. R. Reid, *The Chip* (New York: Simon & Schuster, 1984).
2. James D. Meindl, "Chips for Advanced Computing," *Scientific American*, October 1987, p. 81.
3. Charles and Ray Eames, *A Computer Perspective* (Cambridge: Harvard University Press, 1973), p. 132.
4. "The high-tech commodity," *The Economist* (London), 22 November 1986, p. 88.
5. "Programming the future — a survey of computer software," *The Economist* (London), 30 January 1988. Special supplement, pp. 1–2.
6. Peter P. Luff, "The Electronic Telephone," *Scientific American*, March 1978, pp. 58–64.
7. Robert Noyes, "Microelectronics," *Scientific American*, September 1977, p.64.
8. Eames, *Computer Perspective*, p. 144. Shannon published his findings in "A Mathematical Theory of Communications," *The Bell System Technical Journal*, 22, no. 3 (July 1948): p. 379.
9. Donald Michie, "Turing and the Origins of the Computer," *New Scientist* (London), 21 February 1980, pp. 580–83.
10. For a layperson's description of cybernetics, see Norbert Wiener, *The Human Use of Human Beings: Cybernetics and Society* (Boston: Houghton Mifflin Co., 1950).
11. Eames, *Computer Perspective*, p. 136.
12. "U. S. Looks for Bigger Warlike Computers," *New Scientist* (London), 21 May 1977, p. 140.
13. "The next generation at Cray," *New York Times*, 10 February 1988, p. D–1.

14. "Pushing Chip Technology Towards its Limits," *The Economist* (London), 22 February 1980, p. 83.

15. "Computers from bacteria," *New York Times*, 18 February 1982, p. D–2.

16. "Not-so-superconductors," *The Economist* (London), 13 June 1987, pp. 93–99.

17. Robert C. Wood, "The Real Challenge of Japan's Fifth Generation Project," *Technology Review,* January 1988, pp. 66–73.

18. "Are U. S. companies learning to share?", *New York Times,* 7 February 1988, p. C–5.

19. "A program of shake-up and shake-out," *Financial Times* (London), 30 December 1987, p. 8.

20. "Laser Transmission Takes a Quantum Leap," *Business Week,* 18 April 1988, p. 73.

21. Patricia Holt, "New Ideas from the West," *Publisher's Weekly,* 2 October 1979, p. 32.

22. "Computers let a thousand publishers bloom," *New York Times,* 9 October 1987, p. D–1.

23. "The Third World's paper gap," *Washington Post,* 1 September 1977, p. 1.

24. For a useful survey of the print media, see "Economic Trends in the Print Industry," a series of six articles on various aspects of the industry, *Journal of Communications*, vol. 30, no. 2 (Spring 1980). Also see Anthony Smith, *Goodbye, Gutenberg* (New York: Oxford University Press, 1980).

25. The study is described in Raymond Panko, "Outlook for Computer Mail Sunny, but Dark Clouds on the Horizon Also," *Communications News*, July 1977, p. 32. The SRI researchers asknowledged that their paper flow figures might be off by as much as half, but their basic point remains valid.

26. Transcript of Dr. Clarke's remarks on the television program, "The Mind Machines," in the Nova series, broadcast by the Public Broadcasting System in 1978.

27. Marvin Minsky, "Telepresence," *Omni*, June 1980, p. 45.

28. "Interfutures Report," Organization for Economic Cooperation and Development, Paris, 1979. Quoted in *The Economist*, 3 January 1981, p. 55.

CHAPTER 5

The Economics of the New Age

Any strategy for the information age has to reckon with the powerful economic forces organizing and managing the resources of the new global network. This grid may be the largest construction project ever undertaken. Robert LeBlanc, a leading communications finance expert, once estimated that it will take an investment of $50 billion a year into the next century for foreign countries simply to bring their communications facilities up to current United States standards.[1] Meanwhile, the United States communications grid will continue to expand both in size and in range of services. Economics will be the driving force, primarily in the form of the network market described by Herbert Dordick and others in their research on future United States information patterns.

The communications structure in this country is the result of a complex cat's cradle of uncoordinated, often overlapping, decisions going back a century or more. Marketplace economics have dominated this process, with political and social influence playing a secondary role. This point is important to an understanding of the prospects for a more coherent national strategy in this area. Any such strategy will have to recognize that there is no one focus for decision making, public or private, in the United States as there is in almost every other country because of their centralized government communications agencies.

The previous chapter described how a convergence of technical innovations points to a new physical structure in communications and information. In this chapter, we will look at a similar, if somewhat less precise, convergence of social forces that will also affect future decisions in this field. The pattern was set 150 years ago with the decision to allow the original Morse telegraph system to be built and managed by a commercial firm, Western Union. The government's regulatory touch was light until the passage of the Communications Act of 1934. This legislation created the Federal Communications Commission, the regulatory overseer of a large segment of the communications industry, in implicit exchange for a certain amount of freedom from direct governmental intervention in the industry. This arrangement has held for over a half-century with some modifications, assuring that the communications sector will remain essentially in commercial hands.

"The business of America," said Calvin Coolidge, "is business." This may be a narrow view, but it explains a lot. The United States is the only society whose citizens speak unblushingly about the education business, the business of government, the culture business, and so on. The business of communications and information touches all of these, and more. As the 1977 Commerce Department study of the information economy indicated, it may be the biggest business of all — the "premier industry of our times," as *Forbes* magazine identified it once in a survey of long-term United States economic trends.[2] Reviewing overall economic trends in the eighties, the *New York Times* singled out communications information activities as one of the two most promising fields for expansion in the decade. (The other field was genetics.[3])

Impressive production statistics tell only part of the story. There is a strong case for the proposition that the communications and information sectors will determine the economic directions of the coming decade. In part, this reflects the vibrancy of these sectors themselves. The more important element may be their role in overall United States economic growth, and in particular, in the new emphasis on reindustrialization, the overhauling of the United States economy for more efficient post-industrial tasks. Communications and information are the primary focus of the products and services for this technological turnaround. The changes are already underway: at the end of the eighties, one-fourth of all jobs in this country are dependent on computers. Present-day computers are still relatively conventional machines, often isolated from most of the work force in data processing departments. During the next decade, computers will become more integrated parts of work activities, on assembly lines, in offices, and in other service units. They will not always be the familiar boxes lined up against a wall or on large tables. Most of them will be microelectronic devices embedded in machines with enormously enhanced production capabilities.

Here is where the opportunities lie for reversing the current declines in industrial productivity. In a 1979 Brookings Institution labor productivity survey of 11 industries, only two sectors showed gains in the 1973–1978 period. One was banking, which had turned heavily to automation. The other, significantly, was communications, achieving the highest productivity gains of any industry largely by applying microelectronic technologies. This trend continued through the eighties. Although it is difficult to show causal connections in productivity measures, two factors predominate. One is the labor force itself, and here the hopeful element is the growing professionalization of United States labor, with its promise of an increasing capability to manage the new technologies. Professionals and managers now hold one out of four of the nation's jobs.[4]

The other factor is the upgrading of the machines themselves. Here is where doubts arise about America's ability to maintain its lead in many areas of technology. Spending on research and development as a share of gross national product (GNP) had slipped from 2.6 percent in 1970 to around 2.2 percent in the eighties. Moreover, somewhat over 60 percent of United States Government support for research and development — the largest single slice of the research pie — is tied to defense and space research, two areas where technology does not always translate readily into market application.[5]

Funding for communications and information research and development tends to be higher than for other sectors, primarily because the economic payoffs are usually more immediate and tangible. Innovations alone cannot sustain the reindustrialization effort; the industrial structure is too complex for such simple solutions. However, it is clear that the new productivity effort may fall well short of its goals without significant input from these sectors. Historic trends confirm this, with the telephone industry as a useful case in point. In 1910, AT&T handled six million telephone calls with a staff of 120 thousand; that is about 50 calls a year for each employee. In 1979, the system handled 185 billion calls with less than a million employees, or 185 thousand calls per employee. This productivity trend accelerated even faster throughout the eighties.

There are other hurdles to overcome in the reindustrialization effort. Investment policy, and particularly the persistent low rates of capital formation in recent years, are critical obstacles.[6] Another is the high cost of conforming to environmental and other regulations, as well as the impact of inflation on incentive to invest in innovative (in other words, risky) projects. There is also an amorphous but powerful psychological barrier, the fear of change, particularly when it affects pocketbooks and deep-seated habits. This is reflected in the bloody-minded Ludditism with which people resist the introduction of new techniques through encrusted corporate practices, union rules, or special interest laws. There will be a heavy social cost in the new industrialization cycle, most of it falling on those who are undereducated or otherwise disadvantaged. An important part of any strategy for the information age is to find effective ways of easing social disruption without losing the advantages of technologies that improve productivity and raise overall job prospects.

This will not happen easily. Many recent economic surveys have taken the bloom off rosy predictions about the evolution to an information-based services economy. Although services have led the economy in providing jobs, these jobs usually involve wages that are considerably below those of the manufacturing sectors. One U. S. Bureau of Labor Statistics survey of the largest services sectors — restaurants and retail trade — found average hourly earnings 38 percent below the level in manufacturing. Productivity in the services sectors is, moreover, often flat, or below that of manufacturing. High-tech automation does not necessarily lead to higher productivity. Studies of commercial bank operations indicated an increase of output per employee of only 0.8 percent in the mid-eighties, despite vast investments in computers, automated tellers, and other supposedly labor-saving devices.[7]

As noted earlier, the underdeveloped nations of the next century will be those that choose to ignore the implications of microelectronics and other information technologies. There is a curious, and potentially harmful, tendency in this country to suggest that it cannot happen here. Recent events forcing us to lower our expectations as undisputed world leader should make us realize that we are not — if we ever were — insulated from the consequences of such changes. Our industrial partners in Europe and Japan are responding strongly to the microelectronic challenge. Moreover, a significant group of Third World countries — India, Brazil, and Korea, among others — have made it clear that they will not restrict themselves to making the shirts, shoes, and bicycles that the industrialized West can no longer produce economically. There is no reason why they cannot begin to challenge the West in some areas of high technology. The proof is that they have already begun, with expanding electronics industries that produce an impressive range of communications and information products. These fledgling efforts are useful training grounds for more advanced production projects and a challenge to any complacency we may have about our long-term economic position.

In summary, the communications and information industries need to be considered not only as strong elements in economic productivity, but also as instruments for shaping the overall pattern of post-industrial society. Accepting these premises as true, one might assume that United States economists are engaged in a massive effort to identify the dimensions of the new information-based economy. But this is not the case.

University of Chicago economist George Stigler, once noted that the study of information resources occupied a slum dwelling in the town of economics.[8] Fortunately the subject has been gradually gaining more respectability in recent years. Since Professor Stigler made his analogy, information studies have moved up from the slums at least to middle-class status, largely as the result of the work of younger economists.

Two pioneering studies identify information factors in the new post-industrial environment. The first of these, conducted by economist Fritz Machlup, was a book, *The Production and Distribution of Knowledge in the United States,* written in 1962.[9] Machlup looked at information activities, which he called "the knowledge industries," and concluded that 29 percent of gross national product and 31 percent of the nonfarm labor force were involved in such activities during his base year, 1958. Moreover, he added, the overall annual rate of growth for such activities was considerably higher than the industrial growth rate. His conclusion was logical and direct: information-related activities would eventually outdistance industrial production as the major element in the economy.

Machlup's research focused attention on the role of information in an evolving post-industrial environment. Information and communications activities were classified under the "service sector" rubric in economic analysis until Professor Machlup extricated them from this catch-all category. In documenting their unique, growing role in the economy, he supplied important insights on the shape and content of the new information environment. His approach was broad-brush and did not attempt to analyze the common characteristics of the many "knowledge industry" sectors he identified. It was another 15 years before a precise analysis of the information and communications sectors was carried out, making clear their full impact on the United States economy.

This was done in a United States Department of Commerce research project the results of which were published in *The Information Economy,* issued in 1977.[10] Primarily the work of a young Stanford-trained sociologist, Marc Uri Porat, the study was a massive, nine-volume look at information activities in the United States economy. It confirmed and expanded on Machlup's thesis. It also provided a more sophisticated analysis of the characteristics of the new information economy. The report concluded that overall information activities accounted for 46 percent of gross national production in 1967, the base year for the study. In the same year, half the labor force, earning 52 percent of total income, held some type of information-related job.

These conclusions were both dramatic and debatable. In Porat's words, "Information is the data that has been organized and communicated. The information *activity* includes all the resources consumed in producing, processing and distributing information goods and services."[11] Having set up this standard, the study looked at the characteristics of information capital and information workers. Information capital, in Porat's analysis, included the machines, buildings, and other goods and services, from computers to mimeograph machines, that go into the information economy. Somewhat to his surprise, he found the division between information and noninformation activity relatively easy to define: "Most goods are not ambiguous. A tractor is obviously a member of the food activity, and a seismograph is a member of the information activity."[12]

Information workers cannot be divided as readily. All work involves some component of information processing. Porat approached the problem by looking at each of the 422 occupations reported by the United States Census and the Bureau of Labor Statistics. He asked: Does income from this work category originate primarily in the manipulation of symbols and information? In many cases, Porat found the answer came easily. In other occupations there were complications. Doctors presented a problem: To what degree were they in the information business? After considerable investigation, Porat concluded that a doctor's schedule broke down to about half-time in information activity and half-time in noninformation work.

Whether the information-related activities of doctors can be so accurately determined is, however, peripheral to the Commerce Department study's overall analysis of the information economy. The report was most valuable in providing a more accurate picture of the role of information activities. While the Machlup study lumped these activities together in apples-and-oranges fashion, the Commerce study made some important distinctions. It suggested that the information economy is best understood when it is divided into primary and secondary sectors. The distinction between the two can be determined by asking whether information goods and services are exchanged in the marketplace. The organizations and individuals involved in such exchanges are in the primary information sector. The secondary sector includes all the information services produced by public and private organizations for their own internal consumption. These bureaucracies are repositories of the planning, decision-making, and control apparatus in the economy. By Porat's reckoning, activities in the secondary sector accounted for 21 percent of total gross national production in 1967, almost as much as the 25 percent accounted for by the primary sector.

The long-term evolution of the new information economy is shown in Figures 5.1 and 5.2, which are reproduced from the Department of Commerce study. The relationship between the agricultural, industrial,

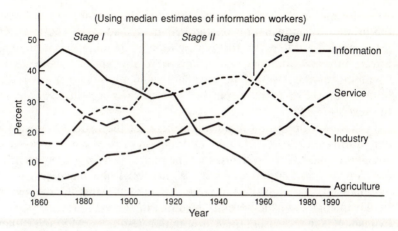

Figure 5.1. Four sector aggregation of the United States work force by percent (1860–1980). (From United States Department of Commerce, *The Information Economy*, 9 vols., Office of Telecommunications Special Publication 77–12, Washington, DC: Government Printing Office, 1977). 1980–1990: Projection by Wilson Dizard.

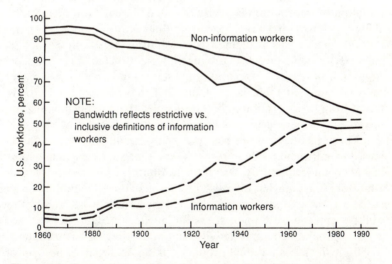

Figure 5.2. Time series of United States labor force (1860–1980). Two sector aggregate by percent. (From United States Department of Commerce, *The Information Economy*, 9 vols., Office of Telecommunications Special Publication 77–12, Washington, DC: Government Printing Office, 1977. Except for 1980 projections, which are supplied by the Bureau of Labor Statistics, unpublished data). 1980–1990: Projection by Wilson Dizard.

and information economies clearly indicates the long-term shift toward the primacy of information-related activities. The other chart, tracing the relative standings of the information and noninformation work forces, indicates that the two groups were roughly in balance at the beginning of the 1980s. The signifiant element to note here is that information-sector employment has leveled off since the beginning of the seventies.

There are important implications here for the United States economy during the 1990s. The new information economy has, in a sense, already reached a level of maturity. The time may have passed when the addition of information resources, both people and machines, would automatically have resulted in large productivity gains. Gains may be harder to come by from here on, resulting in a more cautious approach by managers in increasing their information resources. Moreover, there are indications that expansion is slower within the primary information sector — the market sector — than within the secondary sector, the bureaucracy that, whatever its value, does not directly add to the national product. The result may be to reduce the overall efficiency of the information sector, as more resources are siphoned to its bureaucratic component at the expense of more productive elements.

Inevitably, there were criticisms of the Commerce Department study's methods and conclusions. Some critics have argued that its interpretation of information is overly broad, embracing too many disparate activities. Others have questioned whether information is a commodity that can be as precisely defined as the report suggests. Nevertheless, the study performed a service in rescuing information factors in the economy from their obscurity in the traditional service industries category. Questions remain, but there is no doubt that the information sector is different from the operation of hotels, dry cleaning establishments, funeral homes, and other businesses lumped together as services.

There has been more rigorous analysis and revision of the Commerce Department study in recent years. One such revisionist approach has been undertaken by Dr. John Bermuth, a University of Chicago educator studying what he calls "literacy activities." Defining "literacy" as the exchange of information through the written word, Bermuth went well beyond the traditional stress on language skills. Literacy, he suggests, is a major economic activity, amounting in 1972 to more than one-fourth of the gross national product, taking up about 29 percent of the average worker's time on the job and about 17 percent of the average adult's waking hours. Whether or not Bermuth's literacy format takes hold as a model for clarifying information activities, it and similar new research attest to the continued quest for a more accurate definition of the information economy.[13]

In the late eighties, conventional wisdom about the information economy was challenged by two University of California economists, Stephen Cohen and John Zysman. Attacking what they called "the myth of the post-industrial economy," Cohen and Zysman made the case that a healthy manufacturing sector is central to U. S. economic growth. The myth, they argued, is that services industries alone can compensate for weak industrial performance. Services, including communications and information activities, are directly dependent on manufacturing through what the two economists call "tight to moderate linkage." Economic health, they suggest, depends on recognizing this linkage in ways that strengthen overall national productivity.[14]

There are signs that this is beginning to happen in pragmatic ways. The line between manufacturing and services is getting smudged. Communications, information, and other service activities are being embedded in traditional manufacturing patterns in new, innovative ways. The reasons for this are complex, but a major factor is the search by manufacturers for new forms of marketplace advantage. Such advantage is seen increasingly in terms of product differentiation. This in turn requires production and distribution techniques that allow for *mass customization* of product to meet individual customer needs.

Seventy years ago, Henry Ford and his revolutionary but rigid production line could offer a well-built car "as long as it was black." Product choice was limited. Today's auto firms are fiercely competitive in offering thousands of variations in otherwise standard products. This is possible only through high-tech production, distribution, and sales techniques that are dependent on advanced communications and information resources. General Motors hopes to turn around its laggard performance during the eighties with a global information network, connecting its suppliers, factories, warehouses, and dealer showrooms in ways that provide a new level of competitive efficiency. The key will be a strong emphasis on dealing with the many variations in customer needs. If a dentist in Des Moines orders a pink Buick with green pinstripes and black upholstery, a factory in Michigan will know about it in seconds and begin the customized production process in minutes.

In old-line manufacturing, communications and information activities were regarded as cost centers, the price of doing business. They are seen now increasingly as profit centers. Lockheed, Boeing, and other airframe manufacturers diversified into consumer information services when they had excess capacity on their company computers. A striking example of such diversification is American Airlines. The firm's most successful profit center in recent years has been not the sale of plane tickets but the leasing of time on its computerized reservation service to other airlines. In these and myriad other ways, the early theories about a post-industrial economy are being modified.

While the academicians debate the meaning and extent of the new economy, its superstructure is being built around them by the communications and information industries. As the 1977 Commerce Department report has shown, these industries are part of the largest single segment of the American industrial economy. Their range extends from AT&T down to the latest hopeful one-room firm, betting on a new piece of electronic technology that may or may not catch on.

The communications industry is complex, profitable, and currently in splendid disarray. After decades of relative stability, communications and information firms are being reshaped by economics and technology. New companies with cryptic names like ITEL, UTEC, Racal, and T-Bar are challenging the established giants and the giants themselves are changing. The Bell telephone system may have been, as one wag has suggested, the closest approach to immortality on earth, but it too was losing some of its eternal aura before it was split up in 1984. Semi-immortal or not, the telephone system will be quite a different institution in the 1990s. The long-term impact of the Bell breakup will be crucial in shaping post-industrial patterns in this country. AT&T and other communications firms pass the American pragmatic test — they make things work in exchange for profit. And the profit-oriented market system, battered and berated as it may be, is still a very useful mechanism for dealing with social costs. Despite long-term attempts to wrap itself in the security blanket of government regulatory protection, the United States communications industry is being exposed to the winds of competition and change, as technological innovation is forcing massive shifts in its ways of doing business, and even changing the business it does.

This contrasts with the industry's relative stability of only a few years ago. Then it was stabilized around the voice-telephone network, the first interactive mass communications grid. The network's ability to provide nearly universal service was essentially a political achievement, the result of a decision (incorporated into the 1934 Communications Act) to give AT&T a quasi-monopoly in exchange for the development of a full network. This promise was largely fulfilled. In 1934, only 31 percent of the nation's households had phones; today the figure is well over 90 percent. As sociologist Sidney Aronson notes, the telephone's ring became as "ubiquitous. . . as the ever-present tolling of church bells in a medieval village."

Whatever the corporate faults and failings of the American Telephone & Telegraph Company (and 1,600 smaller systems) over the past half-century, this record of supplying what the engineers call POTS — Plain Old Telephone Service — to such a geographically diverse, economically varied population is unique. Canada aside, no other nation had begun to match it until recent years.

Beyond the telephone grid, the next largest of the old-line telecommunications networks carried data, or "record," traffic — essentially
telegram and telex messages. This grid was designed primarily for business use, and it was dominated for decades by the Western Union Company in this country and by a group of "record carriers" internationally
— International Telephone and Telegraph (ITT), Radio Corporation of
America (RCA), and several smaller firms. The third group of basic
grids was the television and radio networks, reaching into almost every
home with popular entertainment and news programming. The 1934
Communications Act gave a strong measure of political and economic
stability first to radio and, in the postwar years, to television by assuring
them government-granted broadcasting licenses that were, for all in-
tents and purposes, permanent. Although the legislation lays down clear
public service responsibilities in exchange for renewal of licenses, the
Federal Communications Commission, which grants the licenses, has
seldom lifted one for a broadcaster's failure to serve the public interest.
As one critic of the licensing system, former California Congressman,
Lionel Van Deerlin, notes, "If a licensee has managed to stay out of jail,
he is renewed."[15] Given this kind of stability, the New York-based networks and their local affiliates developed both radio and television into
highly profitable merchandising devices for delivering mass audiences
to advertisers.

This was the situation with broadcasting and the other major communications networks through the 1960s. Each network was in its own
groove, applying technological improvements as necessary without
changing its basic operational format. Advanced computers and other
high technology machines based on microelectronics were in the early
stages of influencing communications and information patterns. Future
historians studying our particular part of the twentieth century will be
able to pinpoint more accurately the significance of the technological
shift that took place sometime around 1960 in this country, establishing
the physical parameters of the new information society. They will see,
more clearly than we can at this short distance, a series of converging
scientific developments affecting the entire spectrum of communications
and information activities. This was quite different from developments
in the previous 100 years, when major technical innovations like the
telegraph, telephone, and radio appeared one at a time, allowing a cush-
ion of several decades' time in which to sort out their political and
economic implications.

For the first time, this adaptation process began to occur all at once.
Moreover, the shift involved technologies that provided a quantum increase in quality and capacity of services, as opposed to the slower advances of earlier years. Included among the innovations that came to the

forefront during this shift were satellites, high capacity cables, lasers, advanced microwave techniques, computers, and electronic miniaturization of all manner of technology from the 1950s transistor to large-scale integration (LSI) technology.

The rush of high-tech innovations from the research laboratories to production lines beginning in the sixties has set the pace for the economic upheaval that has marked the communications and information industries since then. Within the United States, the old patterns have shifted radically, culminating in the 1984 breakup of the AT&T monopoly. Seven regional telephone companies were created, each of them big enough to fit easily into the *Fortune* magazine Top Fifty corporate list. New companies have been added to the manufacturing competition, notably Canadian-based Northern Telecom, now a major telecommunications-equipment producer. Old-line leaders such as ITT have had their telecommunications business swallowed up in corporate mergers.

The industry's patterns are still unsettled, with no clear view of the future. The pace of change has increased in recent years, creating unsettling implications for decisions on "freezing" the technologies to be used in the industry's hardware. The other ambiguous factor is the effect of a lack of political and social decision making on the overall pattern of the new information society, a situation that also inhibits economic decision making. We will examine these problems in decision making, particularly as they relate to changes in the three key networks — telephone, data, and broadcasting.

We begin with the phone system, and specifically AT&T. Although the company gave up its most familiar activity — local phone service — in the massive restructuring of its activities at the end of 1983, it remains the standard against which American telecommunications is measured. The events around the divestiture of the local Bell phone companies set the ground rules — and the opportunities — for a new communications framework in this country. The future impact of this divestiture will be examined more closely in the next chapter. Here we will look at the events leading up to it.

In her telephone operator skits, comedienne Lily Tomlin could tweak AT&T's corporate nose by telling her imaginary customers: "We're the phone company. We can do no wrong. We serve everyone from kings to presidents down to the scum of the earth." Most Americans were prepared to accept the Bell System's oft-repeated claim that it provided the best phone service in the world. (In defending its corporate actions during a 1981 court case, a Bell attorney referred to AT&T unblushingly as "the greatest enterprise on earth."[16]) It is probably true that if a decision had been made 30 years ago to entrust the construction of a full-service information utility in this country to AT&T, the system would be completed by now.

A good part of the technology for such a system has come, over the years, from AT&T's own research arm, the Bell Laboratories, certainly the most productive communications research facility on earth. AT&T was never shy in claiming jurisdiction in areas other than traditional voice-telephone service. In the 1920s, it actively sought to become a major developer of radio broadcasting in this country.[17] The company was prepared to move into commercial cable television networking in the 1950s until checked by the FCC.

In each of these instances a political decision prevented or limited AT&T's expansion into areas beyond its traditional service. Meanwhile, technology, economics, and politics were combining to create a new set of operational conditions for the vast Bell System and for a host of new competitors. On the one hand, traditional Bell control of long-distance circuits and the right of the company to install its own equipment was being eroded by government regulatory decisions designed to increase competition in these areas. The Justice Department brought a suit against AT&T in the early seventies over alleged antitrust violations, particularly in connection with the company's manufacturing affiliate, Western Electric. On the other hand, in the seventies, the company took the first steps to develop a strategy for increasing its share of the data communications market, the newest and fastest growing area in the industry. At the time, AT&T president Frederick Kappel declared that the company's revenues from data communications would eventually be greater than those from its traditional voice-telephone traffic. This seemed to many observers a long-shot prediction, but it is now well within the realm of possibility.[18]

In any event, the seventies marked the end of almost a half-century in which Bell's dominance over telephone services was the law of the land. The near-monopoly was raised to the status of dogma by Bell executives and their many supporters. The Bell argument was simple: The telephone system is a natural monopoly, since there has to be a centralized system for connecting phones with each other. Moreover, economics dictate a monopoly since a universal system cannot be built without cross-subsidization between high density profitable and low density unprofitable services.

Given the Bell System's generally commendable record in providing telephone services, it could be forgiven its sentimental boasts, usually spoken with a catch in the corporate throat, about getting a phone line up to the last house on the remotest mountain in the nation. AT&T claimed, several years before the divestiture, that it lost about seven dollars a month on its average telephone customer, a figure disputed by outside observers who suggested that it all depends on who's counting and what's being counted. The facts about telephone economics are very much in the eye of the beholder, an observation raised to high art by the platoons of phone company lawyers, government regulators, and public interest advocates in the interminable rounds of arguments about AT&T's rate structure. Beyond all the graphs and statistics, Bell's primary argument on behalf of its dominant position was that it worked. The claim was incorporated in a corporate slogan, "The system is the solution," widely advertised by Bell companies in the early eighties.

Whatever its virtues, Bell's case in favor of its quasi-monopoly was being passed up by events. A curious but revealing episode in the history of the company's defense of its position took place in 1976 with the introduction of congressional legislation designed to affirm (or as far as Bell was concerned, reaffirm) the company's telecommunications primacy. Known as the Consumer Communications Reform Act, the legislation proposed standards designed to avoid "unnecessary and wasteful duplication" in telecommunications. It specifically required Bell's competitors in long-distance services to prove that they would meet these standards. In other words, they had to prove, before introducing a new service in competition with Bell, that they could do better, a regulatory process that would be expensive and time consuming. It is a tribute to the political clout of AT&T and the independent phone companies that the legislation was cosponsored by 175 representatives and 17 senators. The bill never came up for a vote, which was, in turn, a tribute to the collective ability of the rest of the telecommunications industry to stymie it. The subject eventually moved into legislative limbo, following the introduction of more comprehensive proposals to revise the Communications Act of 1934 — a subject that will be examined in the next chapter.

AT&T was looking for political relief from a technological and economic reality whose time had come. The assault on its near-monopoly began in the late sixties with a series of relatively minor Federal Communications Commission decisions that set the tone for all that has happened since. In the first of these decisions, the so-called "Carterphone case" in 1968, the FCC determined that AT&T could no longer bar the use of telephone equipment of which it did not approve or in effect, any equipment not made by its Western Electric affiliate. The Carterphone was just such a piece of banned equipment, used for mobile telephone units. (With imperial *hauteur*, AT&T referred to such equipment as "foreign attachments.") The Commission ruled that customers could use such attachments, provided they did not harm the network technically. For the first time, other firms could compete with AT&T's manufacturing arm, Western Electric — a major breakthrough that opened the equipment industry to a new range of products and services.

A year later, the Commission allowed a new firm, MCI Telecommunications, to build and operate specialized microwave facilities offering private-line telephone service between Chicago and St. Louis and gave it the right to connect with the local phone company network within these cities. The service was directly competitive with (and cheaper than) AT&T's long-distance service. The FCC later authorized other specialized common carriers to operate similar networks. AT&T protested that these decisions violated its legal rights and, in particular, threatened the economics of consumer telephone service by skimming revenues from its profitable intercity traffic. In the corporate battles that ensued, MCI brought a suit against AT&T charging it with attempting to undermine MCI services by blocking access to Bell System local phones. In a 1980 verdict that rocked the industry, MCI was awarded $1.5 billion in damages by a federal district court.[19]

MCI and the other challengers pressed hard to expand their services in competition with Bell, but the going was not easy. At least one company that started off with high hopes, Datran Corporation, went into bankruptcy after several years. Most of the firms challenging Bell were corporate upstarts, new to the business. However, in January 1979, the Federal Communications Commission authorized an industry giant, ITT, to operate a national long-distance phone network linking 11 major cities from Boston to Los Angeles.

The new competition represented a very small threat to the Bell System's revenues at the time. The odds against the new firms capturing a significant share of AT&T's long-distance traffic were still limited. For example, in 1979, MCI's revenues were $144 million as against AT&T's $23.4 billion for long-distance services.

Nevertheless, the age of competition in telecommunications was plainly at hand. It began with voice-telephone service, but it rapidly expanded into data networking. The stakes were massive, affecting the shape and size of the United States information utility well into the next century. Given their importance in any strategy for the new information environment, the economic factors deserve a closer look.

The look begins with a quick review of the steps leading to the technological marriage of computers and communications. In simpler days, 25 years ago, most computers were "stand alone" machines; computation and communications were separate operations with no electronic links. In the sixties, they began to merge with computers that were linked to outside terminals. The result was the rapid growth of *time sharing*, computer power dispersed to multiple users however remote they may be from the mainframe machines. This was the beginning of computer networks, with terminals interacting with a central computational base. However, computation and communications technologies were still essentially separate and distinct.[20]

These distinctions have been steadily eroding in the past two decades. Computers are being used to switch both voice and data messages. Data processing services are moving rapidly toward *distributive networks*, in which the terminals possess memory and logic of their own, placing greater intelligence capability in the terminal rather than concentrating it in the computer mainframe. Thus, telephone equipment can be programmed to monitor toll usage and to perform billing and accounting functions.

In other words, computer capabilities are being built into the entire communications system. Microprocessors with memory capabilities are now commonplace in telephone exchange and private branch exchange (PBX) equipment. Digital data transmissions services are oriented toward computer uses without requiring *modems* — the attachments to telephones that permit connections to computers. In these and many other ways, the distinction between computation and communications are being blurred to the point that data communications are done by computers and network circuits that are, in effect, a single computation/communications machine.

Communiputers? Computercations? Compunication? Whatever this hybrid is called, it changes most of the old ways of storing and transmitting information. A new kind of business emerged in the seventies, and the rush was on to exploit its possibilities. Conspicuously absent from the initial rush was the Bell System. Critics cited this as another example of AT&T reluctance to shift to more efficient technologies, though many of these technologies were developed in its own Bell Labs. In Bell's defense, it is fair to note that the company was sitting on top of a massive communications network whose upgrading involved complex operational and financial problems. The equipment had to be amortized over a relatively long period of time. Writing it off early could have resulted in higher rates for all services. The arguments and counterarguments are not simply corporate fiscal games, however. The problem of continually outmoded technologies is a consideration in any information age strategy.

Whatever its reasons, Bell moved carefully into the high technology data network competition. From the mid-seventies on, however, the pace quickened. Bell Labs unveiled the so-called *transaction phone*, a credit card verification unit, among other things, that could be viewed as a type of computation device. AT&T also produced a new generation of telephone-connected data display terminals, beginning with "dumb" terminals and moving toward a sophisticated type called Dataspeed 40–4, which had enhanced computational capabilities. Following a series of legal challenges by other firms, Dataspeed was authorized by the FCC as a legitimate — and regulated — part of AT&T's operations.

The company also began promoting "network processing services," its euphemism for a store-and-forward message switch that IBM and other computer firms claimed was part of the data processing services and equipment market. Continuing their euphemistic course, AT&T executives spoke of a dial-up service (for instance, a voice answer-back service for reading bank balances) that, they said, was just delivering a message. Not so, retorted the computer firms. Such a service, they argued, is processing information, which is their bailiwick. Finally, AT&T moved into the satellite communications area, where there was the promise of access to high speed circuits for data communications. This access turned out to be somewhat less than immediate, however. The FCC delayed AT&T's use of satellites for data networks for several years in order to give other firms a chance to establish their own satellite operations without Bell's overwhelming presence. By mid-1979, the restrictions were lifted and Bell was ready to compete for what it regarded as its destined large share of business in the evolving integrated information utility. With classic simplicity, AT&T christened its project ACS — for Advanced Communications System.[21]

The technology to create the utility was available, but the political and economic means for bringing it about were considerably less clear. The 1982 divestiture agreement between AT&T and the Department of Justice was a critical, necessary step in clarifying the future pattern of American telecommunications.

We will take a closer look at this new pattern in the following chapter. Here we will focus on a related subject — the recent changes in the electronic information business where technology is erasing the distinctions between telecommunications and computer processing. The decade of the centralized mainframe computer is giving way to a decade of distributed computing networks. The emphasis is on flexible, lower cost processing of information at the point where it is to be used rather than in a distant computer center. The mainframe data business, providing centralized storage and data bank services, is still very much alive. General Electric was one of the pioneers in this profitable business. Sophisticated variations on networking from centralized data bases will continue to be an expanding business in the nineties.

One prospect, already well advanced abroad, is a videotext service, providing business firms and homes with access, usually via telephone lines, to many sources of data material displayed on a TV set or a computer terminal. Such systems are now being offered as a regular service to the public in Britain, France, Canada, and Japan. The French system, known as Minitel, provides access to several thousand "information providers," as the operators of data banks connected to the system are known. Mass videotext services have gotten off to a slower start in the United States, but they will be widely available by the mid-nineties.[22]

Meanwhile, the industry is concentrating on the immediate prospect of expanding distributed processing networks and services for business. Its goal is the automated workplace, the so-called "office of the future." For all of its oversold future, the integrated electronic office system is on the way. Office-of-the-future enthusiasts are fond of declaring that, while industrial productivity rose nearly 90 percent during the seventies, office productivity went up only 4 percent. Further, they add, average capital expenditure per office worker was only $2,000 compared with $25,000 for the factory worker. The figures are slightly suspect, as well as the apples-and-oranges comparison. It is true, nevertheless, that productivity had declined steadily in offices, which are a major part of the secondary, or bureaucratic, sector in the Department of Commerce's study of the information economy described earlier in this chapter. Whether machines can turn around, or even modify, the bureaucracies' devotion to Parkinson's Law on programmed inefficiency remains to be seen.[23] What is certain is that a multibillion-dollar industry is expanding, with its market focused on sophisticated office word-processing machines, terminals, long-distance facsimile equipment, phototypesetting machines, high-speed printers, and related communications gear. The business is dominated by such old-line equipment manufacturers as IBM, Xerox, and Wang, although there are many newcomers, including Kodak and a very aggressive group of Japanese firms.

This equipment, much of it linked to networks outside the office, is largely an electronic mail and storage system. In fact, over 85 percent of all first class postal service mail can be handled electronically. This includes bills and other business forms that now form the largest share of postal volume. The prospects for an electronic postal service are reinforced every time a piece of the new high technology office equipment is installed. Whether this network will be run by the postal service, by private firms, or by a combination of both is an important issue that has yet to be resolved.

One of the most dramatic changes in electronic mail will take place in the business community. It is called *electronic data interchange* (EDI), designed to reduce the massive amounts of routine business forms that move through the postal system and other channels. Although computers were intended to cut down on paperwork, they have in fact created more since they produce output that people want to see in hard copy.

EDI is designed to reduce this growing paper flow. It does this by standardizing the transfer of routine business transactions — invoices, shipping notices, and even payments — between computers in ways that eliminate, or at least reduce, the need for paper. The result is savings in time, clerical help, cash flow, and overloaded inventories. The Big Three auto makers — Ford, GM, and Chrysler — have embraced EDI enthusiastically, each requiring their suppliers to accept electronic invoices as they move toward on-line computerized purchasing. The U. S. Treasury Department plans to be virtually checkless by the early nineties by dealing with suppliers to government agencies electronically. In 1987, the department's check payments totalled $325 billion at a cost of 26 cents per check. Using its EDI system, this cost is reduced to three cents per check.[24]

Another technology that is challenging traditional postal services is the facsimile (fax) machine, which can send documents (including graphics) to other fax machines across regular telephone lines. An estimated two million of the machines will be installed annually in the early nineties.

The strategic industrial focus of the nineties will, however, be on semiconductors, the tiny chips that are the power modules of the new computers and most other information and communications hardware. They are, one industry expert declares, the crude oil of the post-industrial economy: "From a strategic point of view, this industry is sitting on the reserves that are necessary for the future growth of the economy." Semiconductor production began in the late sixties with a small group of innovative companies playing technological leapfrog with one another in the race to develop more efficient products. By the early eighties, the industry had moved into early middle age and many of the pioneering firms were being absorbed into larger corporations dependent on their products. Only seven of the 36 American semiconductor firms that began operations in the late sixties were still independently owned by 1980.[25]

Foreign competition is also an important factor in this shift. Japanese and European firms, supported by government resources, have mounted a serious effort to displace United States research leadership, eroding the two-thirds share of world markets held by American firms in 1980 to under 50 percent. The stakes are awesome. The electronics industry, increasingly dependent on chips, is now among the leading sectors of the global economy. By the end of the century it is expected to rival automobile production as the world's largest manufacturing industry.[26]

Electronics is also a volatile industry. Semiconductor research and production is readily transferable worldwide. Although American firms have been on the leading edge of semiconductor research, their competitive advantage for any single breakthrough usually dissipates within a year. Variations on their work, often in improved versions, appear on production lines overseas very quickly. Chips are the first truly global technology; no other primary scientific breakthrough has spread so far so fast.

One of the reasons for this is that chips can be made almost anywhere. The industry is not dependent on such traditional factors as natural resources (the basic ingredient is common sand) or transportation facilities — the annual global production can be shipped in a dozen or so cargo planes. The country producing the most semiconductor components at one point in the eighties was Malaysia, an otherwise unlikely prospect for high-tech industry. The reason was that production costs were lower there for American and other foreign firms.

The industry's history over the past two decades has been one of boom-and-bust cycles. Chip technology has gone through a dozen generational changes in that period. Individual companies have risen and fallen dramatically as their original "hot" chip technology is overtaken by another firm's even hotter one. Overall, the industry has been buffeted by erratic demand for its products. In good times, computer companies and other makers of electronic gear have bought chips by the bushel, only to cut back when the market or their product lines changed. The result was huge inventories of unsold chips, and the closing down of production lines. Gearing up for new production was time-consuming and expensive, often involving several years and the expenditure of $200 million.[27]

Complicating this process for U. S. firms was foreign competition, particularly from Japan. The Japanese chipmakers made their first inroads into the American market in 1979, when American producers were caught with low inventories at a time of rising demand. The Japanese quickly captured 40 percent of the domestic memory-chip market. They steadily expanded their position in the eighties through aggressive sales, leading to allegations of dumping at less than the cost of production. The result was to drive many U. S. producers out of the market. By the late eighties, Japanese firms controlled more than 80 percent of sales of memory chips, which are used on a mass scale in computers and a wide variety of consumer electronics products.[28] Their overall share of the American semiconductor market is, however, about fifteen percent.

Responding to industry complaints, the Reagan administration negotiated a 1987 semiconductor agreement with the Japanese government, designed to put a halt to dumping. It also aimed to increase U. S. chip sales in Japan, the only major country where American firms had been virtually excluded from the market. When the Japanese continued their dumping practices, the Reagan White House applied punitive tariffs on Japanese chip imports. This move had the unintended effect of harming many U. S. companies and other institutions that had become dependent on these imports. At one point, a group of state and local law enforcement agencies asked that the tariffs be modified in order to obtain computerized fingerprint identification systems they had ordered from Japan's NEC Corporation.[29]

Protectionist restrictions are usually not an effective way of dealing with trade problems. A more constructive American government action in the global chip competition has been to strengthen the prospects for more competitive semiconductor technology. This was done in 1987 with the founding of Sematech, the semiconductor industry's advanced technology consortium, with a sizable contribution of Federal funds. (Sematech and related developments are described on pp. 85–86.) In addition to the potential economic benefits of the Sematech project, national security factors are involved. A number of government and private-sector studies have warned of the dangers of becoming dependent on foreign semiconductor technology, particularly in its high-tech forms.[30]

The global "chip wars" will continue in the coming years. The Americans and Japanese will be the chief competitors in a market that could be valued at $150 billion annually by the end of the century. The Europeans will become more important contenders, in part as a re-suit of increased high-tech research expenditures by industry, national governments, and the European Communities regional organization. Further down the road, the Koreans are preparing to become formid-able new players in the global chip markets. The mass market for memory chips (DRAMs, dynamic random access memory semiconductors) will be particularly competitive as production shifts from the 256K DRAMs to one-megabit chips, which are four times more powerful.

In the late eighties, there were hopeful signs that the U. S. semiconductor industry had recovered from a 1985–86 slump, and was prepared to deal aggressively with expanded global competition in the nineties. The American advantage will probably be in what the London *Economist* calls ultra-tech research and production — the technological high end of the business.[31] The Japanese will, however, remain formidable competitors. At least one knowledgeable observer, Charles Ferguson of MIT's Center for Technology Policy and Industrial Devel-opment, believes that U. S. industry will have to reorganize itself further, with government support, to match the efficiencies of Japan's vertically-integrated semiconductor firms.[32]

One area in which United States dominance will be maintained for some time is in the collection and storage of specialized information — the so-called "data banks." The reason for this is simple: American firms began to gather up and store such information, as well as to dis-tribute it, usually for a profit, earlier than anyone else. The result has been to make this country the information bank of the world. No one knows how many data banks there are, since the industry's definitions are vague. The banks come in all sizes and purposes. The Medlars bank at the National Institute of Health provides doctors with summaries of the latest medical research, abstracted from over 2,000 journals.

Congress has a data bank to track the progress, or lack of it, for every bill introduced into the House or Senate. The National Technical Information Service in Springfield, Virginia, supplies material on over a million items of research funded by the federal government in recent years. A Canadian researcher has catalogued every known performance of Shakespeare's plays. The list goes on.

The data bank industry is increasingly dominated by a group of old-line publishing companies who have in recent years realized that they are really information handlers. These firms are beginning to put their print products into computers and to sell them as data. The *New York Times* took the lead with its "Information Bank," a computerized version of a newspaper morgue, containing all the information that has appeared in the paper since the late sixties, when the bank began.[33] The Information Bank has been expanded to include the contents of 60 other newspapers and magazines, which are also made available on terminals to customers throughout the country. And in 1981, the *Times* added a special Middle East data section to the bank. Other publishing firms that developed major data bank operations are Dow Jones, McGraw-Hill, Dun & Bradstreet, and the *Reader's Digest*. Meanwhile, other firms not usually associated with information services are moving into the field. One of these, Mead Data General, is part of a paper products company. It operates the Nexis network, an on-line service supplying business firms with a range of full-text material from major United States and foreign news agencies, magazines, newsletters, newspapers, and government publications.

The great unanswered question as these and other services proliferate is how, and when, they will be able to expand beyond the business market into the potentially lucrative home market. The basic technology, in the form of telephones, television sets, and cable systems, is already in place. However, the economic target, namely specific consumer needs, remains elusive. There was a rash of home teletext experiments in the early eighties, each supplying data services aimed to test potential interest. The tests were inconclusive at best.

By the end of the eighties, a number of new and more promising networks were in place. Dow Jones Co., the publisher of *The Wall Street Journal*, was an early videotext provider, delivering financial data and other information to homes and offices. The cable television industry has taken a latter-day interest in videotext services, after years of doubts about whether its customers would pay for them. The solution is to have the services supported by advertising. Small ads appear in the corner of the screen as viewers search out weather forecasts, traffic information, shopping guides, local-events listings, and the like.

One cable videotext channel, *Electra*, is an electronic newspaper, providing news, sports and other services 18 hours a day, seven days a week. Unlike conventional newspapers, Electra is continuously updated. Another cable channel, *Tempo*, is a video version of a traditional stock market ticker, supplying current quotations on 8,000 stocks, including over-the-counter issues. Each listing is color-coded, giving a quick indication of whether the stock is rising, falling, or unchanged.[34]

The steady expansion of consumer videotext is a step in the direction of what is being called "the electronic cottage" or the "smart home." It is a vision of houses wired up for a wide variety of electronics-based services, ranging from burglar-alarm security devices to audio, video, and computer equipment. New external services such as shopping-at-home and information-bank retrieval on television or computer monitors would be delivered by broadcast, satellite, telephone, or cable channels.

The Europeans and Japanese have taken a strong lead in planning for the expansion of smart-home services in the coming decade. The French are promoting *domotique*, their newly-coined word for the home technologies. The European Communities regional organization is supporting an Integrated Homes Systems (IHS) project to insure a common technical standard for home services throughout Europe. One economic survey projects a smart-home market of $12 billion annually in France, West Germany, Britain, Japan, and the United States by the mid-nineties.[35]

Despite these rosy predictions, the full-fledged electronic cottage is still a long-term goal rather than a near-term reality. The concept will develop and flourish as the result of economic competition between several technologies, each capable of delivering massive amounts of information to consumers. In the United States, the competition will involve the telephone and cable-television industries, each seeking to become the primary (and profitable) deliverers of the new services to homes.

New ways of storing and delivering information will add zest to the competition. One of the most promising technologies is the interactive compact disk (CDI). The audio compact disk is already displacing older long-playing records as the standard for music storage. Using the same laser-based digital technology, CDI does this and more, storing prodigious amounts of information in data, sound, and video forms. One small disc can hold the contents of a standard encyclopedia, with specific information called up within seconds, to be seen on a TV monitor or listened to on stereo speakers. Two global electronics firms, Philips of Holland and Sony of Japan, have licensed fifty-five companies to produce CDI hardware and software in anticipation of widespread introduction of their products in the early nineties.[36]

Data banks and other sectors of the information industry will expand rapidly during the nineties. There will be numerous shake-outs as technology and economics combine to challenge the competitive standings of both the old-line firms and the upstarts. The bulk of their business, and profits, will come from sales to other industries engaged in the massive reindustrialization process now underway. A still open question about the future of the information industry is whether there will be a *consumerization* of the market, in which goods and services will be supplied to the home. The answer will have an important effect on another telecommunications area—radio and TV broadcasting.

Until recently, radio and television were secure in their dominant position, supplying news and entertainment to a mass consumer market. Protected from the shocks of outside competition by benevolent government licensing and regulatory arrangements, the broadcasters prospered on their ability to provide advertisers with a range of audiences readily identified by age, sex, and income level in their programming tastes.

The debate on television's beneficent or baleful influences on American life will go on for a long time without conclusive results. What is clear is that the unchallenged dominance of commercial television and radio is coming to an end. During the eighties, the three major networks' share of the nation's television viewers slipped steadily. Television will continue to be a powerful influence in its present form for a long time, but at a slowly decreasing level. The reasons for the shift are complex. Contrary to the self-fulfilling prophecies of television's critics, there are few indications that people are getting bored with television or that their tastes are improving. There are other reasons why they are beginning to spend more time away from the television screen. One significant element, at least for daytime television, is that more women are working outside the home than ever before. Another is that competition for audience attention is being challenged by new communications channels and services.

The big three networks face growing competition from a range of specialized "fourth networks" that rely on satellite distribution of their programs. The most extensive of these grids is operated by the Public Broadcasting System (PBS) and National Public Radio (NPR). Both have used satellites since 1978 to provide their member stations with a broad mix of national and regional programs. The result has been to give local PBS and NPR stations more control over their programming choices, a major objective of public broadcasting. Another specialized network using satellites and microwave relays are the Spanish-language Univision stations serving what is becoming the largest ethnic minority in the nation. Univison (then known as the Spanish International Network) began feeding Hispanic programming to nine stations in 1977; part of its offerings come from Mexico's national network by direct relay from Mexico City. Another satellite network, the Christian Broadcasting Network (CBN), offers fundamentalist gospel programming from its headquarters in Virginia Beach, Virginia, to hundreds of cable systems throughout the country.

A highly successful "fourth network" servicing cable systems by satellite was developed in the late seventies by Ted Turner, a flamboyant Georgian, who controls, among other enterprises, television station WTBS in Atlanta. Turner has transformed WTBS into a "super station" through satellite transmission of its programs to cable systems throughout the country. Within months after he announced his plan in 1977, over 500 cable systems in 27 states applied to carry the WTBS signal.[37] By the end of 1980, the network had been extended to over 800 cable systems. Cable viewers got a new entertainment channel — mostly old films and TV reruns — while Turner's station extended its audience to several million additional households, with appropriate advertising revenue benefits. In 1980, Turner added the first cable news network to his operation. His success led to a number of other "super station" operations throughout the country.

The most dramatic proposal for new national networking involves direct-to-the-home satellite broadcasting. In 1981, Satellite Television Corporation, an affiliate of the Communication Satellite Corporation, was given approval by the FCC to plan such a service, with entertainment and other programming beamed directly to rooftop antennas. At the same time, eight other companies were given permission to develop similar services. The first satellite broadcast service began operation in November 1983 in the Indianapolis area, with others authorized for 1984.

All of these projects failed, primarily because the firms had misjudged the market for their product. Traditional network television was both free and readily available in most locations. Cable television already offered a range of entertainment programs similar to that promised by the DBS (direct broadcasting satellite) broadcasters. Perhaps more important, the DBS firms lost a considerable part of their potential audience through a development that none of them had foreseen. It was the dramatic increase in "backyard dishes," the satellite earth terminals that became a ubiquitous part of the American rural landscape in the eighties. From a few isolated installations at the beginning of the decade, the small terminals expanded in number to over 1.7 million by 1988, linked to homes that had been considered prime targets for marketing DBS services. The hopeful DBS entrepreneurs had lost a significant slice of their potential audience, a loss several new DBS ventures hope to recoup with proposed satellite networks in the nineties.

The backyard dishes were designed to pick up entertainment

program signals being transmitted to local cable systems by such enterprises as Home Box Office and the Disney Channel. Since the transmissions include recent Hollywood films, plus big sports events, the dishes were used as a relatively cheap and easy way to eavesdrop on popular programs. The problem was that the programming firms and cable operators saw this use of the backyard dishes as an illegal pirating of material that belonged to them. They sought legal and legislative relief on the grounds of violation of their property rights. More pragmatically, they proceeded to "scramble" their transmissions to make them unintelligible to the alleged pirates. This led in turn to the proliferation of unauthorized descrambling devices, designed to make the signals intelligible again.

The result was a curious episode involving information rights in conflict with property rights. The backyard-dish owners and their equipment suppliers argued First Amendment rights to pick up electronic signals from outer space. The program providers cited the need to protect their investment, together with compensation by dish owners for the talents of the writers, actors, and other creators of the programs. The issue was partially settled in 1988 by agreement to assure equitable access to scrambled satellite program by dish owners for a fee, combined with a promise by Federal authorities to crack down on the distribution of illegal descramblers.

After years of big promises and false starts, two other technologies — videotape and videodisc — moved into consumer markets in the eighties. The early lead for the vast market was taken by videotape machines, which permitted recording of television programs for later viewing and for showings of the expanding catalogue of old Hollywood movies being recycled once again. With a dozen major electronic companies vying for the business, prices for the recording machines dropped below the $500 mark, opening the prospects for mass market appeal, the results of which could revolutionize television and other home entertainment patterns as well as the film industry.[38] Over 50 million United States homes were equipped with videorecorders by 1988. One result is the increase in sales of blank videotapes used for copying movies. Americans bought tens of millions of blank tapes annually, while the film and television industries fretted about loss of control over their products.

The most important potential challenge to network television has been around, in a different form, for some time. It is cable television — originally known as CATV, for Cable Antenna Television. CATV dates back to the early fifties when hundreds of small systems were installed in suburban and rural areas to provide improved reception of over-the-air television programs from nearby cities. The equipment was simple: a tall antenna to catch the signal and a cable to relay it to subscriber homes. Broadcasters welcomed CATV, since it extended their audience range and, therefore, their advertising-revenue base. However, this CATV bonus has turned into a threat as cable operators began to supply other programming services.

After years of delayed promises of cable programming abundance, cable television services finally became a significant factor in the mid-seventies. The first successful national cable programmer was Home Box Office (HBO). A subsidiary of Time Inc., HBO began distributing current Hollywood films and sports events in 1973 to cable systems. It took the firm five years to turn its first profit, but by 1977 it had 800,000 subscribers on more than 370 cable systems across the country. Its success coincided with its inspired decision to distribute its programs by satellite, cutting its transmission costs significantly and allowing it to reach every cable system in the nation. The pay-television rush was on as other big media conglomerates elbowed their way to sign up cable systems for their films. The boom propelled the industry into an expansion that would have seemed visionary a decade before. By 1988, there were over 3,000 cable systems with over 40 million home "hook-ups." This represents a 50 percent penetration of all United States homes, with the prospect that 60 to 70 percent will be cable-connected by the end of the nineties. In the competitive scramble for cable franchises and home customers, cable companies have expanded their program offerings beyond pay television Hollywood films to other programs and services.

The fortunes of the cable and broadcasting industries in the coming years will be determined in part by their competitive struggle to be the primary suppliers of a new type of video technology. The technology is *high-definition television* (HDTV), a major advance on present-day television. HDTV provides greatly improved picture quality, with a doubling of the present monitor line count. It can operate with stereo sound on larger screens, including wall-mounted flat screens. There will be a data channel for subtitling, teletext, remote computer access, and other services. The primary attraction for consumers will be the near-photographic quality of the HDTV pictures. These features can be delivered to home sets by traditional broadcast stations, by satellite links, cable systems, or by fiber optic telephone lines. The collective futures of companies in these sectors will be profoundly affected by the outcome of the competition to become HDTV suppliers to American homes, schools, and other institutions. The stakes are high. In addition to the multibillion-dollar annual market in producing and distributing

HDTV programs, the American electronics equipment industry will be dealing with the profitable prospect that virtually every television set in the country will be replaced to accommodate the new technology in the coming years. They will face formidable competition from the Japanese, who are, for the present, the leaders in promoting HDTV research and product production.[39]

Cable television networks will probably emerge as a leading supplier of HDTV services. In large part, this will be the result of completing the immense job of supplying their multichannel cables to most American homes. Originally a suburban and exurban phenomenon, cable systems have now moved into the major cities. It has been an expensive transition. Since cable must be installed underground (rather than on telephone poles) in many urban areas, the cost of cabling city neighborhoods has been very high. In the competitive jockeying for market position, the cable industry has witnessed a bewildering pattern of mergers and amalgamations in recent years, prompted largely by the need for greater financial resources to play the urban cable game. Despite many delays, the job of cabling most major cities is now substantially finished.

The significance of this shift goes well beyond the cable industry's day-to-day focus on supplying Hollywood films and covering sports events. The new urban cable networks can help provide the missing links for the development of a full-service national communications utility. This is the information network marketplace envisioned by researcher Herbert Dordick and his colleagues in their studies of the economics of information services that were discussed in Chapter 2. The presence of high-capacity cable facilities in urban areas is critical to the development of an economically viable national network.

Most of the plans for expanding electronic information services to the mass consumer level are still in their early stages. Many of them will fall by the wayside, victims of poor management, inadequate technology, or financial anemia. Cable systems will compete with the telephone companies, the satellite networks feeding into small earth terminals, and other circuit providers in bringing the network to reality.

Success will depend primarily on economic decisions about the viability of the network. A new communications and information infrastructure is being built. The strategies for assuring that it will provide a full range of services, expanding the prospects for an informed postindustrial democracy, are still to be worked out. How does a society make wise decisions in this critical area? The answer is not clear. However, as war is too important to leave to the generals, so the future of the information society is too important to leave to IBM, AT&T, HBO, NBC, and the other private information powers.

NOTES

1. Robert LeBlanc et al., "Changes and Opportunities in Telecommunications," *Telecommunications Industry Monthly*, issued by Salomon Brothers, New York, 1 February 1978, p. 1.
2. "Communications," *Forbes*, 15 September 1977, p. 139.
3. "Technology — Elixir for U. S. Industry," *New York Times*, 28 September 1980, sect. 3, p. 1.
4. Eli Ginzburg, "The Professionalization of the U. S. Labor Force," *Scientific American*, March 1979, pp. 48–53.
5. "America Tries to Cure Its Innovation Blues," *The Economist* (London), 6 September 1980, p. 83.
6. John Dizard, "The Revolution in Telecommunications Finance," *Institutional Investor*, September 1979, p. 143.
7. "Why a service economy is no panacea," *Financial Times* (London), 22 May 1987, p. 10. See also "Services hurt by technology," *New York Times*, 29 June 1987, p. D–1.
8. George J. Stigler, "The Economics of Information," *Journal of Political Economy*, June 1961, p. 213.
9. Fritz Machlup, *The Production and Distribution of Knowledge in the United States* (Princeton, NJ: Princeton University Press, 1962).
10. U. S. Department of Commerce, *The Information Economy*, 9 vols. Office of Telecommunications, Special Publication 77–12, May 1977.
11. *Ibid.*, vol. 1, p. 2.
12. *Ibid.*, vol. 1, p. 3.
13. John R. Bermuth, "Value and Volume of Literacy," *Visible Language*, 12, no. 2 (Spring 1978): pp. 118–61.
14. Stephen S. Cohen and John Zysman, *Manufacturing Matters: the Myth of the Post-Industrial Economy* (Boston: Basic Books, 1987). See also "Manufacturers' gains seen lasting," *Washington Post*, 15 January 1988, p. F–1, summarizing a National Association of Manufacturers survey on the continued strength of the manufacturing sector.
15. Quoted in Gerald D. Rosen, "Communications Dog Fight," *Dun's Review*, June 1977, p. 18.
16. "Government, AT&T Fires First Salvos at Trial," *New York Times*, 16 January 1981, p. D–3.
17. Erik Barnouw, *Tube of Plenty* (New York: Oxford University Press, 1975), pp. 43–50.
18. Mr. Kappel's prediction was reported in "On the Head of a Pin," *Forbes*, 15 September 1976, p. 32.
19. "High Stakes in Bell-MCI Case," *New York Times*, 13 June 1980, p. D–1.
20. Manley R. Irwin, "Where Do Computers Leave Off and Communications Begin?", *Telephone Engineering and Management*, 15 January 1976, p. 30.
21. "Innovation: Key to Bell's Plans," *New York Times*, 16 July 1979, p. D–1. For a history of the Bell System's research activities, see Prescott C. Mabon, *Mission Communications: The Story of the Bell Laboratories*, published by Bell Laboratories in 1975.

22. "Teletext is growing," *New York Times*, 22 November 1987, p. 34.
23. Jon Stewart, "Computer Shock," *Saturday Review*, 23 June 1979, p. 14.
24. Jack B. Rochester, "There's a Rosy Future in EDI," *CIO Magazine*, January/February 1988, pp. 21–27.
25. "Can Semiconductors Survive Big Business," *Business Week*, 3 December 1979, p. 66.
26. Colin Norman, "The International Stake in Microelectronics," *Technology Review*, January 1981, p. 40.
27. "Computer firms hurt by shortage of chips," *Washington Post*, 21 February 1988, p. H–2.
28. "Chip Shop of the World," *New Scientist* (London), 15 August 1985, pp. 28–31.
29. "Many seek exemptions at Japan tariff hearings," *New York Times*, 13 April 1987, p. D–1.
30. "Falling Chips: Is a Big Federal Role the Way to Revitalize Semiconductor Firms?" *Wall Street Journal*, 17 February 1987, p. 1.
31. "High Technology: the Clash of the Titans," *Economist* (London), 23 August 1986. Special supplement on the Japanese-American rivalry in advanced technologies.
32. Charles H. Ferguson, "Sink or Swim With Semiconductors," *New York Times*, 18 August 1987, p. 26.
33. Anthony Smith, "All the News That Fits in the Databank," *Saturday Review*, 23 June 1979, pp. 18–19.
34. "Teletext Use Is Growing," *New York Times*, 22 November 1987, p. H–34.
35. "Home Smart Home," *Financial Times* (London), 22 January 1988, p. 13.
36. "Computer-disc Companies Test New Frontiers," *High Technology Business*, February 1988, p. 18.
37. "Superstation Breakthrough," *Broadcasting*, 30 October 1978, p. 25.
38. "How a Video Revolution is Shaping the Future of Film," *New York Times*, 23 November 1980, p. D–1.
39. "How Soon the Supertelly?," *Economist* (London), 30 January 1988, pp. 70–71. See also "HDTV: Progress Report on Television's Next Quantum Leap," *Broadcasting*, 26 October 1987, pp. 63–74.

CHAPTER 6

The Day All Bell Broke Loose

Future historians trying to date the symbolic beginning of the American post-industrial era will likely do no better than to pick January 8, 1982. On that day, a large part of the pattern of the evolving United States information age was suddenly put in place.

The central event was undramatic, consisting of two announcements from the Department of Justice in Washington. Each described the disposition of an antitrust suit, the first involving AT&T, the second, IBM. Until that cold January morning, the two firms were clearly the predominant forces in American communications and information. They will continue to play major roles for a long time to come. However, the 1982 antitrust decisions have radically changed the form and direction of the U. S. communications and information sectors by opening them up to a much wider array of competitive forces.

Of the two firms, AT&T was more noticeably affected. The company had built and operated the basic national telecommunications system during the 20th century, benefiting from the Communications Act of 1934, which had given legal status to its monopoly position. The 1982 decision ended this particular protection along with the era to which it belonged.

The decision was sweeping. It entailed an agreement (technically, a consent decree) with AT&T on a plan for reorganizing the company. The firm was to be divested of all of its local telephone operations. In exchange, it was allowed to compete in communications and information activities previously closed to it. Moreover, the Justice Department dropped an expensive, long-running antitrust suit against the company. As one wag put it at the time, it was "the day all Bell broke loose."[1]

In a separate but parallel action, the Justice Department dealt with another long-standing antitrust case, the one against IBM. For a generation, Big Blue had been recognized, here and abroad, as the front-runner in the computer industry. Indeed, the antitrust suit against IBM was intended to test whether the company so dominated the industry as to unfairly stifle competition. In the jargon of the times, was IBM a "good monopoly" or not? In its January 1982 decision, the Department of Justice came down on the side of goodness, actually dismissing its own case as being "without merit." In effect, the decision removed the threat that IBM might be split into component parts, ending the integrated operational pattern that had been the key to its success.

At first glance, the two decisions appeared to be countervailing. One broke up the largest company on earth; the other affirmed that an equally dominant firm should remain in one piece. Yet, the decisions were, in fact, compatible and coherent. Taken together, they have given shape to the national framework within which an advanced information utility would be built.

Changing technology forced the two decisions. For years, the nation's political and economic institutions had been straining to cope with the new communications and information technologies, attempting to channel them to meet social needs. But the new communications capabilities were so vast that they did not fit into familiar channels of the policy process. Long-standing ways of dealing with contending political issues did not work. Economic issues arising from the new technologies also made old procedures obsolete. The future of the communications and information sectors was clouded by the lack of policy decision and direction.

In the case of AT&T, the January 1982 divestiture decision represented the culmination of decades of contention over the balancing of public interest concerns with the complex organizational needs of the company. For a short period during World War I, the firm had been nationalized. However, even in those early years, AT&T had sufficient political power to support its claim that it could operate more efficiently as a private firm. It also promised better service of public interests as a privileged firm. This promise was well kept, largely because of the vision of one of the company's early presidents, Theodore Vail. Vail saw the importance of developing the phone network as an integrated national service. He directed the consolidation of hundreds of smaller companies into the Bell System and the development of efficient long-distance service. Alexander Graham Bell may have invented the telephone, but Theodore Vail created the telephone network.

The price of avoiding nationalization was the acceptance of federal and local regulation, together with almost constant probing into phone company operations. During the 1930s, New Deal investigators carried out extensive studies of Western Electric, the Bell System's captive equipment supplier. In 1949, the Department of Justice instituted the first suit to break up the company. The outcome, after years of legal wrangling, was a 1956 consent decree allowing the company to remain in one piece, but stipulating that its operations be limited to essential telephone business. At the time, this decision seemed to favor the company. No one foresaw the later growth of the computer-based data communications sector.

Meanwhile, the Bell system flourished with the postwar economic boom, aided by an impressive range of technological breakthroughs. Most of these research developments came from the Bell Laboratories, the firm's in-house research arm. The Labs were responsible in whole or in part for the transistor, communications satellites, silicon chips, fiber optic cable, and advanced small computers, among other innovations. Despite occasional complaints from government regulators and consumer groups, AT&T's future as *the* phone company remained secure. Throughout this era, AT&T could boast that it provided the best telephone service in the world.[2]

However, events were to modify this placid optimism. First came a series of government regulations curtailing the firm's near monopoly in two major areas, equipment supply and long-distance service. Western Electric, AT&T's equipment manufacturing subsidiary, took the initial blow. In 1968, the Federal Communications Commission decided to permit the use of a piece of non-Western Electric equipment known as the Carterphone in the Bell network. This was a move toward ending the AT&T rule that only Western Electric equipment could be used in the Bell network. A second assault on AT&T's monopoly position came in the area of long-distance operations. In 1970, the FCC voted to permit other companies to compete with AT&T in inter-city long-distance service.

These newly competitive intrusions actually had little impact on the Bell System stronghold at the time. Although the Carterphone decision spawned a new set of competitors, Western Electric maintained its position as the largest producer of telecommunications products in the world. In the long-distance field, competition did not seriously undermine AT&T revenues, despite the aggressive efforts of MCI and the other firms moving into the market.

Gradually, however, subtle modifications in regulations and the gathering momentum in technology changed the climate of operations in information and communications. The change was obvious by the mid-seventies when the corporate perceptions of AT&T and IBM about the new environment began to merge. Previously, the two firms operated in quite separate spheres and each clearly held control within its own. IBM made large computers and dominated two-thirds of the market, leaving the remainder to be divided among a number of smaller manufacturers. (In the industry, this arrangement was known as "Snow White and the Seven Dwarfs.") At the same time, in a distinctly different market, AT&T and its local operating companies were engaged primarily in the business of voice-telephone service. Here, the Bell System (and some independent local phone companies) were responsible for over 90 percent of domestic communications revenues. When IBM wanted communications lines to link its computers, it went to AT&T. When AT&T wanted a computer, it went to IBM or one of the Seven Dwarfs.

What changed the picture was not primarily the result of new government rules or growing competition. Rather, advancing technologies, largely promoted by the two master firms themselves, broke through the bounds of old organizational structures. In the seventies, AT&T and IBM each looked down its respective corporate road, and saw the need for new strategies to match the changed reality. AT&T viewed the prospects for computer-based data networking in its future. IBM, looking in the same direction, saw the need to move into the telecommunications networking business as a requirement for protecting its overall hardware and software marketing interests.

Even before the January 1982 Department of Justice decisions, the two firms began to adapt their strategies to these new perceptions. The decisions reinforced these strategies.

Attempting to head off the threat of a government-ordered breakup in the late seventies, AT&T reorganized its operations into two separate entities — one for its older regulated telecommunications business, and a new one for its ventures in unregulated data communications. The latter would operate without subsidies from the firm's regulated business.

"We are going to draw a bead on the information business," AT&T chairman Charles Brown declared in 1980.[3] The strategy was designed to allow the company to break out of the constraints imposed on it by the consent decree of 1956. The decree had effectively prohibited the firm from dealing in the growing business of "smart" computer terminals or in the data processing field.

The objective was to found a "new Bell," designed by the company itself. However, the proposed reorganization was taking place in the shadow of an antitrust suit filed by the Department of Justice in 1974. Like its 1949 predecessor, the suit threatened to split up the company. Only this time, the company faced a significantly different opposition. In 1949, Bell was up against the government. This opponent was formidable enough, but given the company's rich heritage of political connections and its battalions of lawyers, it was able to avoid dismemberment.

By 1974, conditions had changed. The enthusiasm of the Justice Department's antitrust lawyers for splitting up the company remained undiminished. Now, they were abetted by a steadily increasing number of companies that were, or wanted to be, competitors in the expanding telecommunications equipment and services markets. The lobbying efforts of these ambitious new firms, added to the persistence of the Justice Department, proved overwhelming even for the largest private organization in the world. The final result of the contest was the 1982 divestiture of AT&T, which broke up the company.[4]

Meanwhile, IBM spent the seventies implementing its strategy of moving into the telecommunications business, which it saw as a natural extension of its computer and data processing operations. Big Blue announced its plan for a national data communications network in 1977. Partners in the venture were Comsat General (an affiliate of the Communications Satellite Corporation) and the Aetna Life Insurance Company. Comsat General's participation was based on the network's special use of a new technology: It was the first extensive grid to rely solely on satellite links. Called Satellite Business Systems (SBS), the new venture had an initial capital investment of over $400 million. Its network, inaugurated in 1981, was designed to link small earth station terminals throughout the United States via its own satellites.

Originally, it was expected that SBS's first customers would be big corporations from among the Fortune 500 group, those large enough to make use of the system to facilitate their own internal communications. SBS could give both financial and technical advantages to such corporations in expediting their internal operations. With its all-digital format, the SBS network could handle voice, high speed data, facsimile, and video on an integrated basis. By bundling a wide variety of these services and, pointedly, bypassing both local and long-distance telephone networks, SBS held out the promise of reducing corporate communications costs.

This strategy of concentrating on large customers proved to be a miscalculation. The Fortune 500 group did not come flocking to SBS in the numbers expected. Marketing strategy was, therefore, changed, and the network's services were adapted to attract smaller business customers. Later, even home customers were being sought through a separate consumer telephone service.

Under sponsorship by any group with lesser resources than IBM and its two partners, the SBS project would have been an enormous gamble. For IBM, participation in the project was within the guidelines of its corporate philosophy. Swallowing a natural aversion to government regulation, IBM recognized the need to operate as a regulated common carrier (via SBS) rather than run the risk of losing control over an essential element of its long-range computer market by being dependent on AT&T and other carriers. This reflected the hallowed IBM principle of maintaining total end-to-end control over its operations. In the end, SBS was a major disappointment for IBM. It sold out its essential interests in the venture to MCI.

Even while stretching to claim its place in the new network technologies, IBM was wrestling with changes inside the computer business. IBM's traditional strength in large mainframe machines remained essentially unchallenged, despite inroads by foreign and domestic competitors. The new threat came from the small machines — the minicomputers. This was a market that IBM had not aggressively pursued even when signs showed that low price small machines could begin to replace IBM products at the lower end of its line and also create a new market for office, school, and home uses.

Was Big Blue too big and unwieldy to make the turnaround to mass marketing consumer products and services? The answer was complicated by the Department of Justice antitrust suit, which had been working its way through the court system since the early seventies. IBM faced a possible dismantling of its vertically integrated operations. Competitors argued in favor of breaking up the company on the grounds that its research, production, and marketing practices inhibited competitive growth in the industry. IBM replied that it would be penalized for success if such a breakup should be mandated. The court case dragged on, employing platoons of lawyers and producing literally tons of documents.

Then, on the morning of January 8, 1982, the Justice Department made two separate announcements on the future of IBM and AT&T, and, by extension, the United States information-based economy. For IBM, the decision was simply to drop the case as being without merit. For AT&T, the decision was considerably more complicated.

Years will pass before any balanced judgment can be made on the wisdom of the 1982 decisions. Already, a range of contentious opinions are being expressed. Were the decisions a Reaganite concession to big business, selling out consumer interests? Or did they herald the opening of a golden age, a push-button paradise, as promised in corporate advertising? Whatever the final judgment on them, the decisions are in effect. American society is in for a long period of sorting out the implications at many different levels. The sorting out will take place in political arenas like Congress, as well as the courts and regulatory agencies like the FCC, the Federal Trade Commission, and the Securities & Exchange Commission. It will occur, too, in the financial community, with enormous sums of money going toward expanding telecommunications and information resources in a more competitive environment.

Meanwhile, technology and economics have brought about a convergence of the corporate sightlines of IBM and AT&T. The two firms have become increasingly competitive with one another as each moves on toward more fully integrated communications/information operations. Both are entering uncharted areas of sophisticated equipment and services for automated workplaces — offices, factories, schools, and laboratories. They are also looking at the household market, keenly aware that the average person uses the telephone only 15 minutes a day — a striking underutilization.[5] AT&T, IBM and their competitors are developing strategies for filling the hours of unused capacity with new and potentially lucrative services.

It is useful to look more closely at the ways in which the 1982 Department of Justice decisions have affected IBM, AT&T, the former Bell System local companies, and the rising number of competing firms.

AT&T. When the divestiture agreement was announced in 1982, the company was faced with the formidable problem of a transition from a monopoly of imperial proportions to a new kind of competitive business. By court order, the divestiture had to take place within two years. There were no precedents to serve as guides. The closest parallel was the breakup of the Standard Oil Company early in the century, but the circumstances were not comparable in size or complexity. AT&T's revenues in 1983, its last year as an integrated company, were over $65 billion — more than the individual gross national products of over a hundred nations. The process of breaking up the Bell System underscored the myriad ways in which the system affected every American.

Millions of words have been written about the AT&T reorganization, touching on financial, technical, managerial, political, and social aspects of the event. Each of these aspects is important, but the critical element for AT&T has been the psychological turnaround the company has had to undergo.[6] The Bell System was a service organization with a well-honed tradition of solid reliability. The rumblings of competition preceding the divestiture had the effect of slowly forcing the firm to reconsider its service-oriented philosophy.

Although AT&T maintained its overall dominance in most telecommunications areas, new competitors made inroads in particular sectors. The most notable example of this during the seventies was the lucrative market for PABX office telephone equipment. From a position of almost total monopoly of this market, Bell's manufacturing affiliate, Western Electric, fell to hardly a half market share by the end of the decade, with further declines during the eighties.

As the brisk breeze of the new competition began to be felt, AT&T and the local phone companies discovered marketing. Before the divestiture agreement, the local companies did not have a sales force in the accepted sense of the term. They had "service representatives" who dealt with the public too often with a friendly but firm "Ma Bell knows best" attitude.[7]

The 1982 diverstiture decision gave AT&T what it said it wanted — a chance to compete fully in the expanding telecommunications and information markets. However, its new marketing organization had not advanced quickly enough to match the formidable task of moving the world's largest communications operation into the rough-and-ready competitive environment. Almost every realistic estimate of AT&T's future has cited the firm's ability to make a full competitive turnaround as the critical factor. "The toughest thing to change is corporate culture, and AT&T's corporate culture was not designed for competition," said one former Bell executive in 1983. But there were those who echoed the feelings of another watcher: "Anyone who discounts AT&T and Western Electric is crazy."[8]

By January 1984, when the divestiture agreement came into full force, AT&T had reorganized itself into several basic units.

- *AT&T Communications*. The largest of the new units, managing the traditional long-distance phone business.
- *AT&T Information Systems*. Charged with moving the company into data-related equipment and services.
- *Western Electric and the Bell Laboratories*. Each retained its public identity; this speeds product development and facilitates marketing, both directly and through third parties. (Sears Roebuck, for instance, has become an important outlet for Western Electric consumer products.)
- *AT&T International*. Responsible for global marketing of products and services — an area in which the company had not been active for over fifty years.

The new units were organized to be as self-contained as possible, with the individual research, manufacturing, and marketing resources they needed. The plan looked good on paper, but it soon became clear that it was not working well. Except for the core telephone business, the company was in trouble. The new computer division was losing large amounts of money; the international division's record was similarly unpromising. Most other nontelephone units were not performing up to expectations.

In 1987, the firm's aggressive new chairman, James Olson, tore up the organizational charts and replaced them with a plan that he called the "Single Enterprise Strategy." AT&T would be leaner, meaner, and, above all, more competitive. Most of the firm's operating units were reorganized. There were massive lay-offs, involving 27,000 employees in one short period. The company's 30 separate purchasing systems were consolidated into eight. Six networks, serving 30,000 in-house computer terminals, were replaced by a single network in 1988. After years of confusion. AT&T seemed to be on its way toward its earlier goal of being a full-service competitive player in the new post-industrial economy. Ma Bell, the comfortable personification of the old-line telephone company, had finally been retired.[9]

AT&T Communications — the long-distance phone business — remains the most solid pillar in the new corporate structure. In the early years of the reorganized company, it provided nearly two-thirds of AT&T's revenues and most of its profits. In large part, this is because long distance is a booming business. A generation of Americans has grown up in a communications environment in which long-distance phone calls are taken for granted as a preferred means of casual, daily communication. Long-distance calling is now only a push button away. And for most people, long-distance means AT&T, still the Old Reliable, standing tall above a flourishing undergrowth of young competitors. This traditional image of dependability was the theme of the company's post-divestiture long-distance advertising. Hollywood actors in television ads were seen affectionately patting their phones, and reminding viewers that AT&T was the phone company they could count on to get the message to Aunt Matilda out there in Red Oak, Iowa.

The argument was very persuasive. In the early years after the divestiture, none of AT&T's competitors in the long-distance business could promise to reach every phone in the country. Nevertheless, this disadvantage did not inhibit the competition from full-fledged campaigns to expand their share of the market, the overwhelming bulk of which involved traffic between cities and towns somewhat larger and more easily served than Red Oak.

The divestiture agreement did, in fact, open up important new advantages for AT&T's competitors. Their customers, for example, were no longer required to use the cumbersomely long codes formerly needed to get into long-distance telephone systems. The 1984 divestiture agreement ended this practice. Meanwhile, the challengers stepped up their efforts to capture a larger share of AT&T's long-distance business. To assist them, the Federal Communications Commission authorized a procedure whereby home telephone users would vote for their preferred long-distance company. The results were disconcerting to AT&T's competitors; over 80 percent of those polled chose the Old Reliable. Keeping up with AT&T since then has been difficult for these firms. Their profit margins have often been paper-thin (and in some instances nonexistent) as they adjusted their rates in the wake of the six reductions AT&T made in its long-distance rates during the four years after the 1984 divestiture.[10]

To compensate for their relatively weak showing in the home telephone market, MCI, GTE-Sprint, and other competitors have shifted their market focus toward sophisticated business voice and data transmission — a $36 billion market in 1988 that is growing at almost 10 percent annually. MCI, for instance, took the lead in 1987 in creating a national supercomputer network, linking six National Science Foundation supercomputing centers with other research facilities. Increasingly, the smaller long-distance firms will be competing among themselves and with AT&T for similar specialized services.

The rewards for challenging AT&T's long-distance dominance are substantial. From roughly $45 billion at the time of divestiture, long-distance revenues are expected to rise to $100 billion in the early nineties. In 1984, AT&T's competitors had about 8 percent of long-distance traffic. Eventually, their share may stabilize at about 25 percent. Their gain will result partly from aggressive competition, but it will also be, in part, the consequence of curious twists in the United States antitrust law. In effect, AT&T will have to permit a decrease in its share of the market as proof of its willingness to adjust to a significant level of competition. If the expected decrease should fail to take place, the company could be dragged back into court, charged with violation of the conditions of the divestiture.

No matter how the market stabilizes, no one expects that AT&T will give up more of its traditional telephone business than is necessary to avoid a repetition of the legal battles of the past 15 years. Despite the inroads made by other firms in long-distance markets, AT&T remains a formidable competitor. No other telecommunications organization approaches the research capabilities of the Bell Labs or the manufacturing range of Western Electric. For all its conservatism, AT&T has experimented with almost every technical prospect available in the field.[11]

AT&T's long-term health will depend on how it expands beyond its plain-old-telephone base into high tech communications and information operations. This will take in a wide scope of activities, but the focus will be the company's ability to move in two highly competitive areas — computers and integrated office communications. In the latter field, AT&T's inability to maintain its traditional lead in PABX development was an ominous sign, according to industry observers. However, in recent years, the company has developed advanced office products based on a PABX telephone switch, including word processing, building maintenance controls, and local area networks.

The test of AT&T's information age future, however, will be how it handles its computer strategy. Only IBM has more research and development experience in this area. The inclusion of computer production and related services in AT&T's post-divestiture pattern signaled, more than any other single decision, that the company was challenging the entire information industry. But, as noted above, the firm's computer plans ran into trouble. Industry observers generally regarded as a strategic mistake its decision to entrust its small-computer production to Olivetti, the big Italian electronics firm. Although the product was good, sales were sluggish.

Following the 1987 reorganization, AT&T officials focused their attention on the faltering computer division. Their goal was to position the firm to deal with the changes that will take place in the computer industry in the nineties. For a dozen years, computer data processing consisted of three tiers — the large mainframe machines in data centers, minicomputers for local office needs, and the personal computer on the desk.

In the nineties, the mainframes will continue to be important for organizations with very large computing chores. The use of personal computers will expand, becoming a ubiquitous consumer item in homes, schools, and other locations.

If the best industry strategists are right, it is the minicomputer that will begin to disappear in the nineties. This will be the result of a new convergence of technological and economic forces that are reshaping the computer business from top to bottom. The changes will have particular effect on those firms such as Digital Equipment (DEC) and Wang, which have made their reputations (and profits) in innovative microcomputer products since the mid-seventies. Their success by any standard has been spectacular; in the late eighties, DEC had annual global revenues of over nine billion dollars, and a growth rate of 25 percent a year, a record considerably better than that of IBM.

This pattern is changing as present minicomputer technology is overtaken by more powerful versions, developed by upstart companies that are recent entrants into the computer business. Their product is a new kind of computer, the multi-microprocessor system. Multiprocessing involves closely integrating more than one processor in a machine in ways that expand the range of system performances, upgrade the systems, and do a job cheaper and faster. The primary use of the new machines, at least initially, will be as workstations in businesses such as engineering or chemicals that deal with complex computing problems. John Levinson, chief computer analyst for the brokerage firm of Goldman Sachs, identified 1988 as the year when the new multiprocessor systems began to surpass minicomputers in efficiency. These new systems will take over the market in between the very big mainframes and the personal computers.

This shift in computer technology is forcing major changes in the industry as present leaders adjust strategies and products to new competition. Some established companies will fail; others are forging mergers and other arrangements with former competitors. And all of them are looking at AT&T and IBM to see how they are dealing with the changes.

First AT&T. The company signalled its intention in 1988 to become a major player in the multiprocessor sweepstakes. It announced that it was buying a 20 percent share of Sun Microsystems, a California-based maker of multiprocessor workstations. The decision represented something of a corporate turnaround for AT&T. In effect, it was an admission by the company that it would have to reach out beyond its own considerable research facilities to smaller entrepreneurial firms for technical assistance in the computing field. Sun Microsystems is such a company, with an advanced product (a "hot box," in the industry's phrase), and a proven management record.

Software was a critical element in AT&T's decision to invest in Sun. The California company is one of dozens licensed to use AT&T's Unix computer operating system. Operating systems are described variously as the traffic cop or orchestra conductor directing the passage of data through a computer's central processing unit. Unix can run different software programs on many different makes of computers. Most proprietary operating systems cannot do this. During the eighties, customers were increasingly reluctant to become locked into a single incompatible system. The result was a big push away from proprietary systems toward standardized ones. This happened in personal computers, where almost all manufacturers standardized around the MS-DOS system developed by Microsoft.

This change has happened more slowly in larger computers. Two systems are vying to become the standard. One is OS/2, the successor to MS-DOS. The other is AT&T's Unix. A critical element in AT&T's

decision to invest in Sun Microsystems was an agreement to develop advanced Unix technology solely with Sun. The move was seen by some of AT&T's competitors as an attempt to outflank them in developing and marketing Unix technology. They have been wary, despite AT&T's assurances to the contrary, that the company will make Unix a proprietary product, usable only on AT&T and Sun machines. Meanwhile, most of these competitors (including IBM) are offering Unix-based versions of their products in order to meet customer demands for a proven operating system.

The marketing impacts of these decisions are enormous. One industry estimate is that Unix-based machines will account for a third of the worldwide market for mid-range ($12,000–$350,000) computers by 1992, up from 24 percent in 1987 and two percent in 1982. Unix technology was given an important boost in 1987 when the U.S. Air Force specified it as a requirement for all bidders on a $4.2 billion project to upgrade its computer operations — the largest single U. S. government computer purchase to date. This and similar decisions are making AT&T an even more important force in the world computer industry, 30 years after it developed Unix technology.[12]

Some questions remain about AT&T's ability to compete effectively in new fields. For generations, the firm's reputation rested on equipment designed with all kinds of safeguards against failure. It was an expensive strategy, that could only be indulged in by a protected monopoly assured of its profits. In the new market, most equipment is designed with less concern for long-term stolidity than for short-term consumer appeal. Evidence of this market trend is to be seen in the stripped-down telephones, mostly from the Far East, which have flooded the United States consumer outlets in recent years. Over 20 million telephone instruments were imported in 1983 alone. They are a far cry from AT&T standards, but they are cheap and, after a fashion, they work. Although AT&T has made significant strides in responding to changing consumer demands, it is relying on its reputation for equipment and service reliability to meet the new competition in the coming years.

Another major initiative by AT&T is its decision to move into international markets. The company set its sights high: "We aim to be among the three largest suppliers anywhere we go," AT&T International's vice chairman, James Olson, declared in 1984.[13] There is an element of bravado in the statement since the international telecommunications and services markets play by different rules than those at home. In most countries, telecommunications is a protected sector, with the government operating a network whose equipment needs are met by local industry as much as possible. Consequently, most American equipment companies have not competed vigorously for this business in the past, concentrating instead on the large and lucrative North American market. The exception was ITT, most of whose operations had been located abroad since early in the century.

Although protectionism is still a strong factor in telecommunications abroad, the situation is changing. The United States government is putting pressure on its industrial allies to open their markets to American products and services. Japan — the largest single telecommunications market abroad — has been a target for these efforts, with some initial success. Governments in less-developed countries will need advanced equipment from American firms to upgrade their communications and information facilities. Hence, the overseas market is now of vital interest to the Americans eager for their share of the $1.5 trillion that will be spent on expanding the world network in the next decade. At the same time, American companies are facing increasing competition in this country as foreign telecommunications firms move into the North American market, which is still the largest in the world. Competing in the international market has become a necessary counter-strategy for American companies.

AT&T is the newest major player in this game. Until the late seventies when it set set up its overseas affiliate, AT&T International, it had not operated directly in foreign countries for over 50 years. Such is the global mystique surrounding the company that its entry into the market has had the effect of defining a new era in the way in which the world communications grid will be assembled. For most foreign observers, the puzzling question was why AT&T had not gone into overseas operations earlier. Its Bell Laboratories research strength, Western Electric's production capacity, and the firm's unrivalled financial resources have always made it a strong potential international force. Moreover, the company has had business connections with telecommunications organizations throughout the world as a result of its long-distance telephone operations.[14]

Despite its potential, AT&T's overseas push did not make a strong initial impression. In these early years, AT&T was not a major challenger to the established leaders — ITT, L. M. Ericsson of Sweden, CIT-Alcatel of France, West Germany's Siemens, and the ubiquitous Japanese. This rather slow start reflected the difficulties of breaking into a strongly-entrenched marketing pattern that is not susceptible to easy assault by newcomers, even one with AT&T's resources.

In developing its overseas marketing organization, AT&T started from scratch. To compensate for this initial handicap, the company established links with foreign telecommunications firms that already had global marketing capabilities. The most important of these arrangements was completed in 1983 when the firm announced a joint venture with

Philips, the Dutch electronics multinational. As noted above, the company has an interest in Italy's Olivetti Corp. for both manufacturing and marketing purposes. AT&T also has strong links with East Asian electronics firms, notably in Japan, Taiwan, and Korea. By 1988, the company's entire production of telephone sets, from the Mickey Mouse model on up, had been transferred abroad, mostly to Asia.

In the coming years, AT&T's international strategy will focus on the advanced office equipment market, including computers. It is the fastest growing electronic market, one in which American firms have taken a strong global lead in both technology and marketing. With its new overseas partners, AT&T brings powerful resources to the competition. This strategy also has another intriguing aspect: it puts the firm in direct global competition with IBM, the other dominant American player in this field.

Meanwhile, in this country, the 22 local Bell telephone companies have beeen adapting to the opportunities — and uncertainties — of life beyond their longtime dependence on AT&T. In 1983, they organized themselves into seven regional Bell holding companies, which quickly were dubbed the Baby Bells. Each of the seven was large enough to be included immediately in the top 10 percent of the Fortune 500 companies.

Steadily growing ever larger, local telephone operations will continue to expand rapidly in the coming decade as home consumer demand continues to increase and, more spectacularly, as business data communications experience a spurt in growth. A new high was marked in 1984 when the New York Telephone Company found it necessary to divide New York City into two area codes, with Brooklyn, Queeens, and Staten Island becoming a "long-distance" call from Manhattan and the Bronx. An overload on local circuits had been felt due mainly to heavier business computer traffic over telephone lines. In the Manhattan financial district in 1983, the phone company found that for every person calling another person, there were five computers calling five other computers.[15]

While the regional Bell companies find themselves in a rapidly expanding market, they also find themselves facing new types of competition. The 1982 divestiture agreement, together with other recent government actions, has effectively unwrapped telephone operations from their protective cocoon. Specifically, the FCC authorized a series of alternative systems competitive with the traditional local telephone network. One is a technological innovation called multipoint distribution (MDS), a commercial microwave system that bypasses local phone circuits and offers a range of other services. Another is cellular mobile telephone networks. By FCC decree, the 300 largest metropolitan areas in the country have each been allowed two such mobile phone systems — one operated by the local phone company and the other operated by a competitor. Also, several domestic satellite communications systems are now authorized to transmit directly to offices and factories as long-distance networks, bypassing the local phone networks. Cable television operators are exploring ways of providing home and business services formerly handled exclusively by telephone companies. Finally, many large business firms are setting up their own private communications networks, linking offices and other installations by satellite, microwave circuits, or cables that they own or lease, often bypassing the phone companies' facilities completely.

Despite the new competition, the seven Baby Bells were successful in making the transition from AT&T to independence in the eighties. By their own reckoning, the barrier to even greater success has not been cable systems or the other alternate technologies. It was a feisty Federal judge, Harold H. Greene, of the Circuit Court for the District of Columbia. Under the terms of the final divestiture agreement, Judge Greene was assigned the job of assuring compliance with the agreement by all the parties. In the years after 1984, he was the most powerful individual on the U. S. communications scene. By experience and temperment, he was well suited for the job. A refugee from Nazi Germany, he had worked his way through night law school to judicial eminence. He was, moreover, totally conversant with the telecommunications industry, having presided over the AT&T antitrust case for years. His self-proclaimed goal was to protect the integrity of the American telecommunications system after the AT&T breakup, with special attention to consumer needs.

In particular, Judge Greene made sure that the newly-independent Baby Bells understood that their primary responsibility was to provide efficient local phone service. Under the agreement, only 10 percent of their revenues could come from nontelephone operations. Proposals for nontelephone business required his approval. He granted a large number of such requests, from publishing Yellow Pages directories to operating real estate services. But he was slower to approve an expansion of Baby Bell activities into other, potentially more profitable areas. These included the manufacture of telecommunications equipment, developing long-distance networks, and offering specialized information services to their customers.

The information-services case was particularly important. Such services can cover just about every use of a phone network beyond ordinary conversations — data-bank retrieval, electronic mail, and recording and automatic transmission of voice messages, among other techniques. The

Baby Bells are uniquely qualified to handle such services. Judge Greene was concerned, however, that they would use their monopoly position — control over the wire into almost every house and office — to stifle competition. Similar services were already being provided on a limited basis by other companies. The newspaper industry, in particular, was strongly opposed to phone company expansion into information services, fearing the loss of advertising revenues to "electronic Yellow Pages."

In March 1988, Judge Greene relented on his information-services ban by ruling that the Baby Bells could offer a limited range of such services, including electronic mail and voice messaging. The latter service has the potential for becoming an important new revenue source for the phone companies by replacing the millions of answering machines in U. S. homes and offices. Using a touch-tone phone, a person who plans to step out punches a command to the telephone network to intercept incoming calls with a recorded personal message, take any messages, and play them back when the person returns.[16]

The main business of the reorganized Bell companies will continue to be POTS, plain-old-telephone-service, for a long time to come. Americans make a billion phone calls a day. The telephone has long ceased to be a luxury; its low-cost universal availability is considered a public right. This comfortable assumption was severely tested in the early post-divestiture period, when the tradition of relatively low telephone rates was brought into doubt. Historically, AT&T long-distance toll rates were set to include a built-in subsidy for local service. With the divestiture, the arcane but practical old formulas for distributing costs between local and long-distance operations were no longer applicable.

The in-house subsidy gone, local phone companies proceeded to seek substantial rate increases. In the first year of divestiture, requests for over $6.7 billion in such increases were filed with the regulating government agencies. There were dire predictions that phone rates would triple over the course of a few years.[17] Rates in fact went up, but such predictions proved exaggerated.

At issue was more than an economic question of relief for telephone companies deprived of their former internal subsidies. An important political question was involved, namely the basic concept of universal phone service and, by extension, the matter of equal access to advanced information services. In wired-up America, the personal telephone is an economic and social necessity. But universal access to the network had been achieved only through a highly complex set of formulas that had suddenly been made obsolete.

The search for alternatives to obsolete rate schedules led down thorny paths. At both federal and state levels, politicians and regulatory officials hunted for solutions. The FCC proposed a monthly levy on all telephones to make up for the lost subsidy. Congressional committees put forth counter-proposals. A special assessment on all local telephone use was eventually agreed to. Meanwhile, long-distance rates were free to drop as they no longer had to be set by subsidy-producing schedules. Lower long-distance rates are a welcome relief to AT&T as the company meets the challenge of new competitors in the expanding market. One way or another, however, customers will have to pay the price for separated local phone costs. The ultimate threat is an erosion of universal personal phone service, with lower income families and geographically isolated users in danger of losing easy access. In the new information-based economy, the danger is critical.

Meanwhile, the former Bell System companies have moved, at varying speeds, into the bracing new competitive environment. It will take years to sort out their role in post-industrial America. One thing is certain: they will no longer be just "the phone company." With their technical and management experience, they are expanding well beyond their traditional business into a wide range of new services.

We turn now to IBM — the other company whose future status, along with that of AT&T, was clarified in the January 1982 Justice Department decisions. For IBM, the end of the antitrust case meant that it would continue to operate as an integrated research, production, and marketing organization. The alternative was to have been split up into smaller units. No IBM-watcher doubted that a fragmented company would have survived and thrived. However, most of them agreed that the dynamism that had made the firm a world leader in computers and business machines for most of this century would have suffered in the process.

The antitrust case had, in fact, cast a shadow over the company's future throughout the seventies. Although it was a decade of technical advances and rising profits, computer developments generally appeared to be moving at a faster pace than IBM's ability to innovate, particularly in marketing. The company trailed its competitors in the two biggest changes in the industry since the introduction of large-scale production of mainframe machines in the 1950s. In minicomputers, the small mainframe machines, Digital Equipment Corporation (DEC) set the pace in the early seventies. The other innovation, microcomputers, was introduced by small start-up companies like Apple Computers in the late seventies. The perennial Cassandras among IBM-watchers revived their claim that the company had run its course, that it was fixated on big computers at a time when technology and economics were combining to give smaller machines the largest share of the market.[18]

However, the Cassandras were wrong again. Its future confirmed by the Justice Department's 1982 decision, IBM moved ahead smartly. The company had, in fact, been gearing up for the change for years. From 1976 to 1983, it had invested $25 billion into new plant and equipment. The shift also involved some important intangibles. Fortune magazine, in a 1983 analysis of the new IBM, described it as a cultural change: "To its old motto, 'Think,' IBM seems to have appended the word 'differently.'" The company demonstrated in the eighties its corporate ability to encourage innovation and to act on its consequences.[19]

In doing so, IBM challenged the thesis, beloved of business-school case study exercises, that large corporations cannot innovate as quickly as smaller ones. IBM's approach has been to set up its own independent small venture firms within the company. These are known, in its corporate jargon, as special business units. In the early eighties, IBM created 14 such units to explore opportunities outside its current business. The result was to lead the company into such areas as industrial robots, electrocardiographs, and directory-assistance equipment for telephone companies.

The most dramatic example of an IBM company-within-a-company was the unit set up to design and develop a small personal computer. In the late seventies, this was the biggest gap in its product line, and the gap was becoming more apparent as Apple, Radio Shack, and other firms moved in to fill it. In 1980, the small computer venture was set up in Florida with unusual freedom to bypass the IBM corporate bureaucracy. It was, as one observer noted, the firm's answer to the question: "How do you make an elephant tap dance?" The first IBM personal computer, intended primarily for business use, was put on the market in August 1981. Two years later, a less expensive version was introduced, with the educational and home market in mind. The initial results were stunning. IBM's little machines took the lead almost immediately in an explosive new kind of computer market. In 1984, the value of desk-top computers — machines that were virtually unheard of a decade before — overtook sales of the traditional large mainframe machines in the United States market.[20]

It was the coming-of-age of the American computer industry. From now on, the computer will be a mass-market product. By the early nineties there will be roughly 60 million terminals installed throughout the country. The closest comparable event in United States industrial history was Henry Ford's decision to develop assembly-line production of automobiles early in the century. As with Ford, IBM's achievement was not so much in producing a mass-market product as in setting a standard around which a significant part of American economic and social development would take place.[21]

IBM matched its new product line with changes in its traditional marketing pattern. In previous years, the company had a rather condescending attitude toward its customers. Most of its equipment was leased, with the implication that customers should consider themselves honored by the association. This attitude began to change during the seventies, but it was the introduction of the small computers that marked the full corporate turnaround. Gone were the dignified formal advertising approaches. They were replaced by a promotional campaign centered around a Charlie Chaplin look-alike, spreading the word that even a lovable old tramp could use a computer. There was also a suggestion that owning an IBM machine could be fun as well as profitable. It was a long leap from the firm's traditional starched white-collar image.

In other marketing moves, IBM adopted sophisticated pricing policies, along with new patterns of consumer retailing. In addition to opening its own retail stores, the company struck deals with Sears Roebuck and other large chains to carry its products. Again the walls of corporate tradition were breached, with stunning effect. Sales of the small computers broke the million unit mark in 1984, from a standing start only three years earlier. For the long term, however, one of IBM's most important marketing strategies has been to encourage independent software companies to develop programs for its computers. The net result has been to encourage the widest range of software compatible with its machines.

Despite IBM's dramatic move into small computers, the company was in trouble again in the mid-eighties. Worldwide revenues remained above the $50 billion mark, but profits were down. In 1985, the company suffered the worst earnings drop in its history. In part this was the result of a slump that affected the entire industry at the time. But it also seemed as if IBM — the legendary Big Blue — was beginning to look and act like a tired Old Blue. The competition was looking smarter, and faster in getting new products to the market.

The industry Cassandras revived their old predictions about the decline of IBM. Their analysis centered around the company's continued heavy reliance on mainframe computers. Its big machines accounted for over half the world market, producing 45 percent of IBM's revenues and 50 percent of its total profits. Mainframes were, in fact, a very profitable product, providing gross margins of up to 70 percent for the company.

The Cassandras were right on one score: the mainframe market is being inexorably eroded by smaller machines that can do many, if not most, traditional mainframe tasks. The erosion began in the seventies with increasingly powerful minicomputers. It will be accelerated in the nineties with the largest-scale transition to multiprocessor units.

Although IBM moved into the market for smaller machines with considerable success, there have been troubling quesions about its ability to compete in the new, more competitive environment.

One example is its experience with personal computers. As noted above, the company scored spectacularly with its innovative PCs in the early eighties. Corporate wisdom dictated the quick development of an improved successor. IBM made such plans, but the operational responsibility was shifted from the small maverick Florida unit that developed the original PC to a larger old-line division. In the shift, the innovative momentum slowed down. Scheduled to be introduced in 1985, the new Personal System/2 was delayed two years. It was a well-designed product, eight times more powerful than the company's original personal computer. The delay in getting it to market, however, helped the company's PC competitors grab one-third of its market share.[22]

This and similar events brought IBM's leadership to a moment of truth. In many ways the situation was similar to that faced by AT&T, described above, in dealing with a newly competitive market. In short, the choice was change or decline. Like AT&T's management, IBM's leaders chose change. A new chief executive officer, John F. Akers, took over in 1985 and proceeded to reduce company expenditures. The IBM tradition of never firing an employee was maintained, although there was a net reduction of 16,000 employees over three years through normal attrition and early retirements.

At the same time, the Akers team began to move the company into new businesses. As noted above, IBM had tried earlier to develop a telecommunications capability, with middling success, through its Satellite Business Systems project. In the new Akers strategy, the firm took steps to compete more directly with AT&T through its purchase of a 16 percent share of MCI Communications, AT&T's major long-distance competitor. The move opened the prospect for IBM to become an international force in building voice and data networks, since MCI has network connections abroad with over 50 countries. (In 1988, IBM shifted tactics and sold back to MCI its share in the firm.) IBM also became a competitor in the fast-growing, high-margin supercomputer business.[23]

More changes came about in 1988 with the most sweeping corporate restructuring in the company's history. The role of headquarter executives in day-to-day operations was drastically reduced. Five highly autonomous divisions were created, each with responsibility for all innovation, design, and manufacturing in its sector. The reorganization acknowledged that IBM's traditional strength in big computers could not alone sustain it in a different technological era. The firm will have to compete on all fronts, and in more different ways, than ever before.[24]

The mainframe base will not be neglected. The company's long-term lead in this area will, however, continue to narrow. There is sharp competition in world markets from such powerful Japanese firms as Fujitsu and Hitachi. At home, the loss of business to smaller minicomputers was shared by IBM's mainframe competitors — Unisys, NCR, Control Data, and Honeywell. Unable to compete individually with IBM and the Japanese, several of them have turned to the small-computer market. Here they are latecomers, facing such aggressive firms as Apple, Wang, Digital Equipment, and, of course, their old nemesis, IBM. Unisys and Honeywell, among others, established production links with Japanese manufacturers in order to hold on to their share of the mainframe market.

A major challenge to IBM's mainframe dominance was mounted in 1988 by Digital Equipment, the third largest American computer group. Using sophisticated multiprocessor technology, Digital's VAX 8800 series — an upgrading of its highly successful mid-range computers — was designed to gain entry into the central processing facilities of large corporations, IBM's traditional stronghold.[25]

The immediate target of IBM and its competitors is to share in the electronification of American business. Communications and information technologies are merging in the office at an ever-increasing pace. Internal as well as external needs of business firms can now be dealt with through integrated networks. There were over 20 million computer terminals installed in United States business organizations by 1988, more than triple the 1984 figure. An increasing number of these machines are linked to outside electronic networks via telephone lines or other circuits.

With its longtime experience in business machines, IBM is a primary contender in this market. Its goal is end-to-end equipment and service, including the telecommunications that will link its machines to each other and to a wide array of IBM-compatible equipment across the country. In 1983, the firm strengthened its telecommunications equipment resources by buying nearly 20 percent interest in the Rolm Corporation, a major manufacturer of advanced office private branch exchange (PABX) equipment and other telecommunications products. Once just the hub of office telephone communications, PABX machines have been digitized and computerized to handle data as well as voice. IBM's investment in Rolm will make it more competitive in a market crowded with rival advanced systems.

AT&T will be one of these competitors. The company brings to the market its experience as the basic provider of office electronic communications for over a century. This experience has largely been limited, however, to providing voice communications. AT&T will have to expand quickly beyond this if it is to challenge effectively IBM and other firms, many of whom have a considerable head start in developing and marketing integrated voice, data, and visual systems.

Beyond the office automation market, both IBM and AT&T have active projects designed to bring other advanced communications and information services to Americans. Of the roughly 60 million terminals of all kinds installed by the end of the eighties, about half will be in homes. AT&T is experimenting with a range of videotex services for homes — shopping, banking, community information, general news, and the like. Not to be left behind, IBM in 1988 inaugurated a national videotex network service, offering a full range of information and transactional services for homes and other locations, in partnership with Sears Roebuck.

As noted above, AT&T and IBM will not be the only firms reaching out for these potentially lucrative markets. Xerox, General Telephone & Electronics, Wang, Digital Equipment, ITT, and dozens of other companies are also converging on these new opportunities. Over the horizon, Japanese and European firms have been positioning themselves for a share of the business in this country. By the late eighties, there were over 50 Japanese companies producing personal computers, all with an eye on potential markets in the United States and other countries. The coming years will see a strong marketing push by the Japanese in this area, reminiscent of their earlier successes in exporting television sets, pocket calculators, and hi-fi equipment. Similar efforts can be expected from Korean and other Asian firms.

This prospect raises the critical question of United States international competitiveness in the electronics field. It is an issue that tends to produce more heat than light, as advocates of tighter protectionist controls press their case against the dwindling group of trade-liberalization supporters. The reality is that the United States retains a comparative advantage in high-tech electronic products. The difficulty comes in translating this lead into export sales.

The issue goes beyond trade statistics to the overall position of the United States as a high-tech leader in the new global economy. For 25 years after World War II, roughly 75 percent of high-tech innovation came from this country. The figure is closer to 50 percent now, with the prospect of a drop to 30 percent or 35 percent in the nineties. The shift was, of course, inevitable as Japan and Europe developed independent high-tech capabilities. Nevertheless, there is a strong case for understanding the implications of the shift, and for taking steps to strengthen policies and programs that encourage high-tech innovation.

IBM and AT&T will each have a unique role to play in this global high-tech competition. They are still the pacemakers at home and abroad. IBM's position is well established. Despite the steady pressure of foreign competition, the company has held its own in most overseas markets, the source of about half of its annual profits. The new aggressiveness it has shown in the United States market in recent years is also reflected abroad. It has, for instance, marketed its small computers overseas with the same zeal and success demonstrated in this country.

AT&T's international role is somewhat less clear. Its initial entry into overseas markets after the 1982 divestiture decision was not particularly strong. In part, this reflected the company's priorities at the time, which were focused on the complex job of sorting out its domestic reorganization problems. It would be wrong, however, to underestimate AT&T's long-term impact on overseas markets, and in particular on its role in sustaining United States high-tech leadership worldwide. The firm's lack of overseas marketing experience will be balanced by partnerships it has formed with such experienced multinational marketers as Philips of Holland and Italy's Olivetti.

AT&T's strongest overseas opportunities initially will be in the industrialized countries. Its prospects as an international competitor also include the so-called Third World. Latin America, Africa, and Asia (outside of Japan) have only 10 percent of the world's telephones. The pressure is on to change this imbalance, for both economic and political reasons. Eventually, these developing regions should be able to produce and service a large part of their own telecommunications and information equipment. Until that time, AT&T will be available as the world's unique expert in building and maintaining a mass telecommunications system. The experience will not be totally new for the company. During World War II, its managers and technicians moved all over the globe, setting up communications systems for the United States military. The Third World's transition to adequate communications will occur in fits and starts, but the momentum is already there. AT&T can be an important factor in maintaining it.

IBM and AT&T are, by no means, the be-all and end-all of the newly integrated American communications and information sector. There are thousands of other firms, big and little, ready to compete with them and with each other. One or two of these smaller companies may become the AT&Ts and IBMs of the early 21st century through a combination of technological breakthroughs and managerial skills of the type that have characterized the two leaders over the years. For the present, however, AT&T and IBM are the bellwether organizations against which a good share of the opportunities for a new kind of advanced United States information society has to be measured.

NOTES

1. The best overall account of the divestiture and its implications can be found in "Breaking Up the Phone Company," *Fortune*, 27 June 1983, pp. 60–67.
2. In defending its corporate actions during a 1981 court case, a Bell attorney referred to AT&T unblushingly as "the greatest enterprise on earth." See "Government, AT&T Fires First Salvos at Trial," *New York Times*, 16 January 1981, p. D–3.
3. The goal has been in AT&T's plans since the mid-seventies. In 1976, the then-president of the company, Frederick Kappel, predicted that the firm's revenues from data communications would eventually be greater than those from traditional voice telephone traffic. See "On the Head of a Pin," *Forbes*, 15 September 1976, p. 32.
4. The best description of the complex situation leading up to the divestiture is contained in a congressional study, *Options Papers*, issued by the House Subcommittee on Communications, Committee on Interstate and Foreign Commerce, 95th Congress, 1st session, committee print 95–13, May 1977.
5. "A Strategy for the Telephone," *New York Times*, 18 May 1980, p. D–3.
6. For a useful summary of these psychological factors, see "Cultural Shock is Shaking the Bell System," *Business Week*, 26 September, 1983, pp. 112–14.
7. "The New World of Telecommunications," *Computer Decisions*, 15 September 1983, pp. 95–118.
8. "Changing Phone Habits," *Business Week*, 5 August 1983, p. 71.
9. "AT&T: the Making of a Comeback," *Business Week*, 18 January 1988, pp. 56–61.
10. The problems that AT&T's competitors had in the early post-divestiture period are summarized in "MCI Loses Some Sparkle," *New York Times*, 12 February 1984, p. D–1.
11. "Why Western Electric Has To Hustle," *New York Times*, 17 January 1982, p. D–1.
12. "AT&T's Unix Is a Hit At Last and Other Companies Are Wary," *New York Times*, 24 February 1988, p. D–8.
13. "Can the New AT&T Compete in World Markets?," *Business Week*, 30 January 1984, p. 32.
14. "AT&T's Impact Abroad,' *Data Communications*, February 1982, p. 36.
15. "New York to Get a Second Area Code by Middle of 1984," *New York Times*, 9 February 1983, p. B–1.
16. "Judge Lets Baby Bells Offer Some Information Services," *New York Times*, 8 March 1988, p. D–1.
17. For a good description of the controversy, see "The AT&T Breakup: A World of Confusion," *Washington Post*, 11 December 1983, p. A–14.
18. "The Big Boys Counterattack," *Economist*, (London), 24 December 1983, p. 69.
19. "Meet the Lean Mean New IBM," *Fortune*, 3 June 1983, p. 69.
20. "Bailing Out the Mainframe Industry," *New York Times*, 5 February 1984, p. D–1.

21. "The Colossus That Works," *Time,* 11 June 1983, p. 44.
22. "Big Changes at Big Blue," *Business Week,* 15 February 1988, pp. 92–98.
23. "IBM in Joint Venture on Supercomputers," *New York Times,* 23 December 1987, p. D–1.
24. "IBM Forms Five Autonomous Units," *New York Times*, 29 January 1988, p. D–1.
25. "New Digital Computer Will Challenge IBM," *New York Times,* 9 March 1988, p. D–1.

CHAPTER 7

The Politics of Change

How does a society make wise decisions? How do we determine who we are and what we want to become? How do we organize ourselves and our resources to match these perceptions? These questions are particularly relevant to information and communications policy. A fast-changing society needs access to greater knowledge resources to handle the uncertainties and disruptions that change brings.

Until now our examination of information age strategies has concentrated on technological and economic developments. The United States has already crossed the technological divide into the new age. There are no longer any serious physical barriers to the creation of a full-scale information network utility. We are now crossing the economic divide, as shown in the many recent studies on the information-based economy. The major unresolved issues are in the political arena, involving basic decisions on the form and purpose of the new environment.

This is the most sensitive point in the entire transition. Technology and economics deal largely with immediate problems, focused on particular outcomes in terms of their specific success or failure. As influences on the United States information environment, they are powered by their own internal dynamics. Left to themselves, they could create a post-industrial information structure that would be difficult to modify with public policies in the future, if we should wish to do so. On the other hand, reaching consensus in any area of public policy is difficult, especially in communications and information matters. There are strong contending interests involved, together with a healthy First Amendment tradition against government interference in these areas.

Nevertheless we have arrived at a point at which public decisions are becoming imperative. Technical and economic developments are converging in ways that require a clearer definition of their relationships to overall social goals. Until recently, the pace of technical and economic changes has been a linear progression, spread across many years. The transitions from telegraph to telephone, from radio and television to computers and satellites were marked by relatively long pauses, allowing time for us to sort out their economic and social consequences. Today this time frame is compressed, marked by a convergence of technologies with overlapping decision complexities. As a result, communications and information are regarded as general political issues, instead of, as in the past, the concerns solely of the industry and a few government agencies.[1]

Public involvement in these policy subjects is still fragmentary, but it is there and it is growing. There is a general recognition of the need for a new information resources design that assures all of us the advantages these resources offer. This goal seemed easier 30 years ago, when many of the early prophets of the information age painted a rosy-hued picture of its prospects. This occurred during what might be called the "first computer decade," roughly from 1960 to 1970. Then, the electronic mythos was in full flower, based on the unfolding promise of computers and high-speed communications circuits. There were visions of a new order of data richness and computer-assisted decision making, a more efficient social competence replacing the old disorderly ways of managing issues and events.

It was a heady goal, spurred by the rhetoric of Kennedy's New Frontier and Johnson's Great Society, together with almost uninterrupted economic prosperity. The literature inspired by this vision evoked memories of the earlier technocracy movement of the 1930s with its engineered solutions to social problems. In the thirties, the great dams of the Tennessee Valley Authority were the prototype for future technocratic success. In the sixties, the model was the Apollo space program and its systems-analysis path to the moon. The new computer-based age would bring similar analytic efficiency to such earthbound problems as education, poverty, foreign policy, transportation, and the cities. Writing in March 1967, a team of researchers studying inner city problems in Detroit declared, "We feel that, in a very real sense, the age of the computer has ushered in a new age of urban planning."[2]

Four months later, Detroit went up in flames, urban renewal projects included. The smoky pall that hung over the city for days was a pungent reminder that stubborn social problems were not amenable to computer printout solutions. Civil disorder was followed by escalation in Vietnam, economic setbacks, and the public scandals that culminated in Watergate. The experience with the new information technologies during the first computer decade, however overblown, had its usefulness in defining the limits of computerized shortcuts. The result has been a more realistic view of the role of communications and information — as important but not cure-all resources in reducing economic and social problems.

If there is now a better understanding of what can be done practically, it is also true that we are still only at the beginning of a consensus on how to go about it. The prospect is still a promising one: providing everyone access to a full range of information resources, allowing every person, as Emerson urged, to produce that peculiar fruit each was born to bear. But this objective forces us to face some fundamental questions. Having reached the point where it is technically possible, is full access to information one of our basic rights in a post-industrial democratic society? Or is it simply a desirable long-range goal, whose attainment will be left to the play of economic and social forces, a linear extension — with some technological flourishes — of what we are now doing, with benefits trickling down largely through the workings of the market?

Choices between these options will reflect our contemporary view of the democratic tradition of open information, which supports our need to know, our right to challenge. We have made many public commitments to these ideals in the past two centuries. Those most relevant to our present situation were the decisions favoring universal free public education over a century ago. Our forebears agreed that this was a necessary democratic entitlement, and so, with some lapses, saw that it was provided. Public education moved from one-room school-houses to consolidated schools to our present variegated patterns of learning opportunities. In the post-industrial era, computers and related information devices can be an effective part of a new lifelong learning cycle quite different in style from traditional classroom practices. Will we extend our concept of education to include greater access to these information resources? The response to this question will signal, to a considerable degree, our willingness to evolve to higher forms of democracy in the new era.

The alternative — restricted access — may push us toward a controlled, perhaps even benevolent, authoritarianism in which an elite has effective control over key information resources and uses this power to manipulate a complacent *lumpenproletariat*. An amusing, if somewhat chilling, illustration of this possibility was provided several years ago by a Columbia University professor, Alan Westin. It takes place in the early years of the next century, when an authoritarian information elite, working out of National Databank Headquarters in Philadelphia, controls the rest of society. Their plan is temporarily set back by an assault on their computers by a terrorist group known as the Fold, Staple, Spindle, and Mutilate movement. The elite leaders defeat the terrorists, and take the ultimate step of programming every event in each citizen's life to prevent further disruption. Professor Westin's scenario ends with a surprise twist that suggests that human freedom may prevail. We may never have to contend with such a dire situation, but we do have to face up to the future consequences of present trends pushing us toward an information environment where many questions of access, control, and privacy are still unresolved.

These are political questions, and the answers will come from the untidy, often frustrating give-and-take of political action. The basic issue is the control and distribution of power, enhanced by the ability of the new technologies to permit massive centralization and manipulation of a wider range of information resources than ever before. This issue was identified by Karl Deutsch in his masterful work, *The Nerves of Government,* in which he argued that control of information resources and communications channels was displacing traditional forces — the military and the police — as the measure of power.[3] This has always been true to some extent, but the new technologies vastly enhance the prospect. This fact argues powerfully against our present inclination to leave major decisions in communications and information to the economic and technological sectors. It is putting a burden on those sectors that they are not equipped to handle, and that may be harmful to their orderly development over the long run.

This point was stressed by a former AT&T board chairman, John deButts, several years years ago when he said, "It is not technology that will shape the future of telecommunications in this country. Nor is it the market. It is policy."[4] Mr. deButts made his remarks in the course of presenting his company's ideas on what national telecommunications policy should be. Whatever the details of his advocacy (a unique one, as befits AT&T's special status), he acknowledged — as many of his short-sighted industry counterparts did not — the need for public debate and decision on the future of American communications.

Participatory democracy, an informed citizenry, a strong economy, technologies that serve human needs — these are the stakes in our consideration of the prospects for viable communications and information policies in post-industrial America. It is well to dismiss at the start any fantasies we may have about a tidy master plan for the new information environment. Such an approach would be unacceptable to almost everyone concerned, since no one would be prepared to suspend his or her negotiating rights in the rough-and-tumble of political negotiation of sensitive issues in the interests of a neat, orderly, and probably unworkable system. A more realistic approach is to define minimum guidelines and goals for the near-term, say the next decade. This will be difficult enough, given the obstacles involved.

Any agreed-upon policies will, for instance, have to be grafted onto complex existing structures, controlled largely by organizations that are generally unwilling to trade the promise of long-term gains for present advantages. The changes will have to be nudged, coddled, and cajoled through a political process heavily influenced by interest groups who settle their differences through complex compromises.

Serious consideration of communications and information issues is hindered by the fact that political leaders generally do not regard them as critical. The issues involved seem too abstruse, too wrapped up in technological and economic complexities to attract sustained popular attention. As noted earlier, this attitude is changing as communications and information impinge more directly on people's lives and interests.

Nevertheless, the present lack of any clear-cut public consensus inhibits the development of strategies for dealing with information age issues. Political scientist Harold Lasswell once suggested that an annual balance sheet of "gross enlightenment outcome" of the nation be drawn up so that there would be a measure of necessary knowledge resources. As yet, however, there are no firm indicators of public needs in this area — a handicap to intelligent planning.

The result is a kind of tinker-toy approach; we are trying to piece together bits and parts of a complex structure without knowing quite what we want it to do for us. The results will inevitably be disappointing unless we can agree on a blueprint that combines economic and technological resources with social goals in a workable fashion.

What are the prospects for such a blueprint? The answer begins with the Constitution, that very flexible document that set down the basic guidelines, in law and in practice, for American approaches to communications in only one passage, which deals with the powers of Congress "to establish Post Offices and post roads." The document's most abiding influence in this area, however, comes from the First Amendment prohibition against laws abridging freedom of speech and the press. Any discussion of policy on communications or information begins with, and returns to, this fact. These strictures against government involvement explain why the United States is unique in not having a centralized bureaucracy to directly control or heavily regulate communications.

As a result, communications policy is defined and carried out by a large number of public entities at the federal, state, and local levels. The pattern is confusing, often overlapping, and frequently contradictory. Whatever the faults of this system, it reflects a common agreement to limit government intervention in the communications and information field, particularly in those areas affecting First Amendment rights. The pattern has also been shaped by pressures from the private sector against excessive regulations, that is, over and above the numerous laws and regulations designed to protect its own interests.

The limitation of government activities in the communications field was set early in the telecommunications age. The first federal involvement was to provide financial support for the initial demonstration of Samuel Morse's telegraph system between Washington and Baltimore in 1844, although this support was withdrawn the following year. In the following decades, the telegraph and telephone systems developed under private auspices, with government playing a generally benign supportive role.

The same pattern applied internationally. The United States refused to join the new International Telegraph Union, founded in 1865 to provide needed international standards for the new telegraph networks. The United States' refusal was based in part on the fact that it had few international communications links at the time, but more pointedly on a general suspicion about foreign interference in American communications affairs. It was not until the turn of the century, when the British-controlled Marconi Wireless Company attempted to establish a global monopoly over radio communications, that the United States joined the Telegraph Union to protect its interests and, in particular, to thwart the British monopoly.

Technological developments after the First World War forced a stepping up of government involvement in communications. The Federal Radio Commission was established in 1927 to sort out the chaotic frequency situation caused by an influx of hundreds of new stations. Before the Commission began its work, radio stations gained "authorization" by sending a letter to the Department of Commerce simply notifying it that they were on the air.[5] The Communications Act of 1934 set out more comprehensive legislative standards, including the establishment of the Federal Communications Commission (FCC). The creation of the FCC was an important step in providing a mechanism for sorting out many of the pragmatic problems brought on by the new technologies. However, its authority has been limited to regulating the telecommunications industry. Fast-moving technological developments make it increasingly difficult to define the boundaries of its jurisdiction. A 50-year-old communications act, designed to cope with telephones and radios, does not provide much help.

The bureaucratic process for dealing with communications and information has developed gradually over the years. Until World War II, government communications matters were handled as a part-time concern of the military. The Navy took the lead in the 1920s in helping create the Radio Corporation of America (now RCA, a subsidiary of General Electric) as a United States "chosen instrument" for challenging foreign competition in international communications. The need to set up a worldwide communications network during World War II focused official attention on communications policy matters for the first time. President Truman later appointed a special assistant for telecommunications to deal with the issue. The office and its duties were expanded in a series or reorganizations under Presidents Eisenhower, Kennedy, and Johnson. But these changes still left communications policy as a small-fry concern in the bureaucratic fishpond.

The Kennedy administration became more deeply involved in communications policy in 1962 as the result of a technological breakthrough. The technology was the communications satellite, whose capabilities were demonstrated in July of that year when NASA launched AT&T's *Telstar,* the first active repeater satellite capable of switching incoming and outgoing messages in space. (Previous experiments involved passive satellites, with signals bounced off a balloon.) It was a major technical achievement that raised immediate political and economic questions.

The politics involved problems of organizing a system, both domestically and internationally, for exploiting the new technology. Intelligence reports at the time indicated that the Soviet Union was actively engaged in similar satellite research. In that post-*Sputnik* era, the thought of another Soviet space success, and the prospect that the Soviets might take the lead in organizing a global satellite network, was a sharp goad causing Kennedy administration officials and congressional leaders to move quickly. The result, decided upon in record time for major legislation, was the Communications Satellite Act of 1962, which set up the Communications Satellite Corporation (Comsat) and detailed a plan for organizing an American-sponsored international satellite system. Comsat would be the government's "chosen instrument" for organizing the system and representing the United States in its management.

It was an innovative solution, combining both public and private sector elements, which provided the basic framework for the development of the highly successful Intelsat global system, owned by over a hundred nations. The 1962 legislation was a critical event in focusing American attention on communications policy matters, even though it dealt with only one, albeit an important, aspect of the problem.[6]

A hopeful step toward the development of a coherent policy was taken in the late sixties when the Johnson administration appointed a

Presidential commission to study the subject. The commission, headed by Yale law professor Eugene Rostow, made a thoughtful and controversial attempt at the first national overview of communications issues. It defined communications as a critical issue in United States society and proposed a series of specific actions for strengthening its role in economic and social development.[7]

Along the way, the commission's report also challenged long-standing government and corporate interests. Given the complex nature of these interests, this was perhaps inevitable, as was the fact that the report was quietly relegated to that special Washington limbo for controversial advisory commission reports. Nevertheless, the Rostow study was important because it did attempt to present a coherent view of the future implications of technological, economic, and social developments in communications. It set a basic agenda that is still valid — no mean achievement.

The Rostow study also influenced the new Nixon administration, in 1969, to take a more serious look at the way in which communications policy matters were organized. The result was a decision to upgrade the subject in an enlarged White House unit known as the Office of Telecommunications Policy (OTP) with a charter for coordinating overall government policy and planning on the subject. Setting up OTP was a significant step toward a more rational national approach to communications, but its effectiveness was almost immediately compromised by political controversy. The new office became the Nixon White House's stalking horse for an attack on the alleged liberal biases of the major television networks. Its charges reinforced the fears of the industry and of Congress that the administration intended to use the new office to gain political control over the media in the United States. This, together with the general distrust of OTP by old-line government agencies concerned with communications matters, effectively ended the hope that OTP would bring a fresh approach to national communications planning. The fact that the office performed some valuable services, particularly in funding policy research projects, was hidden in the black political clouds that surrounded most of its history.

In 1977 it was inevitable that the new Carter administration would abolish the unit. With an eye on the political sensitivities involved, the Carter planners rejected suggestions for a replacement that would have a stronger charter for coordinating policy and planning matters. Instead, they redistributed OTP's functions, assigning the bulk of them to a new agency, the National Telecommunications and Information Administration (NTIA), in the Department of Commerce. NTIA was immediately perceived as weaker than the OTP, particularly because it had no direct bureaucratic entrée to the White House, as did the OTP. However, it is a well-established Washington rule that proximity, bureaucratic or otherwise, to the White House can be an elusive benefit.

OTP's effectiveness was destroyed by the political connotations of its direct White House connection. (On a day-to-day basis, the connection was not all that strong.) In its early years, NTIA demonstrated that a lower political profile was, on balance, a help rather than a hindrance in its work. Like OTP, its most important assignment is to provide a coordinating point for the federal government's own communications and information activities. It is also charged with advising the President on overall national policy in these areas. Significantly, for the first time telecommunications and information were newly paired as common policy concerns in one agency, a welcome recognition of the technological and economic realities of the information age. With the advent of the Reagan administration there was an attempt by some of Reagan's more conservative advisers to eliminate NTIA, primarily on the theory that any such federal policy involvement in these areas was undesirable. After some confusion, the administration retained the NTIA structure while at the same time cutting back on its budget, personnel, and policy responsibilities.

If coordination has been the key word in NTIA's mission, it has also been its most difficult task. The image is of a tidy system meant to bring coherence and order to the federal establishment's far-flung involvement in communications and information matters. The reality is considerably more complex, and less neat.[8] The federal government's involvement is a tangle of facilities and operations — from the White House office that instantaneously provides circuits for the President wherever he may be, to Voice of America transmitters in the Thailand jungles, to the dogsleds used by the postal service to deliver mail in Alaska.

The federal government's communications facilities are too far-flung and complex to quantify. One estimate made in the late seventies put its telecommunications facilities alone at $67 billion.[9] Washington agencies control over half of all the radio frequencies assigned in this country under international agreements. The federal government is also by far the world's largest owner and user of computers, although no one is quite sure how many it has.

The agency most heavily involved in telecommunications and information operations is the Defense Department, which uses half of all the frequencies assigned to the government. During the Reagan administration's military buildup, advanced communications facilities were given high priority, involving $18 billion in budget funds in one year alone. Although the military has extensive facilities of its own, it is heavily dependent on civilian communications.

The problems of meshing the two systems came to a head during the 1962 Cuban missile crisis, when serious coordination gaps emerged. This led to the first attempt to develop a strategic communications plan, centered around the establishment of a National Communications System with the Secretary of Defense as executive agent. The case for such a policy was made at the time by Dr. Harold Brown, then Defense Department Director of Research:

> It is...important to recognize that our domestic and international telecommunications systems are critical factors both in our military posture and in our cold war struggle and, indeed, throughout the whole spectrum of conflict. We cannot today consider our communications systems solely as civil activities merely to be regulated as such, but we must consider them as essential instruments of national policy in our struggle for survival and establish policy and organization consistent with our situation.[10]

The National Communications System charter is limited to assuring government communications "under all conditions from a normal situation to national emergencies and international crises, including nuclear attack." The Secretary of Defense is responsible for the daily operations of the system under White House policy direction. Several attempts have been made to expand the system's scope since it was set up, but these have been resisted by other elements in the government's communications establishment.

There are, conservatively, two dozen civilian government agencies with major communications and information responsibilities. The largest of these is the postal service, a hybrid organization operating in a bureaucratic no-man's-land, heavily dependent on government subsidies. The postal service is, for all its faults, a major element in the national information and communications network. Moreover, its future is the subject of considerable debate, particularly concerning its antiquated methods of using high-priced hand labor to carry pieces of paper to tens of millions of homes and offices every working day.

Besides the postal service, there is a conglomeration of other agencies with major communications and information responsibilities. These include the Department of Transportation, which handles air and maritime communications; the State Department, which handles negotiation of international agreements; the United States Information Agency, operating the Voice of America overseas radio network and other media facilities; the National Aeronautics and Space Administration, handling communications satellite experimentation; the Central Intelligence Agency, seeing to analysis of telecommunications developments abroad; and the National Security Agency, a highly classified operation monitoring foreign communications. Other agencies are also involved, though less obviously. The Federal Bureau of Investigation operates extensive files on American citizens and electronic links to local police authorities. Its capabilities, however, fall short of the computerized national crime information network it and many local police departments have pressed for, despite so far successful resistance by civil liberties advocates who claim that such a system could lead to abuses.

Another agency with extensive information responsibilities is the Internal Revenue Service, with its extensive files on what Americans earn and spend. In 1978, as a result of congressional and other pressures, the Carter administration halted the development of an $850 million computer network designed to provide IRS agents with immediate access to the detailed records of taxpayers and corporations.[11] Since then the IRS has expanded its computer capabilities by accretion to the point where its operations have become highly automated. In 1988, the agency announced a computer-based project for eliminating a 40-year-old system that requires 70 million paper forms a year to collect the personal income and other taxes that businesses withhold from employee pay checks — a total of $720 billion in 1987. Beginning in the early nineties, employers will be required to submit such payments information electronically to the IRS.[12]

Less known examples of federal information activities are the scientific and professional services provided by the government both for its internal and for general public use. The medical profession relies heavily on MEDLARS and MEDLINE, the National Library of Medicine's computerized compilation of articles published in medical journals throughout the world. Industry and research institutes make extensive use of the Department of Commerce's National Technical Information Service (NTIS), a computer-based source of technical research done by federal agencies. Educators turn to ERIC, the data base operated by the Department of Education, for information in their field. The Smithsonian Institution's Science Information Exchange indexes about 10,000 research projects a month as part of an effort to keep track of research the federal government pays for.

The overall issue of government-held computerized information has been the subject of intense debate in recent years. The technological prospect that previously independent data banks can be interconnected means that information collected by one agency can be made availabe to many. This led to recommendations that government-held computerized information be centralized in an interconnected data system. The arguments of those stressing the efficiency of such a system have so far been successfully challenged by those who fear its misuse.

The proliferating and jealously guarded division of responsibility over communications and information among so many agencies has at least lessened the threat of Big Brother centralism. But it has also inhibited the development of workable coordinated policy approach to the problems of the new information age.

The National Telecommunications and Information Administration may eventually be able to play a significant role in improving policy coherence, but it has not yet proved its ability to do so. At present, the most important federal influence on communications and information development is the Federal Communications Commission (FCC). The Commission dates from the technologically innocent days of Franklin D. Roosevelt's first administration, at which time its principal duties were to regulate radio stations and telephone companies. The agency quickly took on the usual bias of such commissions, namely a protective attitude toward the industries it was assigned to regulate. For decades it operated in near anonymity in the gray background of Washington bureaucracy.

This situation changed slowly at first, then rapidly toward the end of 1960s, for several reasons. New technologies began to intrude on long-standing regulations based on the older techniques. The combination of advanced technologies and more aggressive economic pressures to expand the industry brought communications and information more into the orbit of political controversy. This situation was exacerbated by an increase in public awareness, particularly in the consumer reform movement, about communications and information matters, from childrens' TV programming to telephone company rates. (After decades of being accorded almost reverential treatment by the public, the phone company found itself facing protestors with bell-shaped buttons labeled "Public Enemy No. 1.")

With its restricted mandate, the FCC was in a difficult situation, straining against the limits of outdated legislation (the Communications Act of 1934) that did not anticipate the regulatory problems raised by satellites, computers, high-capacity cable systems, and other new technologies. For many reasons, most of them having to do with the difficulties of appeasing conflicting economic interests, neither the White House nor Congress were prepared to make controversial policy choices to resolve the conflicts in ways that would benefit the national communications and information structure.

The task has fallen largely to the FCC, which has proved to be an unwieldy agent of change. As an independent regulatory agency, it is not directly accountable to Congress or to the President, although it clearly must take into account signals from both these sources. In the absence of legislated policy, the Commission is a policymaker by default on a wide range of issues. Its failings do not necessarily lay with the Commission or its staff.

The FCC's problem is in coping with the bits and pieces of important communications and information matters in the absence of a clearly articulated national policy. The Commission is less a regulator in the traffic cop sense than a referee without an up-to-date rulebook or even a clear whistle.

Despite these handicaps, the FCC has moved to act on a number of pressing issues in recent years. A good part of this momentum was generated by an activist Commission chairman, Richard Wiley, in the early seventies. A lawyer with little previous communications experience (as he once confessed, "I thought digital communications described something you didn't do in polite society"), Wiley took initiatives over a wide range of Commission matters, adding considerable prestige and authority to the agency. However, his activism — which also had its controversial side — could not make up for the absence of overall national decisions by the White House and Congress on the shape and direction of the new information age. Uncertainty continued to hamper the Commission during the Carter years, although important decisions were made to deregulate many telecommunications services and open them up to the fresh winds of new competition. During the Reagan years, the Commission stepped up the deregulatory pace set in previous years, often with the useful result of eliminating outdated regulatory practices. At times, however, the Commission's actions showed a naive faith in the efficacy of allegedly objective market forces at the expense of legitimate social interests.

A less known but still significant influence on the formation of national communications policies are the hundreds of federal advisory committees, commissions, boards, councils, and other groups that provide, with varying degrees of effectiveness, outside expertise to federal agencies. They are a particularly strong factor in the communications area, where their membership is drawn largely from industry. One survey in the mid-seventies showed that eight of the 11 corporations who contributed the most personnel to all federal advisory groups were in the communications field. In part, this reflects the fact that a considerable amount of expertise — particularly in technical matters — is concentrated in the private sector. It is also an indicator of the outsized role that the industry plays in influencing small parts of a fragmented government policy-planning mechanism, sometimes deterring more effective broader based planning. Although there has been some progress in cutting back the number of advisory groups, the membership of most groups still tends to come from industry. A 1978 survey of advisory group membership showed that AT&T filled 120 positions on such groups.[13]

The absence of overall policy direction in communications and information does not reflect a failure to study the problems in these areas. They have been examined in numbing detail for years. As already noted, the first major study was the Rostow Commission's, reviewing a broad range of policy matters in the late sixties. This was followed by a series of competent research studies sponsored by the Nixon administration's Office of Telecommunications Policy. Also, the independent, congressionally funded National Academy of Engineering and the National Science Foundation have sponsored useful studies on the social applications of new communications and information technologies.

Other projects examined the government's role in developing effective technical information networks — a priority concern for the scientific establishment as well as for American industry in its attempt to maintain a technological lead against increasing foreign competition. Important work in setting standards and recommending actions in this field was done by the Federal Council of Science and Technology beginning in the 1960s. One result of this initiative was the setting up of a central source for all research results produced by federal agencies — the National Technical Information Service.

However useful these studies and the actions resulting from them, they have tended to focus on relatively small parts of the total communications and information problem. None of them recommend a general strategy for public policy in these areas. An exception was a 1976 report to President Ford entitled *National Information Policy*, prepared by the Domestic Council's committee on the right of privacy, headed by Vice-President Nelson Rockefeller. The report's major recommendation was that "the United States set as a goal the development of a coordinated National Information Policy."[14]

Although the document stressed problems of access and privacy, it touched on most of the other major political concerns involved in developing a democratically based information environment. Despite its controversial recommendations, the report had little influence, in part because it was issued in the last, lame-duck months of the Ford administration. Nevertheless, the Rockefeller committee's initiative in proposing an overall national information policy provided an important base from which other studies of this subject can be made.

Any moves toward a new approach to communications and information policy will have to consider the role of Congress. The subject is a sensitive one for Congress, involving constitutional issues as well as the relation of Congress with the executive branch and with important constituencies. This sensitivity explains why Congress has not passed a major piece of national communications legislation in half a century, since the Communications Act of 1934. Nevertheless, the subject is intruding more frequently on congressional agendas. By and large, Congress shares the long-time executive branch predilection for dealing with communications and information matters in a fragmentary manner.[15]

An important attempt to bring the 1934 Communications Act up to date was made in the late seventies. The project was largely the work of a House of Representatives subcommittee on telecommunications, under the leadership of Congressman Lionel Van Deerlin of California and, later, Congressman (now Senator) Timothy Wirth of Colorado. Scores of witnesses appeared before the subcommittee to present their views. The committee staff prepared a massive "options paper" document, outlining the issues involved in adjusting the 1934 legislation to current economic and technological realities.[16]

The committee's hearings were a classic interest-group exercise, with all the affected parties bringing different perceptions and pressures to bear on the attempt to review and rewrite the old legislation. The communications industry was split between those arguing for the status quo and those who saw the benefits of a legislative imprimatur for the new economic and technological forces. Government agencies were generally suspicious of legislation that would affect their prerogatives. Public service groups came to the hearings with expectations of a more consumer-oriented approach to communications problems. The effort to rewrite the 1934 law eventually ended in failure, in part because it was overtaken by events, notably those leading up to the 1982 Department of Justice decision on the AT&T divestiture.

Nevertheless, the House (and related Senate) hearings had their effect. They helped sort out the problems involved and focus them in unique and constructive ways in a forum — the U. S. Congress — that counted. In particular, the hearings identified many of the very real policy issues involved in adjusting economic and technological factors to new information and communications needs. The process was limited in that it addressed itself primarily to the narrow framework of telecommunications. House and Senate committees have been reluctant to address directly the larger issues of the information society, although they have heard considerable testimony on this subject. Telecommunications were regarded as a big enough subject, with enough prickly issues to engage the full attention of the committees. Despite these limitations, the committee hearings have performed the singular service of putting national communications issues on the public agenda and providing a unique forum for airing them.[17]

In the absense of definitive legislation, the courts have played a significant role in defining legal aspects of the new communications and information environment and expanding First Amendment interpretations of privacy and other civil rights implications of the new technologies. The Supreme Court's ruling on the Nixon Watergate tapes in 1974 was the most publicized example of this. Other cases have dealt with data protection, wiretapping, and the limits of electronic surveillance. Outstanding instances of the influence of the Courts on telecommunications policy are the AT&T antitrust suit of the seventies and the complex legal decisions involved in the 1982 divestiture agreement. As noted in the previous chapter, Judge Harold Greene of the U. S. Circuit Court for the District of Columbia has had an outsized impact on American telecommunications policy in his court-appointed role of implementing the divestiture agreement.

Any review of communications policy has to take into consideration the parts played by states and localities. States have had a regulatory role in telecommunications through public utility commissions for many years. Many states and cities are now beginning to see telecommunications and information issues in the wider context of their relationships to such local services as education, law enforcement, library systems, and the like. A number of them have organized special units for this purpose: Virginia has had an integrated telecommunications planning unit for public service purposes since the early seventies. Many large cities are following suit: Los Angeles, Portland (Oregon), Boston, and New York City all have set up local public telecommunications agencies.

In summary, policy questions dealing with the new information environment are moving into the public agenda in a variety of ways and at different political levels. The effort is fragmented, discursive, and complex, reflecting the division of power in a sensitive area of national policy. Meanwhile, the communications and information structure is expanding rapidly, largely as a result of incremental decisions and actions based primarily on their immediate utility to commercial interests. The argument favoring a continuation of this approach is that, by and large, it works. The question is whether this time-tested process can continue to cope with the communications and information requirements of a more complex post-industrial environment. The present lack of answers to this question suggests the need for a more accurate guide to where we are going and what policy options and actions are available in developing a workable strategy in this area.

This strategy must deal with the relationship among public needs, available technology, and economic resources. In part, this involves a more precise allocation of responsibilities between the private and public sectors. In the public sector, more definitive guidelines are needed for meeting overall national requirements in the new environment. In the private sector, industry requires reasonable conditions for meeting communications needs in a period of growing demands for increasingly diverse services.

The allocation of tasks between the public and private sectors is clearly a difficult, sensitive job. Kurt Borchardt has suggested a private/public coordination model based on the Atomic Industrial Forum, which is essentially a systems approach for joint government/industry study and evaluation of the allocations of tasks.[18] There is good reason to question whether this solution would work in the communications sector. It tends to assume that the problem is between bureaucratic policymakers and the industry. There has been relatively little citizen input into the decision making of the Atomic Industrial Forum. This might have been explained — unsatisfactorily, in the view of many — by the esoteric technical nature of nuclear problems. However, a case can be made that more citizen input earlier on in the process might have prevented or modified some of the faulty assumptions made by nuclear planners over the years.

Communications and information policy, by its very nature, requires broad public input. It is a subject that touches everyone at every level. A weakness of our current approach to the new information environment is that decisions are being made, and options closed, every day that should be more open to public scrutiny. Despite the advances in consumer rights practices in recent years, decisions on the consumption of communications and information still tend to be the exclusive province of the bureaucracies — public and private — involved. At a time when we need to take actions to strengthen communications and information patterns in this country through the end of the century, an important element in the decision process is often missing — the views of individual consumers.

A good example of the stakes involved is the future of the postal system. This lumbering giant is currently wandering in the limbo between a respectable past and a highly uncertain future. By any slide rule calculation, there is no question about its future: a drastic cutback in its present mode of operations, including daily mail delivery. The old Norman Rockwell image of the friendly postman, slogging his way through snow, sleet, and rain to deliver Valetine messages will fade into folklore. The reason is that 80 percent of all first class mail deliveries is routine business correspondence, mostly bills being delivered or being paid, which could be handled electronically through the telephone system or cable networks at considerably lower cost.

The trouble with this alternative, as we mentioned before, is that the postal system is not just a business, it is a social institution whose value is not totally measurable in terms of profit and loss. The shift to electronic mail delivery already underway may be both logical and acceptable, but the public deserves to have considerably more involvement in the decision-making process than it has had to date. The alternatives need to be presented clearly, including the crucial question of who should pay the extra costs of maintaining traditional mail services.

The future of the postal system is, however, only a part of the problem of organizing public and private resources for the new information age. Until very recently, the subject was relegated to seminar discussions in a few universities and research institutes. This is changing as more individuals and groups see how their interests are tied to a resolution of the larger public issues involved. For the present, it is largely a sensitizing process, a slow realization that a radically different information environment is taking shape in ways that call for review, and redefinition, of long-standing national goals and purposes.

The need for a broad-based policy debate goes beyond particularistic decisions about computer access, cable television, broadcasting satellites, or the many other issues that have to be resolved. The essential issue is preserving and expanding the sum of two centuries of freedom in increasingly complex circumstances.

In 1787, Thomas Jefferson summed up the case for an open information society in a letter to Edward Carrington during the debates leading up to the adoption of the Constitution:

> The basis of our government being the opinion of the people, the very first object should be to keep that right; and were it left to me to decide whether we should have a government without newspapers, or newspapers without a government, I should not hesitate a moment to prefer the latter.

If Jefferson were debating the principles of a new Constitution today, it is probable that he would have expanded his views on the importance of a free press to include the electronic media and perhaps even open-access computer networks. The principle is the same, whether the technologies involved are 18th century flat-bed presses or modern computers that can print out thousands of words a minute.

How do we organize ourselves to match Jeffersonian ideals with the opportunities opened by modern communications and information technologies? Given the complexity and sensitivity of the subject, the answer does not lie in any master plan but in a range of general approaches, each of which advances the prospect for making adjustments to the new information environment within a democratic framework. The factor they have in common is the need to establish a workable balance between public and private sector responsibilities.

The facile approach is simply to do more of what we have been doing. This assumes that the public sector will neither take the lead in setting comprehensive national goals nor play an activist role in assuring the orderly expansion of communications and information resources over and above its traditional responsibilities for formal education, library services, and the like. The federal government would continue to act as a regulatory balance, brokering between the major economic interests involved and buffering the present communications structure against the instabilities of too rapid change. Given the hundreds of billions of dollars invested in the present structure and the need to amortize these costs over a long period of time this approach is clearly favored by most of the present managers of the system, as well as by that large segment of the public bureaucracy that has a stake in preserving the status quo. The public argument for continuing the present system is a compelling one, namely, that the system works. A second argument is also compelling, that it would be politically impossible to make any major adjustments in the system, no matter what the theoretical benefits might be, given the political and economic power of its present managers.

Despite the realism of these arguments, they are less and less convincing. There are weaknesses in our present approach, particularly in its heavy reliance on economic cost-benefit standards in determining both the form and pace of communications and information development. We are inclined to be impressed by the very real achievements and to miss the gaps. The assumption is that the gaps will be filled in by a trickle-down process. The question, from a social viewpoint, is whether we can continue to rely on this haphazard approach, given the pressure to bring formerly disadvantaged groups fully into the system.

The second, and more radical, approach is to make the public sector a more active participant in developing and managing an expanded communications and information network. The few proponents of this idea argue that only direct public intervention can create an integrated, full-service network, operated as a publicly owned utility. This would be a major reversal in our national style. The fact that other industrial democracies — those of the Japanese and the British, for instance — have thrived with considerable government involvement at this level would have little weight. There are, in fact, interesting examples closer to home of the workability of publicly managed communications utilities. These involve a handful of cities that in recent years have decided to develop their own coaxial-cable utility networks, providing a mix of commercial and public services to homes. Despite the determined opposition of the cable television industry to public ownership, these systems have been well managed and have generally been much more responsive to public service needs than most of their commercial counterparts.[19]

The problem with this alternative is that it is politically impractical. Comparisons with the experiences of the British or Japanese are irrelevant in considerations of the day-to-day performance of a preponderantly commercial system. Justified or not, the idea raises the specter of domination by government in an area where it has up to now largely been excluded, both by law and custom.

There is a third approach, one that tends to get lost in conflicting rhetoric about the virtues of private enterprise against the evils of socialistic centralized government. It is based on establishing, as public policy, a firm commitment to the evolution of a full-service national information grid, augmenting the present fragmentary system in stages. This would require a more clearly articulated division of responsibilities between the public and private sectors.

The basic construction and management of the completed system would be the responsibility of the private sector, which would develop the grid in as many competitive modes as technology and economic considerations would justify. Its performance would be judged by agreed-upon social goals that would be reviewed to reflect the changing communications and information needs of the post-industrial age. There is a solid precedent for this in the Communications Act of 1934, which was, in effect, a social compact between the government and private sectors, establishing regulatory restraints in exchange for the promise of universal telephone and broadcasting services — a promise that, with some lapses, was fulfilled. The situation is vastly more complicated today than in 1934, with many more players, more sophisticated technologies, and greater requirements for communications and information services by individuals and institutions. The basic problem, however, is the same, i.e., the need to form an effective compact between the public and private sectors to assure adequate communications resources.

The public sector's role should be limited largely to providing, where necessary, fiscal and other incentives for encouraging the application of innovative technology. The case for such an approach was made some years ago by Dr. Simon Ramo, then Vice-Chairman of TRW Inc., the electronics firm:

> The modifications of the structure of business and the pattern of all other activities needed to exploit the new information technology will involve massive start-up costs. . . . Despite the potential of economic and social gain inherent in the productivity increase and greater

flexibility the technology will provide, the speed with which this kind of technology can come into being is greatly contingent on a new organizational teaming of corporations and government. The government may need to sponsor large-scale experiments to develop the basic ideas, perhaps seeking improved information flow in government operations as the first proving ground, and be willing to allow, even encourage, the setting up of private industry teams to share risk.[20]

Another expanded public-sector role would be to assure access by individuals and groups to essential communications and information services. The experience of the Rural Electrification Administration in bringing power and telephone services to the countryside is a classic case in point. In the telecommunications sector, there is a strong argument for cutting back government regulatory restraints whose effect, if not intent, is to inhibit the efficient development of a full-service national information utility. The record shows that, on balance, the deregulatory trend of the last two decades has resulted in greater innovation, flexibility, and responsiveness to overall consumer needs. As John Eger, a communications attorney, has noted: "A regulatory commission can do a pretty fair job of curtailing undue monopoly profits, but it cannot issue an enforceable decree mandating alertness to changing market requirements."[21] Nevertheless, there are critical gaps in our attempts to reach the goal of assuring equitable access to basic telecommunications and information needs for all citizens.

The present regulatory system is based largely on three assumptions, one of them valid and two of them increasingly less so. The valid assumption is that there is a need for public regulation and monitoring of technical standards so that the total system is technologically sound. The second assumption, which has eroded over the years, is that regulation is necessary for the orderly economic development of the system. Originally justified largely by the need to amortize the high capital investment needed for communications, regulation became increasingly an excuse for protecting old technologies from new ones. If any lesson in communications regulations has been learned in the past decade, it is that the admirable, if somewhat tentative, FCC decisions allowing more competition in the industry have brought new vitality to the industry, not caused its predicted collapse.

The third assumption, which also is losing some of its validity, is that there is need for public controls over the radio spectrum, a valuable but limited resource. For a long time, government's role in mediating industry demands on spectrum resources was essential, given the steady expansion of spectrum use. The difference now is that the scarcity argument is increasingly less convincing, because of technical advances in efficient use of the spectrum and also because of the increased availability of cost-effective, high-capacity systems such as cable and fiber optic circuits that can conserve radio frequencies. Spectrum scarcity has become a considerably less important barrier to the play of market forces in determining which technology, and which segments of the private sector, can supply the most efficient services in developing a full-scale information grid.

In short, many of the old reasons for government regulation of the communications system are disappearing. Given the economic and political stakes involved, the regulatory structure cannot be phased out immediately. But there is no reason why a national commitment, based on a new pattern of public- and private-sector cooperation, could not be made now to carry us through the transitional phase to a full-service information grid providing low-cost, high-capacity services to every sector of American society.

Conditioned by the onward-and-upward rhetoric of the American electronic mythos, we can easily miss the full significance of this commitment. Certainly the most important outcome can be the fulfillment of First Amendment purposes — the right (*and* the capability) to hear and be heard, to see and be seen, to write and be written about, with due allowance for libel and privacy restrictions. For all our gains, we are still well short of this goal. The late critic of the American press, A. J. Liebling, once noted that there is freedom of the press for anyone with $5 million to buy his own newspaper. (The price is considerably higher these days.) Marshall McLuhan has correctly identified the most revolutionary characteristic of the Xerox and other low-cost copying machines: they make everyone his own publisher, if only on a limited basis. The ubiquitous new electronic circuits can expand our information rights in ways we find difficult to imagine, hemmed in as we are by the present limited range of available communications channels and information sources.

The new circuit-rich environment can be dramatically different. Much of our communication will continue to be private and personal, as in the telephone call and its extension to videophone or data communications, either as two-way or as round-robin conference calls among friends and associates. The major changes, however, will come in the way that wider information services are transmitted and received. This new phenomenon might be called "open electronics publishing." It is the logical outcome of the technological prospects opened up by the new high-capacity communications network and by computers. With the evolution toward channel abundance, supplying a wider range of visual, audio, or print information, competitive electronics publishing will allow any individual or group to offer messages on the new universal information grid. The grid would be a vastly expanded common carrier open to all, no longer restrained by radio spectrum restrictions or other circuit limitations.

This approach would represent a giant step toward the realization of Justice Oliver Wendell Holmes's marketplace of ideas. It would be an *open* market, with high-capacity channels available to all comers, big and small, seeking out consumers willing to pay for access to whatever information or services they want for themselves or what they determine, as a social good, should be made available as a general service subsidized by public revenues.

Electronic publishing would be a competitive enterprise on both a large and small scale. Information producers and consumers would be linked in a network operated as an information utility by commercial common carriers. No general laws would be required other than those already governing publishing such as copyright and libel. Public intervention would be limited to circuit rate regulation and to the setting of technical standards for the utility. Meanwhile, much of the present regulatory structure dealing with telecommunications could be dismantled so as to eliminate most of the present restrictions on information access.[22]

There are many reasons — political, economic, and social — why electronic publishing of the type described above is not an immediate prospect. However, there is no reason the concept of an open market in electronic publishing should not be set as a desirable national goal for implementation by the end of the century. The opening up of the information marketplace is beginning to happen already, with the growth of cable television and independent satellite networks and the beginnings of consumer computer grids. The old-line controllers of limited access, centralized news, entertainment, and other information resources are being challenged and this is all for the better. Their instinctive reaction is to seek government protection for their privileged position, drawing on a wide range of self-serving arguments. Media critic Edwin Diamond has neatly summed up some of the more prevalent myths supporting continued government regulation:

The myth of spectrum scarcity. Since the wavelengths are limited, government has to ration their use to ensure that everyone is heard. Cable television will spell the end of that notion, though it hasn't held up very well in recent years in any case. Newspapers also have limited resources — newsprint, delivery trucks, distribution points — but the private market is allowed to operate without Government control.

The myth that, without government, only the monied interest would be heard. Who's kidding whom? With government now, the richest people in town — the bankers, insurance-company owners, real-estate operators, what Kansas editor William Allen White called the "country-club set" — own both newspapers and broadcast stations (if the even wealthier chains haven't yet taken over).

The myth that government rules ensure diversity of ideas, the airing of controversy, and the chance for "both sides" to be heard on television. In practice, many broadcasters worry about broadcasting *anything* that might interfere with the nice sounds of their ringing cash registers. They don't like controversy because it gets in the way of profits. Also, where is it written that all issues have two sides, and two sides only? There may be more than two sides, or there may be only one.[23]

Although he does not use the phrase, Diamond is defending the concept of "open electronic publishing." His target is the television pattern in this country, our most visible centralized, limited-ownership information arrangement. It is the medium that could be most radically altered in an open electronic publishing environment. In fact, television's period of automatic onward-and-upward influence is already ending, after a profitable 30-year run (1949–1979). The reason is that a new pattern of competitive services — new forms of electronic information — are cutting into the television networks' hitherto unchallenged ability to attract huge audiences. Increasingly, the audience is looking at and listening to a new range of attractive alternatives, such as feature films and information services on cable systems and specialized over-the-air television networks. No one of these new electronic resources is yet able to match the mass audiences of the three big networks. Collectively, however, they are eroding the network audience base, and every indication is that the trend will accelerate in the coming years.

There is enough residual snobbism about television among intellectuals, pseudo and otherwise, to encourage and expand on all reports, however premature, about network television's demise. Their enthusiasm may be somewhat misplaced. Media critic Douglass Cater has noted that, for all its faults, network television and its large audiences have been an important element in maintaining social stability during a particularly rocky passage in the American experience:

Is the fractionalization of audiences a net social gain?...What happens when each minority group can tune in to its own prophets? When there are no more Walter Cronkites each evening to reassure us that despite all its afflictions the nation still stands?[24]

The real problem may be that television, because of its pervasive influence, has been overburdened by too many expectations. Its natural bent is as a news and entertainment medium, yet it has been charged, under the dubious rubric of balanced programming, with being the electronic surrogate for school, church, town meeting, and other specialized institutions. Television cannot, in fact, serve as the equivalent of these institutions, and it would be wise for us to curtail these unrealizable expectations. By sharing its functions more widely with other electronic publishing channels, network television could be freed up very effectively (and very profitably) to carry out its more natural news and entertainment functions, instead of trying to be the electronic Elmer's Glue binding all our interests.

However, the argument for a new pattern of electronic publishing goes well beyond television and other mass media. Its greatest impact will be in the consumerization of electronic networks, providing a full range of text, voice, and visual information services for the general public. Because of costs and technical limitations, such networking has been the province of big business and big government up until recently. A current trend, however, is toward the steady expansion of information networking for smaller organizations and individuals. Two important components of the grid — telephones and television sets — are already in place in over 90 percent of United States homes, as well as in schools and other institutions.

High-capacity coaxial-cable lines are already available to a majority of American families. Until a few years ago, there seem to have been few prospects that another vital element — a low-cost electronic information terminal — would be soon available. However, microprocessor technology makes this possible, either as "black box" attachments to television sets or as separate home terminals connected to telephone and cable lines.

This leaves one significant missing link in the universal grid. It is the consumer-oriented data bases and other services whose product will be useful to the mass audience needed to support a universal grid providing text, voice, and visual services. The grid's full development may hinge on the resolution of a difficult public policy question. A significant group of consumers is clearly identified as a market for any specialized educational and information services. They are the natural information seekers, who are the basic marketing target for commercial electronic information services directed to their homes or workplaces. However, it is a very selective market, one that probably cannot sustain a universal grid. A full network will probably not evolve until there is a clearer definition of responsibilities for educational and information services between the private and public sectors. As long as the grid is limited to commercially salable information, it will have a limited reach. Its full use may depend on public decisions to develop (or, in some cases, expand) public electronic information services, either as direct government services or through subsidies. There are, for instance, some basic decisions to be made about the traditional public library system. Should public libraries continue to be primarily repositories for print-on-paper resources, or should they evolve more rapidly toward a new (and more expensive) mix of books and electronic storage-and-distribution systems?

Though limited, experience with such public services on cable systems to date has underlined the difficulties involved. Cable system operators and other potential information network entrepreneurs are no more or less altruistic than the rest of us. They are developing the basic circuitry and the data bases to serve commercially viable markets. Their circuits will be the infrastructures of what can become a universal electronic publishing network in the coming years. The services provided by the network will depend on economics. The providing of a *full* range of services will depend on social decisions determining that they are a civic necessity. In the seventies, Edwin Parker and Donald Dunn of Stanford University's Communications Research Institute suggested that the public sector sponsor pilot projects within an overall plan for the long-term development of a national information utility:

> Since most of the funds for this utility will come from the private sector, the principal needs for Federal action are in the areas of coordination, policy analysis and assessment, and the funding of pilot projects and demonstrations designed to stimulate the development of new public-sector education and information services.[25]

Such a proposal is part of a long-standing tradition of public involvement in information resources. The public library system is, of course, the most familiar example. Public organizations are the largest single source of both specialized and general information materials in the country, ranging from the products of the Government Printing Office to the Medlars medical data bank and the National Technical Information Service.

There have been some publicly sponsored experiments for information services on cable systems, along the lines suggested above by Professors Parker and Dunn. Many of these were funded by the National Science Foundation. One of the most successful was an interactive cable television information service for the elderly in Reading, Pennsylvania, which demonstrated the social, and emotional, importance of direct access to information for older people, and particularly for those who were homebound. Simple information on Social Security and Medicaid procedures proved to be a critically important part of the services provided. In general, however, government efforts to provide electronic data services have been limited to science and technology subjects, supporting business and professional needs. Such services are, of course, necessary, but they are far removed from ordinary consumer needs.

Efforts to provide consumer services (as in the Reading senior citizen project) are still fragmentary, cautious, and lacking in overall purpose. A good part of the problem is economics: data banks and networking are very expensive operations. A mixed public/commercial coaxial-cable system proposed for the District of Columbia by the Mitre Corporation some years ago put the commercial break-even point for the system at 50 percent of total customers, and the public service break-even point at closer to 100 percent.

This gap is indicative of the economic realities behind the rhetoric that has clogged so many discussions about the new information channels. So-called "free" public services have to be paid for by taxpayers, or through some fee system. Experience with such services on cable systems has been too limited to provide any firm projections of the exact pattern for future services. However, there are indications that they will be tested extensively in the next few years. This will result from the trend requiring that new urban cable systems make specific provision for such services. Some of these systems have as many as one hundred channels. Whether such an abundance of channels will result in a comparable abundance of information and other services, commercial or public, remains to be seen.

The issue deserves considerably more attention than it is now getting. High-capacity communications circuits and data banks are being built largely under commercial auspices. They are efficient, well-managed, and aimed primarily at individuals and organizations who can pay for them. These individuals and groups are the professionals, the trained information seekers. However, this pattern of development ignores the very large group of people who have neither the money nor the opportunities for access to the new resources. As a result, the gap between the information-rich and the information-poor is likely to widen rather than narrow with the introduction of the new information technologies. The question cannot be begged by suggesting that most people don't need, and don't want, access to sophisticated information resources. This reasoning is demeaning, and not particularly true in an increasingly complex society in which the range of information needed for survival is widening.

Post-industrial America cannot thrive in an environment in which there is a new kind of literacy gap based on unequal access to the resources of the new communications and information technologies. Individuals are not all equal as information seekers, but they all seek information for a variety of reasons. We need to know more about these reasons, the kinds of information services people want, and how the new technologies can be adapted to these needs. The information machines, with their flashing lights and mysterious insides, can be intimidating to many people. These paraphernalia of the new information environment should be developed in ways that make them readily accessible, inexpensive to use, and programmed to provide information people need. This will call for a different kind of public sector involvement in assuring access to the new machines. One researcher has suggested that Xerox-type copying machines be subsidized in ghetto areas, where they are generally not now available, as part of an overall information access program.[26] Whether or not this proposal makes social or economic sense is secondary to the fact that it raises a problem — information access inequality — that has not yet been fully faced in considerations of the role of the new high-capacity circuits and machines.

In the absence of a national consensus on the goals of the new information age, economics and technology are now shaping the future. They are the major forces propelling us into the new age. Experience with earlier, less complex technological advances has shown, however, that at least some of the unexpected, unwanted results could have been modified, and perhaps turned around, by some intelligent prior planning. As *Fortune* editor Max Ways noted in a critique of information trends:

> The range of possible consequences presented by the new information technologies is so varied and subtle that no society would be expected to have ready-made solutions to the main problems presented. But as the employment of these technologies continues to spread rapidly, it will be disgraceful if policy questions generated by them are not soon identified, discussed and dealt with.[27]

There are sensitive political, economic, legal, and social issues involved in any attempt to develop a viable national approach to information and communications resources. The participants in the debate tend to polarize their positions. On the one hand there are enthusiasts who exaggerate the influence of the new information machines as solutions, rather than mere necessary supporting resources, for complex problems. At the other extreme are the skeptics who fear, with some justification, that more active public sector intervention in this area could lead to undesirable government controls and erosion of constitutional freedom.

The answer lies, as usual, somewhere in between. The critical issue

is whether everyone in this society — both chief and Indian, the powerful and the powerless — has equal rights to the basic information he or
she needs to survive and thrive. No society has come near this goal. The
United States has come the closest, and our national experience has
shown us that expanding the information base, plugging everyone in, is
the best policy. Moving more rapidly toward this ideal is our biggest
challenge in the new information environment.

NOTES

1. For a useful overview of interrelated communications and information
   policy issues, see Glen O. Robinson, ed., *Communications for Tomorrow*
   (New York: Praeger Publishers, 1978).
2. Harold Black and Edward Shaw, "Detroit's Data Banks," *Datamation,*
   March 1967, p. 27.
3. Karl W. Deutsch, *The Nerves of Government* (New York: The Free Press of
   Glencoe, 1963).
4. John deButts, "Policy, Not Technology, Will Shape the Future of
   Communications in the U.S.A.," *Communications News,* June 1975, p. 47.
5. Erik Barnouw, *Tube of Plenty* (New York: Oxford University Press, 1975),
   p. 39.
6. The dispute surrounding the formation of the Communications Satellite
   Corporation is described in Wilson Dizard, *Television — A World View*
   (Syracuse, NY: Syracuse University Press, 1966), pp. 263–67, and in
   Brenda Maddox, *Beyond Babel: New Directions in Communications*
   (Boston: Beacon Press, 1974), pp. 82–90.
7. U. S. Executive Office of the President, *Final Report of the President's Task
   Force on Communications Policy* (Washington, DC: U. S. Government
   Printing Office, 1968).
8. Anne W. Branscomb, "Communications Policy in the United States," in
   Patricia Edgar and Sayeed Rahim, eds., *Communications Policy in
   Developed Countries* (Honolulu: East-West Center, 1981).
9. U. S. Executive Office of the President, *The Radio Frequency Spectrum:
   United States' Use and Management*, Office of Telecommunications Policy
   (Washington, DC: Government Printing Office, 1975), p. D–18.
10. Testimony of Harold Brown in U.S. Congress, Senate, Communications
    Subcommittee of the Committee on Commerce, *Space Communications
    and Allocation of the Radio Spectrum*, 87th Cong., 1st sess., p. 17. A critical
    description of the evolution of the National Communications System can be
    found in Herbert Schiller, *Mass Communications and American Empire*
    (Boston: Beacon Press, 1971), pp. 63–78.
11. "U. S. Scuttles Plan for IRS Computer," *New York Times,* 7 January 1978,
    p. 1.
12. "Payroll Tax Collectors to Plug Into Computer Age," *Washington Post,* 19
    January 1988, p. D–1.

13. "AT&T Continues to Head Companies on Federal Advisory Boards," *Defense Space Daily* (Washington), 28 October 1977, p. 3. See also "Advisers are Fewer but Expenses Mount," *Washington Post,* 26 March 1978, p. 52.

14. U. S. National Commission on Libraries and Information, *National Information Policy.* Report to the President submitted by the staff of the Domestic Council on the Right of Privacy (Washington DC: Government Printing Office 1975), p. vi.

15. "FCC and Congress Clash Over Proper Role," *Congressional Quarterly*, 27 February 1988, pp. 479–82.

16. U. S. Congress, House Subcommittee on Communications, Committee on Interstate and Foreign Commerce, *Options Papers,* 95th Cong., 1st sess, committee print 95–13, May, 1971.

17. For a useful summary of the checkered history of rewrite legislation, see Manny Lucoff, "The Rise and Fall of the Third Rewrite," *Journal of Communication*, 30, no. 3 (Summer 1980): pp. 47–53.

18. Kurt Borchardt, *Structure and Performance of the U.S. Communications Industry.* Division of Research, Graduate School of Business Administration, Harvard University, 1970, pp. 152–56.

19. St. Paul, Minnesota, and Paterson, New Jersey, are cities that have adopted this option. Municipal ownership of cable systems is, of course, strenuously opposed by the commercial cable television industry.

20. Simon Ramo, "Technology and Resources for Business," *Horizon*, U. S. Information Agency publication no. 4 (Washington DC: 1975), p. 32.

21. Quoted in John F. Judge, "The Complexities of Seeking a Policy," *Government Executive* (Washington), June 1976, p. 44.

22. A strong case for electronic publishing is given in Peter Jay, "The Future of Broadcasting," *Encounter* (London), April 1977, pp. 68–79.

23. Edwin Diamond, "Media Myths That Limit Free Speech," *TV Guide,* 5 November 1977, p. 44.

24. Douglass Cater, "A Communications Revolution?" *Wall Street Journal,* 6 August 1973, p. 18.

25. Edwin B. Parker and Donald Dunn, "Information Technology: Its Social Potential," *Science*, 30 June 1972, p. 1399.

26. The suggestion is made in Susan Krieger, "Prospects for Communications Policy," *Policy Sciences* (Amsterdam), no. 2 (1971): p. 312.

27. The Conference Board, *Information Technology: Some Critical Implications for Decision Makers,* report no. 537 (New York: The Conference Board, 1972), p. 6.

CHAPTER 8

Exporting the Information Society

Fire fighters in Sweden have an ingenious system for assuring efficient responses to fire alarms. A computer data bank keeps records on each building — its construction features, number of occupants, and any special characteristics (combustible chemicals, for instance) that might be important if a fire breaks out. The data bank also records the quickest route from the nearest fire station. When a building catches fire, this information is instantly retrieved on a computer terminal at the station.

The Swedish fire data bank is an imaginative application of computer power. But the project is interesting in another way: the computer containing the data was originally located in Cleveland, Ohio. The 8,000 mile electronic round trip involved in the transmittal of information to and from the Cleveland computer was not a deterrent in awarding the data bank contract to an American bidder, the General Electric Company. The information could be retrieved as quickly as if its source were in Stockholm or another Swedish city. Similar computer data banks are being developed for American fire departments.

The Cleveland computer's role in Swedish fires is only one example of a new phenomenon — the internationalization of communications and information. It was also an example of the problems of electronic internationalism. Despite the fact that the Cleveland fire data base worked efficiently, there were complaints in Sweden about having information regarding Swedish buildings stored in a foreign computer. As a result, the arrangement with General Electric was ended.

When airline clerks make reservations for passengers in Warsaw or Tokyo, they are probably unaware that they are connected to a computer in Atlanta, where a large share of international flight reservations are stored. Nutrition researchers in Rome, searching for technical data on European regional computer networks may not know that they are dealing with a data base in Amsterdam. These networks are, in a very real sense, indifferent to time, place, and distance. They have, as anthropologist Edward Carpenter has remarked, made free spirits of us all, not in a Sunday school sense of having wings or being good, but in the sense of being pure spirit, divorced from flesh, capable of instant transportation anywhere.

Free spirits aside, international computer networks are part of a pattern of dramatic changes in global communications and information resources in recent years. To a considerable extent, this pattern was developed first in this country; most of the rest of the world is only beginning to catch up with us. Over and above the effect this pattern will eventually have on our own information environment, the change represents a strategic new element in the American global equation. The United States needs a strong world communications network to support its overseas interests. Economically, the export of communications goods and services is increasingly important. Politically, communications are the nervous system for the interdependent world order to which this country is committed, and particularly important to this world order are improved links between the industrialized and developing nations.

The expanded world communications network will amplify American ideas and values in a more forceful way than has ever been done before. As in the past, these ideas will evoke reactions ranging from admiration to anger — often at the same time. "What makes America unique in our time is that confrontation with the new is part of the daily American experience," Zbigniew Brzezinski has noted. "For better or for worse, the rest of the world learns what is in store for it by observing what happens in the United States."[1] University of California communications researcher Herbert Schiller, a critic of American communications practices abroad, makes the point that the United States does not simply export products and services in this field. It exports a *system*, including a heavy ideological bent favoring American values and attitudes that in Schiller's view, are not in the best interests of other cultures, particularly those in the developing nations. The evidence Schiller cites to support his observation may be debatable, but this basic thesis has merit.[2]

In assessing the American role, three major trends should be considered. The first of these is the pell-mell growth in world communications and information resources, particularly in the last two decades. Accurate statistics are often hard to come by, but taking one measure — volume of global communications traffic — it becomes obvious that growth is occurring at a rate of between 10 and 15 percent annually, roughly doubling every half-dozen years. Whatever measures are used, communications and information emerge as major growth sectors that have been uniquely immune from the economic turbulence affecting other industries in recent years.

The second trend influencing American interests are the changes taking place in the geographic pattern of global communications. Twenty years ago, this was a neat, orderly business, confined largely to the North Atlantic area and a Japanese extension. By present standards, volume was low, consisting primarily of business traffic passing through government owned or controlled networks. Again, the exception to government control was the United States, whose overseas communication circuits were (and still are) owned by several firms operating under light federal regulation. Nevertheless, the American firms worked efficiently with their foreign government counterparts in what was essentially a gentlemanly division of the world market, dominated by American interests.

Today economics, politics, and technology are pulling these patterns into different shapes. The market is becoming geographically more diverse every year, thanks in large part to the 115-nation *Intelsat* satellite network that provides high-grade communications wherever there is an earth terminal. Among other changes, the satellite network has reduced the importance of the "gateway cities" in Europe, the United States, and Japan through which communications traffic to the rest of the world was formerly channeled. Until the advent of the satellite network, for instance, all international traffic between the east and west coasts of South America was routed through gateway cities in the United States. Similar changes in Asia and Africa have given Third World countries direct communications with each other for the first time, thus lessening their dependence on the industrialized nations. Another satellite development that promises to change old patterns is the regional satellite networks that will operate outside the *Intelsat* framework. The Europeans are operating several such networks now. The Arab states have built a regional system and there are proposals for similar networks in Africa, Latin America, and Asia.

The third significant trend in international communications is the threat of political restrictions on the growth of the world system. The United States has taken the lead since World War II in advocating the elimination of restrictions on communications flow internationally. In the late 1940s, it used its then dominant influence in the United Nations to get international approval for the concept of "free flow of information.'' Our democratic partners approved, while the poorer areas of Asia and Africa were either still colonial states or regarded the issue as irrelevant. Only the Soviet Union and its client states objected, a predictable reaction given their need for tight internal controls over domestic information channels in order to maintain the communist parties in power. Although American advocacy of open information channels reflected deeply held national convictions, it also provided the ideological underpinnings for the postwar expansion of American information influence throughout the world.[3]

Until recently, this influence was welcomed, or at least accepted as a normal consequence of American power and influence. Now it is being questioned in ways that could affect United States interests in international communications as well as overall prospects for an open world infomation order. The reasons for this development are complex, but they center around new perceptions abroad of information as a political, economic, and cultural force. Increasingly, information is being viewed as a strategic resource that, like oil or nickel, is a measurable element in calculations of national strength. As a result, it is a newly contested factor in international affairs. As communications consultant Andrew Aines has noted:

> The battle is to use modern information technology most advantageously. It involves out-and-out espionage, military and industrial. It involves the quest for scientific and technical data of all kinds and for all purposes. It involves the delivery of political information. . . . It involves the United Nations, COMECON (the Soviet economic bloc), the Common Market, military alliances and many other international bodies.[4]

This battle has, in turn, led to a new concept of information sovereignty, defined as the right of a society to protect itself against what it regards as unwarranted intrusion by outside information and communications influences. The concept arose originally during the early seventies when Third World countries complained that their information and communications resources were dominated by American and European interests. The charges originally focused on the influence of Western mass media, particularly film, television, and news agency products. In particular, Third World spokesmen argued that the American free-flow concept did not take into account the massive imbalance in information flows between the West and other parts of the globe. They saw the free-flow thesis as a rationalization for what they regarded as cultural and economic imperialism. The debate went beyond rhetorical charges and countercharges. In recent years, Third World countries have taken a series of steps to gain more control over foreign influences in their domestic telecommunications and information affairs.

The information sovereignty question is also being seriously discussed by European nations, although their perspectives and motives are generally different from those of Third World countries. Confident that they can hold their own in this field, Europeans are considerably less worried about American cultural influence. Their concern is to protect themselves against what they regard as inordinate outside (that is, American) control over their information resources, particularly in computerized data banks and circuits. American companies have been particularly successful in marketing goods and services to industrial nations abroad. Some analysts estimate that between 50 percent and 60 percent of European *domestic* data records are processed by American companies.[5] This ratio has been lowered in recent years since most European countries have taken actions to strengthen their domestic data resources.

Information sovereignty issues still worry the Europeans, both in terms of personal-privacy rights and the newly perceived strategic importance of information and communications as a national and regional resource. This has led them, as we shall see, to consider regulations on controlling transborder data flow. At another level, the Europeans are also concerned about the strong American lead in computers. They have taken steps to improve domestic computer production through government subsidies and other programs. The European Communities (EC), the Brussels-based regional economic organization, has sponsored development of a regional computer data network. Taken together, these moves reflect a recognition that in the future, as an Organization for Economic Cooperation and Development (OECD) report on European industry has stated, "information and knowledge, rather than capital and production of manufactured goods will become the central issue around which sharp competition will develop."

These world trends toward protectionism and control of information flow across borders have not yet reached a critical stage. However, they are a potentially serious problem for the United States in advancing its political, economic, and cultural interests favoring an open global information pattern. Not only are other countries taking a closer look at their own national interests in this area, but the subject is being debated here. A 1976 Defense Department study suggested that the United States was too libera' in sharing its science and technology know-how with other countries. The report declared that a significant "leak" in this area was created by the large number of foreign students in American universities. According to a 1986 National Science Foundation report, of the 300,000 students from abroad then enrolled in universities and colleges, 60 percent were majoring in technical studies. While it is improbable that the United States would ever adopt general policies restricting information exports, over and above longstanding controls on technology flow to Communist countries, there is increasing concern about the rate at which certain technologies are exported, cutting into the competitive edge for American products.

Rapid growth, changing patterns, challenges to American leadership — these are the conditions that will set the agenda for United States strategy in the global information and commmunications field during the 1990s. American decisions in this area will be an important element in determining the future pace and scope of world communications growth. No other country has the technological and economic strength, or the political will, to assume the lead in this area. The Soviets are ideologically incapable of taking a major role, given their own inhibitions about information and communications matters. The Europeans have been slow to develop a consensus, much less take actions, in this area. The Japanese look upon the issue primarily in terms of trade.

If the United States takes on a greater leadership role, it will first have to address the fact that it does not now have an articulated national policy in this area. Its primary interest in the past two decades has been, with good reason, to provide support for the international expansion of the American communications and information industries. Government policy has essentially reacted to commercial needs. In most cases this has been done successfully and in one instance, it was done brilliantly — in the Communications Satellite Act of 1962, which provided the legislative authorization for America to develop a global satellite system. The legislation was a triumph of pragmatism over a formidable list of reasons why it couldn't be done. However, no effective attempts have been made to develop a long-range policy approach in other global communications matters since then. One effort to develop such a policy in the late sixties, by the presidentially appointed Rostow Commission on communications discussed earlier, was unsuccessful because some of its recommendations clashed with strong communications industry interests in this country.

As in the domestic policy area, international communications responsibilities are divided among a number of federal agencies. The overall responsibility in the executive branch rests with the State Department. Within the department, however, this authority had been, until recently, fragmented among a number offices. Although the Federal Communications Commission's (FCC) primary responsibilities are in the domestic field, it has become increasingly involved in international matters in recent years as a result of the expanded foreign activities of the domestic companies it regulates. This wider involvement led former FCC chairman Richard Wiley to propose that the commission be authorized to negotiate agreements on communications matters directly with foreign governments — a function normally carried out by the State Department. The department did not take kindly to the proposal and the matter was dropped.[6]

A dozen other agencies have fragmentary roles to play in overseas communications matters. The Defense Department, manager of its own large global communications system, carries weight in any discussion of the subject involving its many interests. The Department of Commerce, the Federal Aviation Agency, NASA, and the Central Intelligence Agency contribute their particular interests. The United States Information Agency has a mandate to advise the President and foreign affairs agencies on foreign communications matters. The National Telecommunications and Information Administration (NTIA), created in 1977, also has international responsibilities as part of its charter to coordinate overall government communications policies. Its authority is limited in practice, however, by the resistance of other agencies, notably the Defense and State Departments, to NTIA activities in areas traditionally assigned to these agencies. NTIA also is inhibited by its bureaucratic location at the second level of the Department of Commerce.[7]

The overall fragmentation of United States Government responsibilities was summarized several years ago by Senator Ernest F. Hollings, then chairman of the Senate Communications Subcommittee: "No single agency of the United States government has comprehensive authority over international communications, nor was the distribution of functions among several agencies the result of planned allocation. Rather, it grew like Topsy, responding to particular technical or industrial problems as they arose."[8] A significant step to correct this situation was taken by the House of Representatives' Subcommittee on Information Policy in a 1980 report suggesting the establishment of a top level office for communications policy in the State Department, and a White House-level interagency coordinating mechanism.[9] After much pulling and hauling among agencies attempting to defend their bureaucratic turfs, a permanent office designed to coordinate United States government international policies was set up in 1983 in the State Department. Diana Lady Dougan, a communications executive from Salt Lake City, was appointed first head of the office, with the rank of ambassador.

Meanwhile, the controlling factor in United States overseas communications is that these communications are private sector responsibilities, with government in only a minor supportive role. This is unlike the situation in most other countries, where governments control or tightly regulate all international communications. A significant exception to private sector dominance in this country was made in 1962, in a decision to make the Communications Satellite Corporation (Comsat) a government mandated "chosen instrument" to exploit the then American monopoly on advanced satellite technology. The Comsat exception was a compromise between competing claims within private industry on how best to manage the satellites commercially.[10]

In the absence of any grand design for public policies, the communications industry is the prime mover of American overseas interests. It is big, wide-ranging, and cockily confident of its capabilities. It has the advantages of operating from a strong domestic base, the biggest market in the world. Until recently, almost half of total global communications equipment production was absorbed by the United States market. This ratio dropped to about 40 percent by the late eighties, still an advantage no foreign competitor will come close to matching. American industry had a running start in the early postwar decades, before competitors in other industrialized countries had geared up. Riding the technological lead provided by their research and development laboratories, American firms dominated most segments of the overseas communications field. Competition is more rigorous these days, and the American lead is narrowing in the three key sectors — equipment production, message distribution, and information products and services. Since United States industry plays such a dominant role in world communications, it is useful to take a look at its place in these three sectors.

Providing reliable overseas commmunications circuits has been a complex, risky business since the 1850s when Cyrus Fields attempted to lay the first transatlantic cable — a primitive telegraph wire wrapped in guttapercha. The cable snapped, and Fields and his associates went bankrupt. A later project was successsful, providing the first oceanic link in what has become a cat's cradle of international circuits throughout the globe. The first cables were simple wires that were later supplemented by unreliable radio circuits. This changed in the 1950s with the development of high-capacity submarine cables and, in the 1960s, with satellite microwave links. Thus the technical base for a dramatic expansion in global communications was opened.

American firms were in a strong position to exploit this advantage. In early 1960s, when expansion began in earnest, over half of all international communications originated in this country. Yet, international telephone and telegraph traffic was, and is, only a small part of the American communications pattern. Overseas traffic accounted for only about five percent of total national service in the eighties.[11] These figures do not accurately reflect the quantum jump in American overseas communications in recent years, paced largely by business requirements as American firms expanded abroad. Telephone calls are a good indicator. In 1950, the annual number of overseas calls was one million; by 1975 this had jumped to 42 million (excluding Canada and Mexico). By the late eighties, the number of calls exceeded 500 million. Because Americans make more international calls than they receive, the United States has a trade deficit in the overseas phone business. In 1987, AT&T — the dominant overseas carrier — paid a record total of $1.2 billion to foreign carriers for handling the extra calls.

The American share of the international telephone and data markets is split among a half-dozen firms. In the telephone market, AT&T's long-term monopoly has been modified in the past decade as a result of FCC deregulatory decisions. AT&T now has competition for overseas telephone traffic, primarily from MCI and GTE-Sprint. Nevertheless, in 1987 AT&T collected 95 percent of American international telephone revenues. Its circuits, along with those of its competitors, are linked to 99.5 percent of the world's phones, one half of which can be dialed directly.

During the nineties, direct-dialing capabilities will become nearly universal abroad, in part because of the introduction of a worldwide dialing code developed under the auspices of the International Telecommunications Union. A world telephone number has up to fourteen numbers, making it possible to reach any dial phone anywhere. Taken together with rapid telephone growth abroad, the result should be a massive increase in global voice phone traffic.

The fastest developing area of international telecommunications traffic is in data communications, with typical annual growth rates of 10–15 percent. Starting out with traditional telegraph services in the last century, data communications to overseas points expanded rapidly in the post-World War II years. The emphasis was on telex traffic. (Following the domestic trend, the international telegram business is headed for extinction.) Telex will be an important element in international data flow for a long time, because it is a relatively cheap service and is accessible in most countries over ordinary telephone lines.

The long-term expansion prospects in international data flow, however, lie in the development of high-speed computer-to-computer services. AT&T and IBM have become major entrants into this competitive field since their antitrust cases were dropped in 1982. One result has been a realignment of the four "international record carriers" that had previously dominated the overseas market — RCA Globcom, Western Union, ITT Worldcom, and MCI International. In 1988, ITT Worldcom was bought up by Western Union as part of a massive reorganization of the latter company. At the same time, MCI International purchased RCA Globcom.

The international telephone and data transmission markets are clearly in transition these days from the low-volume elite services of two decades ago to new kinds of mass communications networks. The changes have sharpened the competitive edge of the American firms involved, battling for market shares not only among themselves but also with foreign firms such as Britain's Cable & Wireless, whose international facilities are greater than those of any American carrier.

International networking trends point upwards; the question is how far up? An important part of the answer depends on the willingness of foreign governments to provide, through the telecommunications structures they control, the facilities that American companies need to extend their services abroad. During the seventies and early eighties, government-controlled post, telegraph, and telephone agencies (PTT) were cool, and sometimes hostile, toward American proposals for new services. Traditionally conservative, many PTT's were in no hurry to upset their highly profitable telecommunications operations (which normally subsidize money-losing postal services).

This situation is changing rapidly. The pressure is on overseas telecommunications authorities to loosen up their stodgy operations, and, in particular, to expand faster into new services. In large part, they are being pushed to reform by domestic forces, primarily business organizations that need these services to compete more efficiently at home and abroad. But a significant part of the pressure has come from the overall success of efforts in the United States to deregulate the domestic telecommunications system in ways that have vastly expanded its range of services. The 1984 AT&T divestiture was only the most dramatic example of liberalizing decisions that have been taken over a 20-year period. This American experience has demonstrated the overall efficiencies that can result by moving away from regulated monopoly patterns to a more openly competitive environment in telecommunications.

These changes have had a strong impact abroad. Great Britain was the first country to move toward a variation of the American deregulatory model. In 1984, the government licensed a new network, Mercury, to compete with British Telecom (BT), the newly privatized successor to the previous government telecommunications monopoly, known quaintly as the British Post Office. The Japanese followed suit in 1985 with a somewhat different privatization of Nippon Telephone & Telegraph (NTT), the government telecommunications system, also permitting the entry of new companies that would compete with NTT in providing specialized services. As a result, by the end of the eighties, three of the world's five largest telecommunications networks (AT&T, BT, and NTT) were privately owned in a competitive market environment. NTT is by far the most affluent of these firms, with a 1988 market value of $300 billion, ten times more than that of AT&T.

Other industrialized countries are taking similar measures. By and large, they are retaining government control over the basic telecommunications network, while permitting greater private competition in a range of specialized services such as electronic mail. The French government, long a textbook example of centralized telecommunications controls, has been a leader in developing this new pattern of competition in so-called value-added services. In order to carry out these plans, the government set up a deregulatory agency in 1986 with the wonderfully Gallic name of "Commission on Communications and Liberties."[12]

The most dramatic project for liberalizing communications and information services abroad has been sponsored by the Commission of the European Communities (EC), the 12-nation regional economic organization. The initiative has been part of the EC's overall program to bring about a "Europe without frontiers" in 1992, i. e., the ending of all major trade barriers among its member states. In February 1988, the Commission reached essential agreement on a proposal for all its members to dismantle the barriers that have impeded the development of a European-wide competitive telecommunications market.[13]

Building a full-scale world communications network will require a staggering amount of new equipment, from satellites in space to telephones in African villages. Large segments of the network are already in place, but most of it still has to be built. Telecommunications Industry Research (TIR), a British market-forecasting firm, estimates annual global telecommunications equipment expenditures of $156.8 billion in 1990, rising to $243 billion by 1995.[14] Such growth projections involve educated (and usually conservative) guesses; what is more certain is that the locus of world telecommunications growth will shift from the United States, which, until a few years ago, accounted for half of all global communications equipment production and use. The American market will still be the largest, but major growth will take place in other industrial countries and, increasingly, in the Third World.

Equipment markets were dominated handily by American manutacturers in the early postwar decades. This is no longer true; European and Asian firms are now stiff competitors. The ability of Japan and other Asian countries (Taiwan, Korea, and Singapore, among others) to produce cheaper, quality consumer goods has resulted in a net deficit in the United States communications equipment balance of trade in recent years. The American industry's strength is in high-technology products, but even here the advantages provided by innovative research, quality engineering, and patent protections are shrinking. "The world is regressing to the speedy technological transfer of the 15th century, when patents did not exist," the London *Economist* notes. "Electronics, where patenting is nearest to collapse, is recreating that vanished age. In electronics, the technological lead time is usually only 18 months."[15]

The result is, increasingly, a global free-for-all as telecommunications firms (and the many governments that subsidize their efforts) scramble for bigger shares of an expanding market.

The market involves a bewildering variety of products, but most of them are grouped around two familiar items — telephones and computers. A century after Alexander Graham Bell's invention, the rest of the world is moving into the telephone age. The phone has been an elite instrument until now in all but a handful of countries — the United States, Canada, Sweden, and several others. Despite its advanced industrial status, West Germany did not have phone service for 40 percent of its families in the late seventies. Moving down the economic ladder, telephone services range from the inadequate to the near-hopeless in most Third World countries. What phone services exist in these countries are patchwork systems, often in an advanced state of decay.

Another group of countries deserves mention for their new attention to telecommunications development. They are the Soviet Union, the People's Republic of China, and their client states. China has taken aggressive measures in recent years to upgrade a rickety communications system. With a population of over a billion, it has about five million phones; only one person in 250 has access to a telephone. Telecommunications expansion was given a considerably higher economic priority in the seventh five-year plan adopted in 1985. The plan calls for the addition of 10 million new phones, more long-distance lines and 20 new satellite earth stations to serve the domestic communications satellite network being planned by the government to reach remote areas. These projections are probably optimistic; one element in their favor is that the Chinese are actively seeking outside help, primarily from Japanese and American companies, in developing the equipment and other services needed to expand the system.[16]

The Soviet telecommunications system is similarly in urgent need of upgrading if it is to support the ambitious plans for economic modernization proposed by General Secretary Mikhail Gorbachev. The USSR has the lowest per capita distribution of telephones among the industrialized nations — 10 per 100 citizens. Most other civilian communications resources are equally poor.

In the early years after the Russian revolution, Leon Trotsky reportedly proposed to Josef Stalin that a modern telephone system be built in the new Soviet state. Stalin brushed off the idea, saying, "I can imagine no greater instrument of counterrevolution in our time." He opted for tight Party controls of all communications channels instead of the country's broader social and economic interests.

In Mikhail Gorbachev's Russia, pragmatic needs are forcing a new look at the dilemma between information controls and economic efficiency. In part, this has been set by the much-publicized *glasnost* campaign, aimed at providing more credible content in the Soviet media and the arts. Equally important, though less publicized, are the steps being taken to expand telecommunications and information resources as part of the economic restructuring effort.

A significant start in this direction has already been made. According to Western estimates, the Soviet Union spent the equivalent of $9.8 billion on telecommunications equipment in 1987, an increase of 17 percent over the previous year, putting it in second place after the United States ($24.3 billion) among industrialized countries. Following a 1985 decision by the Central Committee of the Communist Party, an increase in overall telephone facilities by about one-third was decreed in the 1986–1990 five-year plan. Another component of Mikhail Gorbachev's Soviet-style "information revolution" is the expansion of computer terminals and networks, including the large-scale introduction of personal computers. Over and above the impact that this may have on strengthening Soviet economic development, there are critical questions about the longer-range effect of these new resources on the government's controls over communications and information.[17]

Meanwhile, in the noncommunist world, the rush is on to expand communications systems as scores of countries, both the haves and the have-nots, realize that a good telephone system is not only a national status symbol but also an economic necessity. They want their new systems quickly, and they often opt for the latest models, which means expensive, computerized, all-electronic equipment. (In the case of technology-poor countries, this high initial expense can make sense since electronic exchanges, with fewer moving parts, are easier to maintain with small trained crews.) Building a minimally adequate world telephone system in the coming decade — amounting to roughly 1.4 billion phones, compared to half that number now — will be one of the biggest construction projects ever undertaken.

American industry will provide equipment and services for large parts of this expanding network. The Big Three equipment firms are AT&T, Northern Telecom, and GTE. All three begin with the advantage of serving a strong United States market. Although this country may seem to have become telephone saturated, with over 95 phones per hundred households, the market continues to absorb more. In a recent year, 6.5 million new phones were installed, more than there are in all of Africa outside of South Africa.

The overseas market is big, and competition from European and Japanese manufacturers is sharp. Working in Third World countries is difficult. Technicians who are used to neatly phased domestic construction programs find themselves enmeshed in management and technical nightmares compounded by strange political, economic, and cultural customs that, in theory, have nothing to do with building a phone system. One experienced United States executive compares the experience to wrestling with a jellyfish.[18]

Despite these difficulties, the Third World represents a major area of telecommunications growth in the coming years. With some notable exceptions, the communications deficit in Asia, Africa, and Latin America is acute. The disparities between these areas and the more developed countries were highlighted in a 1986 report by the Maitland Commission, an international group sponsored by the International Telecommunications Union to study practical ways to speed up the pace of Third World telecommunications development. "More than half the world's population lives in countries with fewer than 10 million telephones between them and most of these are in the main cities," the report noted. "Two-thirds of the world population have no access to telephone services. Tokyo has more telephones than the whole of the African continent, with its population of 500 million people."[19]

As a result of the Maitland Report and similar efforts to bring attention to the problem, telecommunications has been increasingly recognized as a vital part of economic and social development in Third World areas. The United Nations has set as a goal the provision of telephone service within an hour's walk of every village in the world.[20]

Some Third World countries have begun to move more quickly toward this goal than most. They are the so-called NICs, newly industrializing countries such as Brazil, Mexico, South Korea, and Taiwan. One of their common characteristics has been to focus resources on more adequate domestic communications systems. For some of them it is a formidable task: India, with a population of over 760 million, has only 3.7 million phones. The most successful NICs have been in East Asia, were Korea, Taiwan, and Singapore have made stunning progress in developing internal communications resources and in producing equipment for export.[21]

In this latter effort, they have been aided by linkups with American and Japanese firms. During the eighties, there was a large-scale movement of U. S. production facilities abroad, largely to the East Asian NICs, lured by lower labor and other production costs. Seventy-five percent of the first IBM personal computer consisted of foreign components. In the late eighties, AT&T stopped making telephone instruments and other consumer products in the United States, transferring production largely to East Asia. A 1987 survey by the National Association of Purchasing Management noted that 88 percent of American manufacturers now use foreign components.[22]

Another important shift has been the expansion of foreign telecommunications equipment firms into the American market. One reason for this was the provision in the AT&T divestiture agreement that effectively ended the monopoly that the company's manufacturing arm, Western Electric, had in selling equipment to AT&T's local phone companies. This opened an enormously profitable market to competition, of which European and Japanese firms quickly took advantage. Many of them have built production facilities here to be close to their American customers. Siemans, the giant West German telecommunications firm, had 46 manufacturing and assembly plants in 19 states by 1988, producing $2.3 billion annually in goods and services.

This globalization of the telecommunications industry has changed the international prospects for American firms. They continue to win big contracts abroad; they often lose bigger ones. The classic confrontation took place in the late seventies over modernizing the Saudi Arabian system, a project that involved a series of contracts totaling over $4 billion. All of the major American firms were involved in the biddings as were Sweden's L. M. Ericsson, Germany's Siemens, and Japan's Nippon Electric. The struggle was epic in its proportions, involving low intrigue and high diplomacy. The final contracts went to a consortium of Ericsson, Philips of Holland, and Northern Telecom, a Canadian company.[23]

During the eighties, there were growing doubts among some U. S. economic experts about whether American firms were being aggressive enough in the competition for the overseas equipment market. Many of them were concentrating their efforts on the domestic market, still the largest in the world though its growth rate is slower than the offshore markets where there is more pent-up demand. In a 1980 survey of American prospects in this area, *Business Week* noted that the American firms' superiority in technology was offset by weaknesses in the marketing of their products abroad.[24] Furthermore, American sales were often hampered by tariff and other measures designed to protect local manufacturers. This led to a special effort by the Reagan Administration, through the White House Office of the Special Trade Representative, to negotiate more favorable conditions for United States electronic exports. The initial target was Japanese restrictions, which had virtually closed off opportunities for many American firms seeking to sell in that lucrative market. Despite these efforts, the United States had an unfavorable trade balance of over $1 billion annually in telecommunications products in the late eighties.

The U. S. government has also tried to strengthen free-trade prospects for American companies in other negotiations. An important breakthrough was the completion in 1987 of a treaty liberalizing trade with Canada, America's largest trading partner. The result, beginning in January 1989, is the virtual elimination of tariffs and other restrictions on cross-border trade in the $5 trillion North American market. Telecommunications trade between the two countries will be an important beneficiary of the agreement. At another level, the American government has pushed hard to reduce barriers to trade in telecommunications goods and services in the so-called "Uruguay round" of negotiations for a revised General Agreement on Trade and Tariffs (GATT) by the early nineties.[25]

The economic stakes are equally high for American firms in another equipment area — computers. Here the Americans took an early lead and have kept it. Computer power is a new index of national strength. American dominance is, for the present, still formidable. The reasons are not hard to find. Much of the technology was developed here followed by a strong investment program during the fifties and sixties. The major companies have large distribution and servicing organizations here and abroad. The domestic market gave them a strong starting point for what has been, almost from the beginning, a major international market. Finally, American computers have, by and large, set the world standard, making foreign competitors follow in their technical footsteps. As a result, by 1976, United States computer equipment firms accounted for 87 percent of the sale of the world's computers, by value. By the late eighties, the American share dropped to less than three-fourths of the international market due to increased foreign competition.[26]

This is still a healthy lead — but it is also one that will be increasingly challenged. No longer can the United States computer industry automatically count on its technological and merchandising superiority to win international orders. The industry also has to cope with foreign government policies designed to curb dependence on American computer equipment and to build up national capabilities. The result, as with telecommunications equipment, is a complex series of steps, — involving subsidies, mergers, cartels, quotas, and restrictionist devices — directed at limiting American computer products and services. A decade ago, these moves were aimed primarily at IBM.

"Watching the movements made by companies and governments in the computer industry worldwide is like watching 15 chess matches going on at the same time," international computer expert Angeline Pantages noted. "Every match has one thing in common, though. IBM seems to control both queens on every board."[27] If most computers had a "Made in U.S.A." label on them, they usually also had the clinically efficient IBM logo. The company share of the world computer market started at more than 50 percent in most major countries; it has been almost totally dominant in many smaller markets. Half its sales and half its profits normally come from overseas. With over 130,000 employees abroad, 21 plants, and 10 laboratories, it has had a worldwide reach and flexibility unmatched by any other firm. For example, a new model, the 3033, was introduced in 1977 with a $3.38 million price tag for the smallest version and simultaneous production at factories in Pough-keepsie, N.Y., Havant, England, and Yasu, Japan. The project was typical of the kind of global strategy that has given IBM such a strong lead in research, manufacturing, distribution, and servicing of its products.

IBM now faces new problems in maintaining its international position. In Europe and Japan, a combination of government and private strategies have been developed to reduce the company's dominant position. The first moves were made in the sixties in France, prompted by President Charles de Gaulle, who cited both French *gloire* and economic realities as the reasons why IBM's near monopoly of the French market had to be ended. This resulted in a cycle of mergers, licensing deals, and other arrangements, all designed to create a workable domestic alternative to IBM.[28] The results are mixed: IBM's long lead has been cut back, but it still is a dominant factor in the French market. In 1976, the newly elected President, Giscard d'Estaing, ordered a comprehensive look at the entire French communications and information structure. (His motivation, in part, was to redeem an election promise to improve the French telephone system, whose condition was summed up in the popular complaint, "Half of France is waiting for a telephone; the other half is waiting for a dial tone.") The resultant government study, the 1978 Nora Minc Report, was a prescription for transforming France into a modern information society.[29] The code word was *télématique*, the integration of communications and information resources into a powerful strategic national utility. The immediate result of the report was a dramatic improvement in the French telephone system. Within five years, subscriber lines were doubled and a host of high-technology innovations were introduced.

However, computers were the main focus of the Nora Report. The future of France as a political and economic power, the report said, rested on decisions in this area. IBM was, predictably, portrayed as the villain, the most formidable factor in American domination of French computer resources and of the data banks on which French industry and research facilities were forced to rely for specialized information. France had to develop its own resources in these areas in order to maintain itself as a healthy society. Although the report concerns technological and economic matters primarily, it includes valuable sections on the cultural implications of the *télématique* society that offer many insights useful for our own American dialogue on the new information environment.

The Nora Report also encouraged a series of French Government initiatives in advanced communications, including increases in subsidies for research and development, and a renewed attempt in 1981 by the new Mitterand government to reduce the large American minority share (held by Honeywell) in the biggest domestic computer company, CII-Honeywell Bull.[30] President Mitterand nationalized the major French electronic firms as part of an effort to develop a strategic base for strengthening national resources in this area. His efforts were hindered by a stubborn recession, labor union opposition, and a continuing wary attitude on the part of the *patronat* — French big business — toward government controls. Despite these difficulties, the French are positioning themselves to play a strong role in world telecommunications through aggressive marketing of advanced high-tech products.

In the meantime the European Economic Community was also taking steps to counter the influence of IBM and other American firms in the Common Market, motivated by the fact that the EEC accounted for only 15 percent of the West's production of computers and 26 percent of consumption in the early eighties. The negative European trade balance in electronic products went from $200 million in 1970 to $6.5 billion 10 years later.[31] At a 1980 summit meeting in Dublin, the EEC determined that its members should aim for a third of world communications and information resources, both in production and consumption by 1990. In 1983, the EEC announced a $1.3 billion program, code-named Esprit, to encourage regional cooperation in advanced computer research.[32] Funds have since been appropriated to extend the program into the nineties.

More recently, both American and European attention has been focused on a new competitive force in the high-technology international markets — the Japanese. A more than symbolic turning point in Japan's role as an information power occurred in 1980, when IBM's leading place in computer sales within the country was overtaken by Fujitsu Ltd. The shift also signaled Japan's entry into world markets, competing against the Americans and Europeans both on their home grounds and in the export trade.[33] The aggressive Japanese push in computers will be an increasingly significant factor in the next few years. The more important Japanese impact may involve the basic microelectronic module, the semiconductor chip, with Japanese firms challenging the hitherto massive United States dominance of the field, both technically and economically. In California, the Japanese firm, Nippon Electric, built what was then the most advanced semiconductor plant in the United States in late 1981.

The Japanese challenge has its roots in a 1971 Ministry of International Trade and Industry "white paper" on information and communications.[34] The report set goals for the conversion of Japan to an information-based economy, with due attention given to high-technology electronics. Large-scale government assisted research and development during the seventies paid off in a wide range of technologies. When United States manufacturers could not meet the demand for microelectronic chips in the late seventies, Japanese manufacturers jumped in and captured 40 percent of the United States memory-chip market by the end of 1979.[35] The Japanese also moved actively into Europe, staking a claim to the growing microelectronics market there. In the process, they forced Common Market economic experts to adapt their strategies to a new non-American challenger.

The United States electronics industry reacted vigorously to the Japanese initiative in the early eighties. Capital spending to expand facilities rose to record levels, as did investments in research and development. Major firms began pooling their research and development efforts, usually under university sponsorship, modifying their previous practice of individual research competition in this area. This shift moved American firms closer to Japanese and European methods of pooling technological resources. The best-known of these efforts is Microelectronics and Computer Research, the joint research entity set up in 1983 by a consortium of leading computer and semiconductor companies. A related development was the formation of Sematech, a joint industry/government microchip research group in 1987. In addition, the University of Minnesota's Microelectronics and Information Science Center was underwritten by Control Data, Honeywell, Sperry, and other firms; IBM, Xerox, and Burroughs were among the companies jointly underwriting basic microelectronics research at the California Institute of Technology.[36] In the meantime, the industry pressed for political action, in the form of advocating protectionist trade legislation.

However, the strongest weapons United States firms have in meeting Japanese and other foreign trade challenges are still aggressive competitive merchandising and a leading edge in technology. Two leading American firms — IBM and Intel — have demonstrated this dramatically by expanding their operations in the Japanese market against formidable local competition.[37]

These developments reflect the high stakes involved in the future of the United States semiconductor industry. Its health, both economically and technologically, will directly affect any American strategy for the information age, since it is essential to a productive electronics industry whose annual output will soon reach $400 billion.

Despite challenges from overseas competitors, United States electronics equipment manufacturers will continue to have a large, though diminishing, share of the world market for some time to come. The pattern will change as more competitors enter the field and as the market itself changes to accommodate the new minicomputer, micro-computer, and microprocessor technologies. Not all the competition will come from Europe and Japan. Many ambitious Third World nations want a computer industry in much the same way that they had originally sought steel mills, airlines, and Hilton hotels.[38] Brazil, in particular, has developed firm national policies for building up a computer industry, including protectionist measures against foreign competitors. Other developing countries have invited Western manufacturers in to develop joint venture projects. In some instances, countries have sought to take over majority control of local foreign plants. Almost all of ITT's Latin American production facilities were nationalized or placed under local majority control during the 1970s. IBM pulled out of India in 1978 after refusing to accept 60 percent Indian ownership of its local subsidiary, as the country's government had ordered.[39]

Beyond hardware, there is a new and rapidly expanding export market in information services. Selling (or giving away) information is an old American habit. The United States is the largest information market in the world, a condition that has had incalculable consequences for our political structure, economy, and culture. We have not been shy about sharing this resource with others: until recently over half of all international communications originated in this country. Three major changes have taken place in this pattern in the past two decades. First, the United States share of this information transfer has decreased as other nations build up their information resources and make them available internationally. Secondly, a larger share of information is moving electronically across borders and increasingly between computers. Finally, the volume of this information is expanding exponentially, probably at an annual rate of 10 percent.

The net result has been the creation of global information networks of all sizes, patterns, and purposes. One of the largest is the World Meteorological Organization's massive world weather watch, which gathers information from thousands of stations on earth as well as from weather satellites in space, analyzes the results, and retransmits them all over the globe. Another is the United States government's Medlars network, a computerized data base of over four million research reports from 3,000 medical journals and other sources. Medlars is "searched" a million times a year by doctors and hospitals in North America and abroad, either by mail, telex message, or direct on-line access.[40] Another United States government information facility, the National Technical Information Service, makes available reports on all research funded by the government. It is heavily used by foreign governments and institutions for its access to a significant portion of United States technological and scientific research.

These and similar public data banks are made available without cost, or for a relatively small service fee. They are an important part of the new electronic information services. Even greater expansion is taking place in the commercial sector. Information is a highly salable item, and this country has traditionally held the lead in making technological data available for a fee. The United States is responsible for almost half of the global trade in the licensing or sale of technical know-how.[41] This is sold in many different forms, but increasingly it is moving as data between computers.

This has spawned a new sector in the information industry that provides access to specialized data resources stored in computers for a wide variety of customers. These include systems operated by such firms as Lockheed, Control Data, Systems Development Corporation, and General Electric. Most of them provide time sharing arrangements, where the customer pays by usage, although many variations for obtaining their information have been developed. The General Electric network can be accessed from local telephones in over 400 cities in North America, Europe, Japan, and Australia. The network information industry has moved up over the billion dollar sales mark with international sales accounting for about one fifth of the total.

Another category of networking is composed of private corporation circuits, heavily used by the big multinational firms for their internal communications around the globe.[42] The Bank of America's telecommunications network stretches from Hong Kong to Vienna, involving circuits on three separate satellites. The system provides voice, data, telegraph, and interactive computing services in ways that give the bank's central headquarters in San Francisco instantaneous access to its operations on four continents. Citicorp, the largest United States bank, has a computerized global network that links its operations in 95 countries. Over 2,000 of the world's major banks belong to a network known as SWIFT, an acronym for the Society for Worldwide Interbank Financial Telecommunications. SWIFT's global reach allows its subscribers to buy, sell, lend, and borrow throughout the world, getting an acknowledgment back five or six seconds after the transaction is made. The process is a big business version of what will eventually be a consumer-oriented electronic banking system in this country, handling similar transactions for bank customers in their homes. In New York, an electronic clearing house for international payments known as CHIPS processes several hundred billion dollars in transactions on a normal business day.

These changes in financial networking are leading to a new phenomenon — the round-the-clock global money market. It is a development that came into sharp focus during the October 1987 Wall Street crash. For the first time, financial markets throughout the world reacted almost instantaneously to violent shifts taking place in one market. The reason was the electronic interlinking of the markets by high-capacity telecommunications networks. Stock exchanges in Tokyo, London, Paris, Sydney, and Hong Kong, among other places, each played a direct role in the turbulent events taking place in New York. National financial regulatory controls over the markets were overwhelmed by the global scope of the events. One result was a call for developing international rules to deal with the new electronic markets.[43]

The nineties will see a continued expansion of electronic global markets. Worldwide automated trading systems, known as "screen trading," will become more important. These involve 24-hour trading with orders entered, matched, and cleared by simply punching buttons on a computer keyboard. A prototype system, managed by the Reuters news organization, was developed in 1988 for the Chicago Mercantile Exchange.[44]

There has been a similar expansion on non financial networks. The best-known of these are Tymnet and GTE's Telenet, both of which provide domestic and international electronic mail and other communications services. The future of this sector of the information services business will be set largely by the relationship between AT&T, IBM and the Xerox Corporation, all of which are developing advanced telecommunications networks that may bring information service grids down to the consumer level in this country, eventually to connect with similar networks abroad.

The rapid expansion of information networks has led to the dispersal of international business to locations where there are low taxes, good communications and few restrictions on data transfer. Two such locations, popular with banks, are the Bahamas and the Cayman Islands in the Caribbean. As early as 1977, the Bahamas had 263 banks, most of them foreign, with assets of $70 billion; the tiny Caymans had 260 banks with assets of $12 billion. Basically, these islands are offshore tax havens, where, thanks to good communications circuits, business can be transacted as easily as if banks were in a traditional financial capital.[45]

But not all international business can be transacted on lush Caribbean islands, whatever the tax advantages. The bulk of it is still done in the old locations, where stricter regulations apply. Foreign governments are becoming increasingly concerned about the vast amounts of computer-based data information moving in and out of their territories, affecting their economies and often their political interests. The result has been a move, particularly in Europe and Canada, toward regulatory guidelines on transborder data flows. The Canadians are concerned that too much information about their economy, and their citizens' private lives, is stored in computers in the United States. In Europe, most countries have developed legislation imposing specific restrictions on the electronic transfer of personal information about their citizens to other countries. The first country to approve such restrictions, Sweden, has a national data control board that must approve all such transfers. On a regional basis, the Organization for Economic Cooperation and Development (OECD) has drafted guidelines for assuring the compatibility of such privacy legislation, and is also studying more general questions of the economic impact of international data flows. The United States has been publicly sympathetic to concerns about privacy of information — which it also protects through its own legislation — but is also worried that the expansion of restrictions on transborder data flow may affect American economic interests.[46]

The most controversial area of United States information sales abroad involves the mass media — film, television, publications, and news agencies. Here the American information age is made visible to literally billions of people abroad in ways that are brash, colorful, and immensely popular. It will be generations before the impact of contemporary United States mass culture on the rest of the world can be measured. Will it be judged as the raucous noise of a flash-in-the-pan society, as critics claim, or will it be seen as the transmitter of ideas and values that created a new democratic world order? For the present judgments are mixed, but there is little dispute about the ubiquitous influence of American mass culture abroad.

In the last century, an English cleric, Sydney Smith, asked, "In the four quarters of the globe, who reads an American book? Or goes to an American play? Or looks at an American picture or statue?" It is a different story now, when American influences have been instrumental in establishing the first world cultural style. There are many sources of this impact, but a large share of it comes from the Hollywood film industry. In the 1920s, the industry produced and distributed most of the world's films establishing the medium's artistic, technical, and economic standards.[47] This production dominance was cut back in later years as film industries developed abroad, but Hollywood continued to set the pace. It was an envious Stalin who once told a visitor, "If I could control the American film industry, I could control the world." However, entertainment rather than ideological enlightenment was what drew huge audiences to Hollywood films. Even now, when American production is down to 10 percent of the world total, Hollywood films dominate foreign markets with total international revenues in 1988 of over $2 billion.

When film production fell off in the fifties, television programs took its place. As films had done in the twenties, American television shows provided a large share of world production in the sixties and seventies.[48] Although these products are still a healthy export market for United States syndicators, they face increasing competition from foreign producers. In Latin America, once an unchallenged market for United States television, Mexican, Venezuelan, and Brazilian producers now have the largest export share. American syndicators also face restrictions in the form of quotas on the amount of foreign programs shown on overseas stations. Many countries now have such restrictions, generally designed to encourage local production as well as to counter criticism that too many foreign (that is, American) programs are shown, with allegedly baleful effects on local cultural patterns.[49]

The oldest segment of American media involvement abroad is the news business. The two large American press agencies — Associated Press (AP) and United Press International (UPI) — dominate international news flow, although there is strong competition from European agencies, particularly Britain's Reuters organization. Reuters has taken a strong lead in transforming itself from an old-line news agency to an electronic information network, particularly in supplying financial information to corporations and, more recently, directly to individuals via cable systems. By 1984, Reuters was providing 47 specialized news services to these subscribers in 74 countries.[50] A more uncertain challenge is the prospect that, within the coming decade, one or more large news agencies may be organized in Third World countries. Similar proposals have foundered in the past. In the late seventies, a nonaligned news pool, largely under Yugoslav sponsorship, was set up for news exchanges among Third World countries. The initial results were professionally unimpressive, but the motivation behind the idea was strong enough to suggest that some form of permanent organization might develop. In 1983, after four years of preparation, a Pan African News Agency, sponsored by Black African countries, began operations.

This motivation was a combination of political and cultural factors. Culturally, it involved a desire to break away from dependence on Western press agencies as news sources allegedly biased against Third World accomplishments and values. Proponents of this view invoked the concept of "information sovereignty," contending that Western agencies were only interested in reporting political unrest, earthquakes, and *National Geographic* type exotica from their countries. However justified these charges, there was also a strong underlying political motivation to curb Western reports on Third World political and economic troubles. The nonaligned news agency's output in its early years consisted largely of Propaganda Ministry handouts from its member countries. The experiment raised doubts as to whether an indigenous Third World news-reporting system — a laudable enough project — could be developed soon. In the meantime, the American news agencies and their European competitors will continue to be the dominant force in international news flow.

Another influential segment of United States international media influence involves print publications — from the *Reader's Digest* to scholarly books and journals. *Reader's Digest* is an international media phenomenon in its own right, with editions printed in 13 languages and in 31 countries. The international editors of *Time* and *Newsweek* reach relatively small but significant elite audiences in every country. *USA Today*, the London *Financial Times*, and *The Wall Street Journal* are now global newspapers, thanks to satellite delivery of their editions to all parts of the world. The American book industry, with over $8 billion in annual sales, relies heavily on its export trade, particularly in the technical field. United States publishers have been successful in developing cooperative production and marketing arrangements with local firms in Third World countries since the abrogation in the seventies of a long-standing arrangement that gave British publishers preferential access in large parts of the world.

The weakest area of American media influence abroad is radio. Before World War II, a number of attempts were made to develop commercial shortwave broadcasting from this country, with emphasis on transmissions to Latin America. The war halted these efforts. The only private United States stations now broadcasting to foreign audiences are evangelical-type religious stations, most of whose transmitters are located abroad. International radio is largely a government responsibility, with particular emphasis on reaching audiences in communist countries where outside news and information sources are restricted. Three government financed stations — Voice of America, Radio Liberty, and Radio Free Europe — provide almost continuous round-the-clock transmissions to these areas.

In summary, the United States is a major player in the business of international communications and information — from building satellites for the Arabs to selling *Reader's Digest* in Brazil. Although American activities cover a wide range, they share three characteristics. The first is that American firms have a strong position in each sector. The second is that each sector is becoming more competitive each year; the easy postwar days are over. The third is that, in each sector, American products and services face, in varying degrees, threats to their access to foreign markets.

Harvard University information resources expert Anthony Oettinger sees information access as a major policy issue for the United States in the coming years. He uses a simple chronological progression to illustrate his point: in the fifties, American strategic interests centered around access to real estate for military bases; in the sixties the emphasis shifted to economic access for the worldwide expansion of United States industry and banking. He believes the problem has now shifted to threats to information and communications access, the connectors between an increasingly information-dependent American society and other nations.

A former Oettinger colleague in the Harvard information resources study, William Read, has suggested that we may come to a world "information crisis" roughly comparable to the oil crises of the early seventies.[51] This may seem to be a worse-case scenario, given the fact that the trend toward more communications circuits, and more information openness is running strong. There is, however, a dark side to this trend, based on the imbalance of world information resources. By and large, this imbalance has favored the United States. As foreign nations begin to perceive communications and information resources as national security factors, American strength in this area is seen in a different light. This shift lies behind the "information sovereignty" argument, or in simpler terms, good old-fashioned political and economic protectionism extended to a new field.

Fortunately, the problem is not yet generally regarded in such rigid, black-and-white terms. Information is not oil, a resource that can be easily bestowed or denied by turning on a tap. However, it would be risky not to recognize the potential of greater political control of information flow. The Soviet Union has demonstrated, over a period of seven decades, the relative ease with which a determined authoritarian regime can control information flow for its own interests. The new information technologies, from the computer on down, have no ideology. They can be manipulated for various purposes. The threat is there, and occasionally it surfaces in direct form. In 1983, a number of Arab banks decided to boycott the SWIFT international payments transfer network because 10 Israeli banks had joined the system.[52] In 1978, British telecommunications workers voted not to handle any international traffic to South Africa, in protest against racial policies there. The ban lasted only a short time. It is possible to imagine a similar ban against traffic to this country because of the way it voted on a certain issue in the United Nations, or because of some other political event.

The United States has indicated on at least one occasion that it would be prepared to take such action. Shortly after United States Embassy officials were seized as hostages in Tehran in November 1979, the White House ordered a study of the possibilities of cutting off all communications between Iran and the outside world. The study concluded that a complete cutoff, particularly of satellite communications, was not feasible for legal and other reasons, and the project was dropped.[53] The world communications and information networks are fragile instruments, easily disrupted by terrorist attacks. Whereas terrorists and other revolutionaries used to seize radio and television stations, they have now begun to turn their attention to computers and other information facilities as a way of seriously disrupting a society.

These kinds of assaults on electronic networks that link our social and economic activities will be increasingly common events in the coming years. Another less violent prospect will be the taking of political actions to restrict communications products and information flow. As noted earlier, this is already a problem for American firms in such areas as data communications, television exports, and computer machine exports. In each case, the aim has been to restrict rather than to eliminate American products and services. The initial effects have been economic, resulting in some loss for American industry. This is an important enough consideration, but it should not mask the overriding political issue involved. The United States is in no position — lingering superpower mythologies to the contrary — to impose its will in such matters. It does, however, have a leadership role to play in the evolution of a world communications system whose emphasis is on openness rather than protectionism and outmoded concepts of sovereignty. Clearly this will benefit our trade interests, but the United States should not be so preoccupied with short-range economic problems that it does not recognize the need for sharing information and communications resources, particularly in correcting the massive imbalance between industrialized and developing countries.

This will be a difficult, complex job. It will be viewed with suspicion by those with more narrow-minded economic interests as a do-gooder approach, one that limits their options. There is, in fact, no reason why a policy encompassing our long-run economic and political interests cannot be developed. At present, the United States lacks the coherent guidelines needed to undertake this task, over and above a cycle of tactical moves that represent reactions rather than initiatives designed to create a more stable overall environment for global communications development.

Part of the problem, noted earlier in this chapter, is the absence of an effective mechanism within the American Government to coordinate these issues. Policy decisions are spread across a dozen major agencies and departments. The problem is not how to group them in one agency — this would be an impractical and probably impossible venture, given the bureaucratic passions involved. A more realistic approach might be to establish a coordinating mechanism that operates under clear-cut Presidential directives and has strong liaisons with the private and public interest sectors. In any event, both public and private policymakers need to establish better consultative arrangements, within and between each sector, if they are to identify and implement the decisions required for a full American role in the global communications environment. Since 1981, a number of bills authorizing a Cabinet level committee to oversee United States policy and operations in this area have been introduced in Congress.[54]

A strengthening of the United States Government apparatus remains a prerequisite for handling the more difficult problem of how to improve international consultation on communications and information issues. Any domestic consensus on how to proceed will depend for its success on how it relates to negotiations with other nations, either individually or in groups. Our traditional preference has been for bilateral negotiations, where the problems (and their solutions) are usually more narrow and clear-cut. However, the trend is toward multilateral negotiations as communications and information problems spill over into regional and wider international concerns. This means that the United States will do more of its negotiations through the United Nations and related international organizations.

The number of international organizations claiming stakes in these subjects increases annually. For many of them, communications and information are trendy subjects they can invoke to extend their bureaucratic empires with correspondingly bigger budgets. Other agencies have more legitimate claims. These include such relatively small organizations as the Universal Postal Union, the World Meteorological Organization, and the International Atomic Energy Authority, each of which has performed useful, quiet service in global information cooperation. The two world agencies with the most direct interest in the subject, however, are the International Telecommunications Union (ITU) and the United Nations Educational, Scientific, and Cultural Organization (UNESCO). Most of the critical multilateral negotiations in communications and information during the nineties will be held in these two agencies.[55]

In Chapter 3, we examined the ITU's role in developing and administering global standards for telecommunications, including the equitable use of a major natural resource, the radio spectrum. The Union is a one-nation, one-vote organization, and the new nations of Asia, Africa, and Latin America make up the majority of the membership. These nations are prepared to use their influence to seek redress for what they consider, almost without exception, to be an unequal distribution of international telecommunications resources. This pressure comes at a time when the older industrial powers have need to expand their own use of these resources for post-industrial requirements.

These pressures came to a head at the ITU-sponsored 1979 World Administrative Radio Conference (WARC), which reviewed and made decisions on the radio spectrum pattern for the rest of the century.[56] (The conference, which caused hardly a ripple in the world media, was the largest international conference ever held. It had 2,000 participants from 145 countries, 15,000 proposals to consider, and ran in Geneva for three months.) The 1979 WARC tested the world's ability to deal with its expanding communications requirements within the finite limits of the radio spectrum. This goal is technically reachable. The critical question is whether ITU's members, particularly the new nations-in-a-hurry, can resist confrontational political and ideological temptations in the interests of maintaining an orderly telecommunications framework.

The United States has its own set of temptations in the form of strong domestic pressures from industry and from public claimants on spectrum resources. By and large, the 1979 conference held to its technical agenda, avoiding political confrontation and reaching agreement on most issues. Some of the more sensitive problems were, however, postponed until a series of specialized conferences held during the eighties. This had the effect of making spectrum issues the subject of almost continuing negotiations throughout the decade. These negotiations were a stringent test of the ITU's ability to preserve its role of maintaining a technical order in international telecommunications.[57]

The other major international forum for communications and information issues is UNESCO. Founded with idealistic hopes after World War II, UNESCO has a checkered record of achievements and failures. It has settled down to bureaucratic middle age in its Paris headquarters, peopled by an international staff who grind out documents written in a corkscrew international dialect that may, if everything goes wrong, someday become the world linguistic standard. In its early years, UNESCO was dominated by the conflict between the Europeans' esoteric cultural concerns and the Americans' pragmatic interests in literacy campaigns, scientific cooperation, etc. The organization is now dominated by Third World concerns, reflecting the majority of its members.

Communications and information issues are high on the current agenda. Developing countries see UNESCO as a useful forum for airing policies and programs to correct the communications imbalance. A corollary to this is the effort of underdeveloped countries to curb the "cultural imperialism" resulting from the current heavy flow of Western films, news, publications, and other media to their countries.[58] These concerns fall under the Third World rubric of a "New World Information Order." UNESCO was the spawning ground for the concept of *information sovereignty*, or the right to protect one's cultural heritage from harmful outside influences. This led to a move to overturn UNESCO's long-standing support for free flow of information, a concept sponsored by the United States in the organization's early years, in favor of a new emphasis on the right to communicate and on a more balanced information flow. The need to correct the imbalance was acknowledged by the United States and other democratic nations. The debates became sharp, however, when proposals for imposing international restrictions on news flow were put forward under the "New World Information Order" slogan. The subject was extensively documented in a UNESCO-commissioned report by an international committee headed by former Irish foreign minister, Sean McBride, issued in 1980. The report was, from the American viewpoint, a mixed bag. It supported the concept of open information flow and also put forward a number of restrictive proposals, which had the effect of compromising this concept. Nevertheless, the United States supported the report during UNESCO's 1980 general conference in Belgrade. At the same time, the American approach has been to urge UNESCO members to call an armistice on the cyclical ideological debates in favor of practical programs for improving Third World information and communications resources. To this end, it sponsored a proposal for a UNESCO project on international communications development programs that was approved at the Belgrade meeting.[59]

Despite these and other attempts at pragmatic solutions to global information imbalances, Third World countries maintained their ideological pressures on the alleged information imperialism of the United States and other Western powers. Their grievances were summarized in an extensive resolution passed by the United Nations General Assembly in its 1980 session. In December 1983, the United States took the unusual step of informing UNESCO that it intended to withdraw from the organization within a year if significant changes were not made in the way in which the organization handled information issues. A year later, it made good on its threat. In 1988, after the installation of moderate leadership at UNESCO, the United States took initial steps to return to the organization.

Both UNESCO and the ITU are weak reeds on which to build an international policy structure for communications and information. Each agency is buffeted by pressures that often prevent it from acting effectively, even in relatively simple matters. However, both are preferable to any of the occasional proposals for a supranational organization to guide overall global network development — a proposition that would neither serve United States purposes nor, in the long run, anyone else's.

There is one limited example of a successful supranational agency in this field. It is Intelsat, the operator of the 115-nation satellite grid that has reshaped global communications in the past 25 years. By the late eighties, Intelsat operated over 100,000 circuits, double the number in 1981 and three hundred times the number of cable circuits that were the only reliable intercontinental connections in 1964 when the first Intelsat *Early Bird* was put into orbit.[60]

Intelsat also represents a significant political achievement, a dramatic step in the exploitation of a major technology through international cooperation. The Intelsat innovation combined profit motives, a pragmatic division of power, and a willingness by its owner-nations to forego short-term political and ideological advantages in the interests of a workable system. Intelsat's owners are diverse, ranging from the People's Republic of China to South Africa to the Vatican State. (The Soviet Union is the only significant nonmember.) Collectively they generate over 95 percent of all international traffic.

The Intelsat system was started by the United States and managed by it, through the Communications Satellite Corporation, for a dozen years. The American voting share, based on system usage, dropped from over 60 percent in 1965 to below 25 percent in the late eighties. The surrender of American control was not the result of unalloyed altruism by any means. It was the price the United States paid for creating a network management system acceptable to other nations. Intelsat now faces different problems as satellite technology opens new service opportunities and as the needs of its member-owners grow. The organization's success raises questions about its role as a model for other global communications ventures. It is an intriguing idea, but the Intelsat experience is probably not readily transferable to other areas. The organization was a unique creation of its time, involving a technology that would not work without a high degree of political cooperation. The technology was, moreover, a monopoly of one country — the United States — that had the resources, the imagination, and the will to allow its monopoly to erode gradually in the interests of a long-term viable world system. Such circumstances cannot easily be replicated in the foreseeable future.[61]

Intelsat's status as a virtual global monopoly in satellite communications is being challenged by newer forces. International fiber optic cables are providing major economic competition. A number of countries have constructed regional satellite systems that will become separate but compatible networks under the Intelsat umbrella. In addition, several United States commercial satellite firms applied to the FCC in 1983 for permission to operate their own satellites, servicing the lucrative North Atlantic area in competition with Intelsat. The applications set off a fierce policy battle within the American government between officials who saw benefits in a more competitive international satellite environment and those who feared that such competition would harm

Intelsat's economic viability. The pro-competition group won, with the result that the first international private satellite system began operations in 1988, competing against Intelsat.

New technologies like Intelsat's satellites are deceptive in their promises. They encourage visions of instant hookup, of plugging everyone in. It is a peculiarly American vision — the old electronic myth updated. Why shouldn't there be a princess phone in every Hottentot hut and Eskimo igloo, not to mention a television set and a tabletop computer? Despite the new technologies, however, the world information network is going to be built through the slow, patient activities of a wide variety of organizations, techniques, and economic programs.

In summary, we have seen that the United States has a major stake in the development of a strong global communications system. Its own information society can be a general model for a new kind of post-industrial democratic evolution abroad. Access is the measure — access to information and communications resources in terms of their availability, the ability of people to pay for them, and their freedom to use the information for personal enrichment as well as community needs.[62]

Assuring international open access may be the most difficult United States information policy issue of the nineties. It is not a new problem, but it will take different forms in the coming years. Many other cultures do not put as much of a premium on open access as we do, including otherwise like-minded societies in Europe. And the Third World is suspicious of our tendency to be aggressive in both giving and receiving resources.

A primary United States resource in promoting these interests is its industrial productivity. A world grid will not be built by UNESCO resolutions or other pious incantations. It will be built by good technology, sensible economics, and stable political conditions. This is an elusive combination, in short supply in most parts of the world. American industry has the ability to provide the goods and services needed for the network, as do its European and Japanese competitors and the new communications industries of the Third World. Assuring a reasonably open market for these United States products is an important part of overall American strategy. It should complement the major thrust of our strategy — our commitment to an open information order, one in which adequate information and communications resources are available to everyone.

NOTES

1. Zbigniew Brzezinski, *Between Two Worlds* (New York: Viking Press, 1970), p. 31.

2. For a summary of Schiller's views, see his *Communications and Cultural Development* (White Plains, NY: International Arts and Sciences Press, 1976).

3. Anthony Smith, *The Geopolitics of Information* (New York: Oxford University Press, 1980), pp. 19–40.

4. Quoted in Jonathan Tourtellot, "A World Information War," *European Community* (Washington), January/February 1978, p. 12.

5. *Ibid.*, p. 14.

6. For a summary of the controversy, see *Telecommunications* Report, 18 July 1977, pp. 2–5.

7. A useful compendium of Congressional and private sector attitudes on government policy and organization in international communications and information issues is given in U. S. Congress, Senate Committee on Foreign Relations, *The Role and Control of International Communications and Information*, Report to the Subcommittee on International Operations, 95th Cong., 1st sess., June 1977.

8. *Telecommunications Report*, 18 July 1977, p. 5.

9. The basic proposals of the subcommittee are summarized in U. S. Congress, House Committee on Government Operations, *International Information Flow: Forging a New Framework*, House Report, no. 96–1535, 96th Cong., 2nd sess., 1980, pp. 55–59.

10. For a description of the debate, see Wilson Dizard, *Television — A World View* (Syracuse, NY: Syracuse University Press, 1966), pp. 263–67.

11. U. S. Department of Commerce, *U. S. Industrial Outlook 1976, with Projections to 1985* (16th ed.) (Washington, DC: Government Printing Office, 1976).

12. For a useful survey of recent European communications trends, see Ian Mackintosh, *Sunrise Europe*, (New York: Basil Blackwell, 1986).

13. The EC plan is described in *Towards a Competitive Community – wide Telecommunications Market in 1992*, Document COM (88) 48, Commission of the European Communities, Brussels, 8 February 1988. See also Tom Kerver, "Europe moves towards deregulation," *Global Communications*, January 1988, pp. 20–26.

14. "World Outlook 1988," issued by Telecommunications Industry Research Center, Barnham, West Sussex, United Kingdom, December 1987.

15. "Where are Britain's Capital Venturers?," *Economist* (London), 23 July 1977, p. 73.

16. "Chinese Telephones: the Waiting Giant," *Economist* (London), 11 January 1986, p. 81.

17. See Wilson P. Dizard and S. Blake Swensrud, *Gorbachev's Information Revolution*, (Colorado Springs: Westview Press, 1987).

18. "The Great World Telephone War," *Fortune*, August 1977, p. 144.

19. "The Missing Link," report of the Independent Commission for World-wide Telecommunications Development (the "Maitland Commission"), issued by the International Telecommunications Union, Geneva, January 1986, p. 13.

20. For a useful review of the impact of telecommunications at the village level in the Third World, see Heather Hudson, *When Telephones Reach the*

Village: the Role of Telecommunications in Rural Development (Norwood, NJ: Ablex Publishing Co., 1984).

21. Singapore, with minimal natural resources but possessing an educated population, is a textbook example of a newly developing country adapting to information-age conditions. See "Wafer-thin: Singapore's high-tech industry": *Economist* (London), 28 November 1987, p. 45. Korea's spectacular progress as the world's fastest-growing economy in the late eighties is described in "Anything Japan Can Do...," *Economist* (London), 20 February 1988, pp. 19–22. The problems of adapting computers to Third World needs are surveyed in "The Computer Tangle," *South* (London), July 1987, pp. 9–17.

22. "Two hard-to-quit habits sustain trade deficit," *New York Times*, 14 January 1988, p. D–1.

23. "Blanketing the World With Phones," *New York Times*, 2 February 1980, special section on international economic developments, p. 12.

24. "Data Communications: A Market Where the U. S. Lags," *Business Week*, 11 February 1980, p. 57.

25. For background on how the negotiations may affect international telecommunications trade practices, see Russell Pipe, "The Ultimate Bypass," *Datamation*, 1 August 1987, p. 60–61. The impact on information services trade is discussed in Peter Cowhey, "Trade Talks and the Informatics Sector," *International Journal*, XLII, Winter 1986–87, pp. 107–37.

26. American Federation of Information Processing Societies, *Information Processing in the United States: A Quantitative Summary* (Washington), 1977, p. 14.

27. Angelina Pantages, "The International Computer Industry," *Datamation*, September 1976, p. 56.

28. For a description of the complex maneuvers involved in the attempt to reduce IBM's share of the French computer market, see "Western Europe's Computer Industry," *Datamation*, September 1976, pp. 65–75.

29. Simon Nora and Alain Minc, *The Computerization of Society* (Cambridge, MA: MIT Press, 1980).

30. Guy de Jonquires, "French Telecommunications — The Wired Society Gamble," *Financial Times* (London), 1 October 1980, p. 14.

31. "The European Community prepares to close the widening technology gap," *Data Communications*, September 1983, p. 54.

32. "Why Europe Is Not an Open Market for Computers," *The Economist* (London), 5 April 1980, p. 83. See also "European Strategies to Fight IBM," Business Week, 17 February 1979, p. 43, and "Telematics Are Here: European Community Working on a Common European Strategy," *Europe* (Washington), May/June 1981, pp. 5–7.

33. "Computers: Here Comes Fujitsu," *New York Times*, 11 November 1980, p. G–1.

34. Ministry of International Trade and Industry, *The Plan for an Information Society* (Tokyo: Jacudi, 1972).

35. "Fighting Off the Japanese," *The Economist* (London), 7 June 1980, p. 80.

36. "Joining Hands Against Japan," *Business Week*, 10 November 1980, p. 108.

37. For a description of the two firms' successful strategies in Japan during the eighties, see "IBM's Big Splash in the Land of Electronics," *Business Week*, 1 August 1983, p. 35, and "Why Intel is Winning Big in Japan," *Business Week*, 19 September 1983, p. 48.

38. Louis Turner and Stephen Woolcock, "Emerging Nations Compete with the Industrialized World," in German Marshall Fund, *Transatlantic Perspective*, no. 3 (September 1980): pp. 21–24.

39. "Computing the Loss of IBM," *The Economist* (London), 1 December 1979, p. 77.

40. In 1980, at least 10 countries had full or partial on-line access to Medlars. See "Information Biomedical Communications — the Role of the U. S. Library of Medicine," *Health Communications Informatist*, 1980, p. 212.

41. "The Trade in Technology," *The Economist* (London), 21 April 1979, p. 48.

42. For an overall description of American corporate networking abroad, see "A Scramble for Global Networks," *Business Week*, 21 March 1988, pp. 140–48.

43. "A Push for International Market Rules," *New York Times*, 23 November 1987, p. D–3.

44. "Future Markets Will Let Their Fingers Do the Dealing," *Economist* (London), 19 March 1988, p. 77.

45. "A Boom in No-Strings Banking," *New York Times*, 2 February 1980, special section on international trade, p. 2.

46. For useful background on this issue, see "Transborder Data Flow," special issue of *Stanford Journal of International Law*, 16 (Summer 1980).

47. William Read, *America's Mass Media Merchants* (Baltimore: Johns Hopkins University Press, 1976), pp. 39–44.

48. Read, *op cit*, pp. 144–79.

49. The point is documented, with some ideological bias, in Jeremy Tunstall, *The Media Are American* (London: Constable, 1977).

50. "Reuters plans to go public after bonanza," *Washington Post*, 13 November 1983.

51. William Read, *Foreign Policy: The High and Low Politics of Telecommunications*. Program on Information Technologies and Public Policy, Harvard University. Publication P–76–3, February 1976, p. 2.

52. "Arab bank boycott of data links," *New York Times*, 17 February 1983.

53. "No Go for Satellite Sanctions Against Iran," *Science*, 16 May 1980, p. 20.

54. "Bills to Establish Review on FCC Clear Hurdles," *Wall Street Journal*, 17 May 1981, p. 6.

55. For a useful description of the international agencies involved in communications and information policy, see Edward Ploman, "The Whys and Wherefors of International Organizations," *Intermedia* (London), July 1980, pp. 6–11.

56. The political and technical aspects of the conference were extensively examined in 10 articles grouped under the overall title, "The U. S. Faces WARC" in *Journal of Communication* 29, no. 1 (Winter 1979): pp. 143–207. For a review of the conference results, see Glen O. Robinson,

"Regulating International Airwaves: The 1979 WARC," *Virginia Journal of International Law*, 21, no. 1 (Fall 1980): pp. 1–54.

57. A useful survey of proposals for reforming the ITU over the years is contained in J. Henry Glazer, "Infelix ITU — The Need for Space Age Revisions to the International Telecommunications Conventions," *Federal Bar Journal*, 23, no. 1 (Winter, 1963): pp. 1–36.

58. This development is summarized in Jonathan F. Gunter, ed., *The United States and the Debate on the World Information Order* (Washington, DC: Academy for Educational Development, 1979), pp. 44–53. See also "Third World News and Views," *Journal of Communication*, 29, no. 2 (Spring 1979): pp. 134–98.

59. Philip H. Power and Elie Abel, "The Third World vs. the Media," *New York Times Magazine*, 21 September 1980, p. 116. For a useful summary of the Third World agenda in communications and information matters, see United Nations, General Assembly, Special Political Committee, *Questions Relating to Information*, Annex to Agenda Item 59, December, 1980. An American-initiated critique of attempts to curb information flows can be found in *Voices of Freedom*, the working papers of the World Conference of Independent News Media, Talloires, France, 15–17 May 1981, published by the Edward R. Murrow Center for Public Diplomacy, Tufts University, 1981.

60. For background on Intelsat, see Joseph Pelton, *Global Talk* (Rockville, MD: Sijthoff Noordholf Publishers, 1981).

61. Marcellus Snow, "Intelsat: An International Example," *Journal of Communications*, Vol. 30, No. 2 (Spring 1980), pp. 147–56.

62. Anthony Smith, *The Geopolitics of Information* (New York: Oxford University Press, 1980), pp. 148–73. See also Glen Fisher, *American Communication in a Global Society* (Norwood, NJ: Ablex Publishing Co., 1979), pp. 141–57.

CHAPTER 9

The Open-Loop Future

The British historian, Arnold Toynbee, once suggested that the 20th century is the first time that mankind can seriously consider the welfare of the entire race. If this is true, it is in large part because of the ideas and events described in this book. They mark the evolution toward a universal electronic communications network, the nervous system of a new information-rich global society. Given the political will and the economic resources, this unique development can be achieved in the first half of the next century.

We are inclined to be impressed most by the physical aspects of the network — the satellites, computers, high-speed cables and other devices that will form it. The more significant impact, however, will be on our understanding of how these facilities can affect the prospects of a changed world order in which, for the first time, we can reach out directly to the minds and emotions of men and women everywhere, and in turn be reached by them.

American ideas, resources, and actions will have an outsized influence on this prospect. This does not mean that our particular domestic pattern for dealing with information-age realities will or should be copied. Nevertheless, our actions will be watched closely by other societies as they consider their own approaches to the new age. Like the rest of the world, Americans face an open-loop future, in which it will be increasingly difficult to identify guideposts that can point us in the right direction. As physicist Robert Oppenheimer once noted:

This world is a new world. . . . One thing that is new is the prevalence of newness. . . so that the world alters as we walk in it, so that the years of a man's life measure not some small growth or rearrangements or moderation of what he learned in childhood but a great upheaval.[1]

Communications and information are driving forces in this new environment. Their technologies are no longer constrained by the linear pattern in which innovations were previously introduced over a period of many years. The telegraph, telephone, wireless radio, and other machines evolved slowly, strengthening economic productivity without disrupting social order in an expanding democratic society. In the present age of converging technologies and greater social complexity, the balance between economic productivity and social harmony becomes more difficult to maintain.

The balance is threatened by a dilemma. Technology as a productive force rolls on, while its contribution to social stability grows weaker. And as the distance between technological promise and social effect widens, confidence in technology is eroded. The situation underscores the warnings of Jacques Ellul on the contrary effects of rapid change. Other observers, like Jay Forrester of MIT's System Dynamics group, suggest that we may have to impose what were formerly unacceptable restrictions on personal and collective freedoms to cope with the consequences of this imbalance. It is a conclusion they reach not because they are antidemocratic but because they see such control as the only alternative to social collapse.[2]

Whether right or wrong, these critics are generally wary of facile post-industrial or information society labels. Their point is valid — but only to a point. The United States is not stepping over some imaginary line in time, from materialistic industrialism into a golden epoch of white-collar ease. Such boundary drawing is simplistic, given the still fragmentary evidence of the changes taking place and our own distorting proximity to them. Nevertheless, once we get past the exercise of labeling ages and epochs, we face the fact that the current shift appears increasingly to be a departure from the dynamics that drove our agricultural and industrial past.

Agriculture is still a vital sector of the United States economy, but it is no longer a major force for innovation or for shaping social values and goals. Similarly, a loss of inner dynamism is becoming evident in the industrial sector, although this is masked by a continued high output of goods. Less than a quarter of the United States work force is now involved in primary industrial production, a ratio that reflects a steady decline in the amount of human energy being put into the production of goods in recent decades. Technological change has profoundly altered the nature and centrality of industrial activity in our society. Growth in agriculture and industry is no longer the major impetus of social development, but is being replaced by a still undefined force. This is an information-based thrust that draws on human resource capital to transfer knowledge into many forms of physical and social activities, to generate wealth in new ways, and, in the process, to profoundly alter goals and values.

Is this a permanent shift, or simply a fluctuation in our national energy that will someday subside into a familiar pattern? Improvements in information production and distribution, after all, have been part of all general economic and social advances throughout the agricultural and industrial ages. James Beniger of the University of Southern California makes an important point in tracing the roots of the current information society back to the 19th century.[3] Then, however, the information factor was subordinate, in terms of applied resources, to physical activities. The shift taking place now, the one we need to know more about, is moving us toward an environment in which information production and distribution will overshadow material production.

This may be a unique moment in human history, one we cannot observe clearly because we are too close to it. Astronomer Carl Sagan has given the concept a cosmic twist with his suggestion that within the past generation we have turned a corner, developing a replication of the information coding and storage capacities of primitive life via the computer. It is, he argues, a quantum leap in the creation and storage of intelligence *exosomatically*, that is, outside the body. For the first time we have machines whose information-handling capacity is roughly comparable to the genetic memory of a living organism — the single-celled paramecium.[4]

This point is sharpened by a comparison of the progressive power of various information storage methods during the past 40 centuries. The measure is the number of binary digits, or bits, representing information that can be stored in one gram of each device, beginning with the first permanent information records developed in the ancient Middle East:

Sumerian cuneiform table	10^{-2} bits or .01 bit.
Paper with typewritten words	10^3 bits or 1,000 bits.
Electronic magnetic tape	10^6 bits or a million bits.
Ultrafine silver haloid film on which information is placed with microbeams through a demagnifying electronic microscope	10^{12} bits or one hundred billion bits.[5]

Such a leap in high-technology information and communications capacities leaves us disoriented. The familiar road markings are smudged or missing. In Marshall McLuhan's analogy, we move into the future looking through a rearview mirror.

Comforting old assumptions can no longer be taken for granted. Heirs to the electronic myth, we like to assume that information and communications factors will continue to raise our level of economic productivity and social progress. There are disturbing indications, however, that such information-based productivity gains may have reached a plateau. The introduction of more resources may not advance the gains of recent years at the same fast pace.

There is growing evidence to suggest that communications and information resources will have to be reassessed if they are to realize their full potential in the current reindustrialization effort. Recent studies indicate a flattening of growth curves, indicating a point of diminishing returns with respect to investment in information goods and services. This is one of the important implications of the research carried out by economists Michael Rubin and Mary Huber on current trends in the information economy.[6]

Although the information sector is now larger than the agricultural and industrial sectors combined, the costs of its labor intensive activities may outweigh the productivity gains made possible by more sophisticated technology. In particular, economists have identified the braking effects of a nonproductive public and private bureaucracy, the fastest growing subsector of the information economy despite perennial attempts to control its spread. In the eighties, office work has accounted for over $800 *billion* in annual expenditures in the United States economy, 70 percent of which involves salaries and other personnel costs.[7] To reduce the burden of labor intensity in information growth, problems of management conservatism and other obstacles must be overcome first. Better application of existing technologies may be more productive than an accelerated pace of technical sophistication.

Beyond the question of production levels is the matter of social balance in the new information environment. Heavy infusions of information historically have had a disruptive effect on societies. The current flood of new data, increasing at a rate of about 10 percent annually, is unprecedented in any age. It is unclear how much of this is useful information, contributing to social productivity and maintenance, and how much simply adds a potentially unmanageable physical and psychic burden to what Alvin Toffler (*Future Shock*) and other analysts characterize as "information overload." In a society that gives the broadest legal protection to the most questionable fact and the most wrongheaded opinion, there is no acceptable way to evaluate information as useful, useless, or superfluous. Justice Holmes's open marketplace of competing ideas remains our ideal, whatever it lacks in standards for selection.

How much information do we need? There is an analogy between the broad information requirements of our evolving society and the specific needs of the Wright brothers in the development of their first successful airplane. Theirs was an unstable machine, designed with barely sufficient information input to allow it to move successfully through a turbulent three-dimensional environment. The analogy remains apt for the perilous passage we have to navigate toward a more complex level of democratic order.

Optimism is difficult to sustain in the face of current trends. One might better take the stance of a pessimist, defined by an anonymous Polish wit some years ago as an optimist with better information. Realistically, the likelihood is that in the near future American society will be marked by higher levels of uncertainty, a blurring of values and priorities, rising mistrust among large sections of the population, and a resulting inability to adapt private and public institutions quickly enough to cope with current problems, let alone adequately anticipate future ones. Expanded information and communications resources will tend, in the short run at least, to magnify these factors rather than reduce them to manageable proportions.

A striking analysis of this prospect is to be found in a 1978 French Government study of the effects of computerization on French culture.[8] Known as the Nora/Minc report after the two civil servants who were its principal authors, the survey was given fairly wide publicity in this country because of its strong attack on the alleged American computer dominance of the French economy. The report's sober analysis of the long-term effects of *informatisation* on French society was largely ignored here. This was unfortunate since a significant point made by Messrs. Nora and Minc was the need to face up to the negative effects of the new computer-based environment, particularly the threat of greater social alienation and erosion of traditional values. The report was a best seller in France, and the focus of continuing debate there.

We may not be able to replicate the neat Cartesian, and somewhat authoritarian, way in which the French approach problems of orderliness, but we need a better understanding in our own context of the issues raised in the Nora/Minc study. The United States faces essentially the same situation — a massive technocratic drive, threatening to go out of control unless its potentially dehumanizing antidemocratic effects are understood and reined in. If this is not done, there is a strong possibility that broad masses of people will be cut off from adequate participation in the technological mainstream, swept along as a kind of information-poor *lumpenproletariat*.

To expect these groups to accept such a position docilely would be dangerously shortsighted. One of the paradoxes of information and communications technology is that, although it seems to benefit primarily those in power, it also provides the means for organizing previously scattered and powerless challengers into strong constituencies.

One example, yet to be adequately documented, is the role played during the Vietnam protest movement by a simple technology — the telephone — in organizing groups who reversed a major national policy. Platoons of researchers have concentrated their efforts on the role of television for having "brought the war into the American living room." Though television played a role, it was essentially a passive one.[9] As a readily available two-way technology, it was the telephone that gave politically motivated groups the means for organizing against an establishment that had infinitely more communications resources available for its own purposes. Whether or not the protest groups served overriding national interests is still debatable. Their success, however, is an effective example of the chances a democratic society will have to take in the new information environment in which established power groups may be tempted to limit access to communications channels and information resources to protect their interests.

The risks of open access are substantial. Yet everything in our tradition tells us that the risks are worthwhile, that we must embrace error. A strong reaffirmation of democratic values and actions will be needed to assure social balance and, ultimately, national survival in the new information age. A pluralistic democracy such as America's needs to provide sufficient shared information, beliefs, and assumptions for its members to function as self-governing groups at many levels. "The way to prevent error is to give the people full information of their affairs" — the words are those of an 18th century optimist, Thomas Jefferson. They are a reminder that a fully responsive national communications and information system is not a luxury but an imperative if we are to survive and thrive as a vital democracy.

How can our complex society come to decisions and act to make high-technology communications and information responsive to its goals? We are handicapped by the lack of an overt information or communications crisis or of a coercive fact of the kind that a pluralistic society usually requires to mobilize itself for action. Moreover, we are restricted by a special sensitivity to policy enforcement in this area. A good healthy dose of First Amendment protection buffers us from self-appointed guardians of what is right. British communications scholar Anthony Smith has identified the paradox present in any discussion of the management of communications and information resources in a free society:

We have acquired a double conundrum: what happens to freedom of communications when the necessary instruments are concentrated inside a small elite of professionals? What obligations has a society towards policing its mass culture when that culture can exercise an influence over the attitudes, the morals, the emotional security of the mass audience? We have already lived with this debate long enough to know that these are not simple organizational questions capable of simple organizational answers. The problems are buried very deep inside our culture and like such problems in past generations they cannot be solved, only replaced with new problems and new formulations of old ones. . . . The only undisputed effect is the dilemma which it poses for all modern societies.[10]

The reality of this dilemma should be a check on any facile approach to a national strategy for communications and information. This caution applies particularly to recurrent proposals for using technocratic methodology to solve sensitive social problems. Such proposals abounded in the wake of the "optimal control" techniques used in the Apollo manned-space-program during the sixties. If computers could be used to identify a path through space that optimized manpower, fuel, and other resources, why not use them to develop policies and programs that optimize the performance of whole societies? The analogy was grossly inexact when applied to a complex civilization whose strengths lie, paradoxically, in an unwillingness to optimize its future by formula. As Nigel Calder notes, it is a wise society that believes the future is too interesting and dangerous to be entrusted to any predictable, reliable agency:

We need all the fallibility we can get. Most of all we need to preserve the absolute unpredictability and total improbability of our connected minds. That way we can keep open all the options, as we have in the past.[11]

This does not argue against prudent planning. It does suggest hedging our bets against unknown or unforeseen factors. If we choose a rigid course and are proved wrong, we all go down. Americans are steadied by a pattern of checks and balances that, in spite of some dangerous tilts, has kept us on a relatively even keel for more than two centuries. This stability will be tested severely in the coming years as we adjust our institutions and attitudes to information-age realities.

It is a point that is underscored by the Harvard Business School's Shoshana Zuboff in her 1988 study, *In the Age of the Smart Machine*, detailing the ways in which information technology is transforming the nature of work in America.[12] She is particularly critical of management's tendency to see the new automation primarily in cost-cutting terms rather than as a larger opportunity to strengthen the skills and commitment of the work force. The result of this shortsighted approach is a widening of the gap between managers and workers, leading to alienation, disorientation, and eventual erosion of the benefits, that automation can bring to the production process as well as to the lives of the men and women involved.

Our ability to deal with these and similar social changes will depend largely upon decisions we make on the distribution and use of power in the new age. In *The Nerves of Government*, political scientist Karl Deutsch documented the power inherent in high-tech information and communications resources. He argued that the groups who control the nervous system of modern society, the information networks, can control the society. If democratic liberties are to flourish in the new high-tech environment, there must be more adequate checks and balances against the misuse of information resources.

Deutsch's thesis is both persuasive and prescient. At the political level, its importance was reaffirmed in recent years by the events surrounding the Iran-contra scandal in the Reagan administration. Information manipulation played a major role in the abuse of constitutional procedures for decision making in foreign policy by a small group of officials. The deliberate withholding of information, as well as its falsification, was an important element in their plans. Other administration officials, Congress, and the public were kept in the dark about critical decisions and actions.

The White House conspirators were eventually caught in an information web of their own making. Despite their attempts to shred documents containing incriminating data, they were unaware that the White House computer storing this data was programmed to maintain backup records of their activities. The culmination of the affair was a series of nationally-televised Congressional hearings where details of their botched plans were revealed.

The Iran-contra incident demonstrated both official manipulation of information resources as well as the ability of a free society to counter such activities through public disclosure. There will be similar examples of such abuses and, hopefully, of corrective actions as we move deeper into the information age.

Future incidents may, however, be more subtle. As information power increases, the instruments for misusing it are becoming increasingly sophisticated. New electronic surveillance devices can invade our lives softly and invisibly without, so to speak, leaving fingerprints or other incriminating evidence. These devices can be used for legitimate purposes such as burglar alarm security systems. At the other extreme are their uses for malevolent purposes, reminiscent of those employed by Orwell's Big Brother. In between lies a wide grey area, a seemingly innocuous monitoring of routine activities that is carried out in the name of efficiency or safety but is capable of violating personal rights. Such electronic intrusions will be hard to measure and harder to resist, since they will often involve quiet, discreet functions whose potential threat to civil liberties is not evident.

Such Orwellian scenarios are not all hypothetical. Communications and information technology, unchecked by democratic restraints, can be concentrated in the hands of a distant, anonymous elite bent on restricting innovation and protecting its own power, nominally for some higher purpose. The efforts of any such elite will eventually fail because the new technologies are not that controllable. We have begun to see how modern anarchists, the new breed of political terrorists, can manipulate television, radio, and the telephone system, as well as the traditional print media, for their purposes. Such latter-day guerrilla tactics are, as defense authority Ian Smart has remarked, a lateral evasion of traditional social restraints. This capability is a new form of power, and it can be very effective. The physical fragility of most communications networks — wires, towers, and the like — make them particularly susceptible to terrorist actions that can paralyze a city or an entire region. Terrorist actions will be increasingly directed against computer installations — the newest, and highly vulnerable, form of information resources. This can involve the introduction of a software "virus," a type of computer program that can be secretly spread from computer to computer and potentially modify or destroy stored data.

Threats from small activist groups cannot be ignored, but they are peripheral to the problems that have to be dealt with by the majority who accept the premises, and the promise, of the new information age. The central issue is power and its disposition. At this critical time in America, an awesome amount of power is concentrated in complex information technologies and the economic efforts behind them.

Can we handle this expanded power through adjustments in present policies or linear extensions of current practices? Or is a new strategy needed for a different dimension of political power? Are information trends more than a progression of technological and economic adjustments? Do they constitute a fundamental shift in the patterns and purposes of United States society? If communications and information resources are in fact pushing us toward a radically different environment, a new political consensus on their use may be needed.

A strong case can be made against a radical change in strategy, for both pragmatic and ideological reasons. The pragmatic arguments stress that the communications and information structure is naturally evolving as an open system through the dynamic interplay of economic forces. In the new competitive environment, the United States is moving toward a universal information utility that is accessible to more people more quickly than even the sunniest optimist would have predicted a decade ago.

There is a large measure of truth in that argument, but it is false to assume that technological and economic forces, however dynamic, can by themselves assure a fully accessible system. There will be gaps in isolated geographic areas and among disadvantaged groups who are by-passed for economic or other reasons. Those who are left out will not, in this day and age, be willing to accept second class status until market forces trickle benefits down to them. In a complex, interdependent post-industrial society, the risks of excluding them from mainline benefits may be too high.

The history of communications and information development in this country shows that there has been public intervention at critical points to insure a broadening of benefits. The list is long and distinguished: Congressional funding of the original Morse telegraph experiments, the Morrill Act providing assistance for land grant colleges, federal intervention to assure wireless radio development after World War I. The example most closely paralleling the current situation was public intervention to assure the development of the world's first mass interactive communications systems — the American telephone network — in the 1930s. This decision was incorporated into the Communications Act of 1934, which gave AT&T unique legal protections in exchange for providing universal telephone service, a commitment largely fulfilled. The legal decision 50 years later to break up the AT&T empire will have reverberating effects for some time to come. Meanwhile, there remains a continuing need for public study and consensus on future communications and information patterns in this country.

The ideological argument against political intervention rests on the First Amendment and its protection of individual expression. Rights of free expression, and their support in law and custom, cannot be abridged without compromising the democratic character of the new information age. In simpler times, the definitions of those rights were relatively clear-cut. These distinctions have become fuzzy, however, in the new information environment, with its complex levels of economic and political power wielded by governments and private interests, often in collusion. The line between public and personal rights blurs to the point where civil liberties arguments become a smoke screen for policies and actions that work against individual freedom.

The debate on political principles for the information age is just beginning, together with a new sensitivity to the distinctions (and similarities) between public and private interests. "After all," notes communications lawyer Glen Robinson, "interest conflicts do not disappear simply by chanting the words 'public interest' three times, and, indeed the public interest is not something grandly aloof from the amalgam of different private interests that lie beneath it. . . . Yet there must be something more in governance than simply the arbitration and settlement of private conflict."[13] This "something more" is the elusive and necessary component of a coherent national communications and information policy. Essential personal freedoms must be protected against arbitrary political and economic power without sacrificing the social dynamics that have given American society the most open communications system in the world.

The outlines of a democratic strategy for the new age begin to emerge. These do not constitute a centralized master plan, but a new social compact that will provide the basis for needed policies and actions in the expanding area of information and communications. How can a consensus for identifying and realizing these needs be formed? Agreement will be difficult to bring about in a society in which much of political action is determined by organized interest groups seeking to protect and enlarge group entitlements. New approaches to democratic political strategy are needed, approaches that are not limited to problems of communications and information but recognize their central role in the process. Interest group politics has been given new force by the sophisticated use of communications in ways that often seem to favor direct self-serving actions over the more difficult, slower processes of consensus. Constructive decisions on the future of communications and information may, in fact, be compromised by an anachronistic approach to policy making. It is time for us to reevaluate the ways in which we approach our long-range planning.

The lead has to come from the top. In the American political structure, this means the federal executive branch, and specifically the White House. Communications and information strategies should be put on the priority agenda of critical issues requiring deliberate policy attention. At present, the subject is still relatively low on the political list, if only because there isn't any compelling pressure from major public or private interests. This may be an advantage for the time being. It reduces the prospect that the issue will be "discovered" for some temporary crowd-pleasing purpose. The usual result, in such cases, is to prevent any serious attention to the issue, once the clarion calls for action, the prestigious advisory commission, and the other paraphernalia for crisis politicking are set in motion.

Long-term strategies for communications and information will be better served by a less frenetic, more deliberate approach, involving the participation of major interest groups. One way of doing this could be a presidentially appointed Communications and Information Policy Council for the purpose of defining problems, goals, and strategies. The council should not have a large bureaucracy attached to it, but it should have sufficient funds to carry out necessary research in preparing its recommendations. A credibly refreshing precedent would be set if the council's funding were shared by federal government, industry, labor, and consumer organizations represented on the council. Participation and funds should also be provided by state and local governments, a generally overlooked sector that has an important stake in communications and information strategy.

The council's primary purpose would be to serve as a sort of communal radar, tracking the implications of communications and information developments out on the horizon and making the results of its deliberations, including those concerning minority views, available to the President, to Congress, and to the public at large. It should strive for consensus, not in the spirit of surface unity, but rather in an ongoing attempt to set the agenda of issues. It should seek cooperatively to identify and address information age realities. No one public organization can encompass all these realities. However, the council could provide a highly visible public forum for identifying and developing long-range national goals and policies in this area.[14]

Meanwhile, certain policies and actions require immediate attention. Priority should be given to the ways in which communications and information matters are now organized within the federal structure. Each administration since the mid-fifties has attempted, with only partial success, to develop procedures for handling communications and information issues within the executive branch. The Carter administration's decision to consolidate many federal programs in a single National Telecommunications and Information Administration brought some order to the subject but did not succeed in providing a strong coordinating point for policy action decisions. At least 18 federal agencies, plus the independent Federal Communications Commission, remain involved in major communications policy and operational activities. In 1981, the Reagan administration moved cautiously in the face of conflicting recommendations from interest groups to eliminate NTIA. Fortunately, the changes were not made, with the result that NTIA has been allowed to play a constructive role. Nevertheless, there is a strong case to be made for providing a better coordinated approach to both policy making and operational needs in this area.

There are three related areas where policy initiatives are urgently required, whatever new organization structure is developed. The first of these involves both Congress and the executive branch in the problem of modernizing national communications law to reflect information age changes. Significant decisions to move the country in this direction, taken by the FCC and the White House in recent years, have been slowed down by the inability of Congress to pass comprehensive supporting legislation. Until Congress can act on many of these developments, the arbiter will be the courts, which by their own admission are unable to provide clear decisions in the absence of specific legislation. Efforts to bring the Communications Act of 1934 up to date have resulted in legislation only partially responsive to the need. This partial mandate is inadequate; only a comprehensive set of legislative actions can accomplish for the new technologies what the 1934 legislation did for telephone, telegraph, and broadcasting systems.

The second area in need of policy initiatives is the economic sphere. The impact of communications and information as vital industrial sectors in themselves and also as key elements in the current reindustrialization effort must be recognized. The Department of Commerce study on the information economy discussed in Chapter 5 described the dimensions of that impact. Economic policies in this area will be critical in determining the overall growth of the economy through the end of the century.

The third priority policy area involves America's international role, with particular attention to economic factors. Information and communications make up the third largest element in the United States export pattern, after agricultural products and aviation. America's high-technology resources in this area gives us a strong competitive edge, an advantage that is being challenged by our industrial allies in Europe and Japan. This is a welcome challenge, in fact, since it is in our overall strategic interest that these countries develop comparable strengths in these sectors. Nevertheless, it is not a healthy sign that the United States now has a chronic trade deficit in telecommunications goods. It needs to respond with a more aggressive trade program to capitalize on our present advantage in microelectronic-related products. Specifically, we need to see that increasing indications that we have been slipping, due in part to complacent business-as-usual attitudes, are reversed.[15]

Our international concerns should also extend to the development of more stable policies in the political area. Communications and information have become more sensitive issues as nations identify them as strategic subjects, affecting political, economic, military, and cultural affairs. We have been inclined to ignore, and on occasion denigrate, overseas concerns about the dominant United States role in these sectors. Such attitudes, and the policies that sustain them, have to be revised if we are to take a constructive lead in the development of an open global information system. In particular, we need to work more closely with our European and Japanese allies in developing long-range strategies and operations for strengthening communications and information resources in the Third World.[16]

Our responsibilities abroad are a natural extension of the democratic forces that have impelled us to develop an open information society at home. Decisions to continue to support and expand this approach, in a new era of technological abundance, are basically political. We will make them by conscious positive efforts or by default. Either way, they will be made.

The information age is only a convenient phrase to describe the climate of change in which we live. We cannot understand its full significance, however, simply by analyzing the economics, politics, and technology involved, or even by understanding the interaction of these elements. The evolving information environment is part of a larger shift, a shift in the powerful intangibles of values and purposes.

We have gone through two centuries of extraordinary change, beginning in the North Atlantic region and spreading more and more rapidly around the globe under the rubric of modernization. Modernization has many aspects, but its dynamics spring from the scientific revolution. A vision of an inflexible, precise natural order first drove this revolution and then was absorbed into social ideas. The transition was subtle, facilitated by the assumption that, having learned the rules of nature, we had only to apply them to society. Thus the valid precepts of such men as Newton and Darwin were extended beyond their original contexts.

This misapplication of scientific theory pushed us toward the brink of anarchy. We will not survive another two centuries if we continue to pursue the same social chimeras, inspired by myths of scientific and technological certitude. Fortunately, we now sense that something is wrong, and the new perceptions of science confirm our doubts. In physics, Einstein and quantum mechanics shattered the supposed order early in this century. More recently, biology has challenged the extremes of Darwinian social views and now offers some hopeful analogs about our human destiny.

Biologist Lewis Thomas has noted, with grace and clarity, the ways in which new studies have questioned older concepts of evolution as primarily a record of open warfare among competing species, with survival limited to the strongest aggressors. He points out:

> Now it begins to look different. The tiniest and most fragile organisms dominate the life of the earth. . . . [The] urge to form partnerships, to link-up and form collaborative arrangements, is perhaps the oldest, strongest and most fundamental force in nature. There are no solitary free-living creatures; every form of life is dependent on other forms.[17]

These observations from the new biology parallel the realities we face in coming to terms with the information age. The vision of thousands of Einsteins whose talents are liberated by computers, as suggested in Chapter 1, will not be fulfilled if computers are used simply as sophisticated storage and calculating machines. Their greatest potential is in creative simulation — not as "artificial intelligence" but as a powerful augmentation of our own imaginations. And this means combining the computer's power with our own power of serendipity — the seemingly formless way in which the human animal arrives at its most enduring ideas, not by proceeding directly and infallibly in doing the essential business of our kind, as other species do, but by leaving well-trodden paths and exercising our gifts for ambiguity.

It is by appreciating this marvelous inherited gift that we can begin to fit the new communications and information resources into a more mature reordering of our personal and collective purposes, not as deterministic evolution but rather as a more harmonious melding of the many-colored strands of our common humanity. British scholar George Steiner has noted the importance of molding communications systems in ways that do not sacrifice diversity to the uncertain benefits of a bland global culture. He cites the role of the world's 10,000 languages in this process:

> Each and every tongue is a distinct window into the world. Looking through it, the native speaker enters and emotional and spiritual space, a framework of memory, a promontory on tomorrow, which no other window in the great house of Babel quite matches. Thus every language mirrors and generates a possible world, an alternate reality.[18]

We may some day shape a world order in which unity not only in language but also in other ways prevails. This prospect, however, is a long way off. For the present, our best interests lie in preserving freedom through competing diversities. This is the objective Americans must keep in mind in shaping our society in a new age. Other cultures will judge us, and identify their own interests, as they see fit. It is, in the last analysis, the one sure path to expanding human freedom, permitting each of us, as Emerson urged, to produce that peculiar fruit we were born to bear.

NOTES

1. Quoted in Max Ways, "The Era of Radical Change," *Fortune*, 11 February 1980, p. 201.

2. The counterargument to these attitudes is presented in Ithiel deSola Pool, *The Technologies of Freedom* (Cambridge: Harvard University Press, 1983), particularly in Chapter 9, "The Policies of Freedom."

3. James Beniger, *The Control Revolution* (Cambridge: Harvard University Press, 1986).

4. Carl Sagan, *The Dragons of Eden* (New York: Ballantine Books, 1978), p. 25.

5. James G. Miller, *Living Systems* (New York: McGraw-Hill, 1977), p. 12.

6. Michael Rubin and Mary Huber, *The Knowledge Industry in the United States: 1960–1980* (Princeton, NJ: Princeton University Press, 1985).

7. "Death Sentence for Paper Shufflers," *The Economist* (London), 27 December 1980, p. 56.

8. Simon Nora and Alain Minc, *The Computerization of Society* (Cambridge, MA: MIT Press, 1980).

9. Michael J. Arlen, *The Living Room War* (New York: Viking Press, 1969).

10. Anthony Smith, "The Management of Television in a Democratic Society." (Paper presented at the Symposium on the Role and Management of Telecommunications in a Democratic Society, Munich, June 24–26 1974).

11. Nigel Calder, *The Life Game: Evolution of the New Biology* (New York: Viking Press, 1975), p. 32.

12. Shoshana Zuboff, *In the Age of the Smart Machine* (New York: Basic Books, 1988).

13. Glen O. Robinson, "The New Communications: Planning for Abundance," *Virginia Quarterly Review,* 53, No. 3 (Summer 1977), p. 397.

14. A useful first step was taken in this area by a White House Conference on Libraries and Information held in October 1979 in Washington. Its report recommended a broad series of initiatives for making information available to all citizens through the new technologies. A follow-up conference, reviewing progress since the first meeting, is planned for the early nineties.

15. This has been particularly true of the manufacturing sector, where the United States has had a net trade deficit in telecommunications equipment since 1983. The services export picture is considerably better. See "The Bright Future of Service Exports," *Fortune,* 8 June 1987, pp. 32–38.

16. The basic document for an American initiative in this area is "Toward an American Agenda for a New World Order of Communications," a report issued by the U. S. National Commission for UNESCO (Washington, DC: Government Printing Office, 1980).

17. Lewis Thomas, "On the Uncertainty of Science," *Harvard Magazine,* September/October 1980, p. 19.

18. George Steiner, "The Coming Universal Language," *Atlas World Press,* October 1977, p. 26.

Selected Bibliography

Abramson, Jeffrey, Arterton, Christopher and Orren, Gary R. *The Electronic Commonwealth: The Impact of New Media Technologies on Democratic Politics.* New York: Basic Books, 1988.

Arlen, Michael. *The Living Room War.* New York: Viking Press, 1969.

Barnouw, Erik, *The Sponsor.* New York: Oxford University Press, 1975.

———. *Tube of Plenty.* New York: Oxford University Press, 1975.

Bell, Daniel. *The Coming of Post-Industrial Society.* New York: Basic Books, 1973.

Beniger, James. *The Control Revolution.* Cambridge: Harvard University Press, 1986.

Benjamin, Gerald, ed. *The Communications Revolution in Politics.* Proceedings of the Academy of Political Science, Vol. 34, Number 4. New York, 1982.

Bolter, J. David. *Turing's Man: Western Culture in the Computer Age.* Chapel Hill: University of North Carolina Press, 1984.

Brock, Gerald. *The Telecommunications Industry.* Cambridge, MA: Harvard University Press, 1981.

Brodeur, Paul. *The Zapping of America.* New York: W. W. Norton & Co., 1977.

Brzezinski, Zbigniew. *Between Two Worlds.* New York: Viking Press, 1970.

Calder, Nigel. *The Life Game: Evolution of the New Biology.* New York: Viking Press, 1975.

Clarke, Arthur C. *Voices Across the Sea.* London: Luscombe Publishers, 1974.

Codding, George and Rutkowski, Anthony. *The International Telecommunications Union in a Changing World.* Dedham, MA: Artech House, 1982.

Cohen, Stephen S. and Zysman, John. *Manufacturing Matters: The Myth of the*

Post-Industrial Economy. New York: Basic Books, 1987.

Compaine, Benjamin, ed. *Understanding New Media.* Hagerstown, MD: Ballinger Publishing Co., 1984.

Demac, Donna, ed. *Tracing New Orbits: Cooperation and Competition in Global Satellite Development.* New York: Columbia University Press, 1986.

Deutsch, Karl W. *The Nerves of Government.* New York: Free Press of Glencoe, 1963.

Devoutzis, Michael and Moses, Joel, eds. *The Computer Age: A Twenty-year View.* Cambridge, MA: MIT Press, 1980.

Dizard, Wilson P. *The Strategy of Truth.* Washington, DC: Public Affairs Press, 1961.

_____. *Television: A World View.* Syracuse, NY: Syracuse University Press, 1966.

Dizard, Wilson and Swensrud, S. Blake. *Gorbachev's Information Revolution: Controlling Glasnost in a New Electronic Era.* Colorado Springs: Westview Press, 1987.

Dorfman, Ariel. *The Empire's Old Clothes: What the Lone Ranger, Babar and Other Innocent Heroes Do to Our Minds.* New York: Pantheon, 1983.

Eames, Charles and Ray. *A Computer Perspective: A Sequence of 20th Century Ideas, Events, and Artifacts from the History of the Information Machine.* Cambridge, MA: Harvard University Press, 1973.

Economist, The (London), 30 January 1988. Special supplement: "Programming the future — a survey of computer software."

Edgar, Patricia and Rahim, Sayeed, eds. *Communications Policy in Developed Countries.* Honolulu: East-West Center, 1981.

Eisenstein, Elizabeth L. *The Printing Press as an Agent of Change.* New York: Cambridge University Press, 1980.

Ellul, Jacques. *The Technological Society.* New York: Alfred A. Knopf, 1964.

Estabrook, Leigh, ed. *Libraries in Post-Industrial Society.* Phoenix, AZ: Oryx Press, 1977.

Evans, Christopher. *The Micro Millenium.* New York: Viking Press, 1979.

Feigenbaum, Edward A. and McCorduck, Pamela. *The Fifth Generation: Artificial Intelligence and Japan's Computer Challenge to the World.* Reading, MA: Addison-Wesley Publishing Co., 1983.

Ferkiss, Victor C. *Technological Man: The Myth and the Reality.* New York: George Braziller Inc., 1969.

Fisher, Glen. *American Communication in a Global Society.* Norwood, NJ: Ablex Publishing Co., 1979.

Forester, Tom. *High Tech Society.* Cambridge, MA: MIT Press, 1987.

Gunter, Jonathan F., ed. *The United States and the Debate on the World Information Order.* Washington, DC: Academy for Educational Development, 1979.

Hamelink, Cees. *Cultural Autonomy in Global Communications.* New York: Longman Publishers, 1983.

Hammer, Donald P., ed. *The Information Age: Its Development and Impact.* Metuchen, NJ: Scarecrow Press, 1976.

Hudson, Heather. *When Telephones Reach the Village: The Role of Telecom-

munications in Rural Development. Norwood, NJ: Ablex Publishing Co., 1984.

Innis, Harold A. *Empire and Communications.* Toronto: University of Toronto Press, 1972.

International Telecommunications Union. *The Missing Link.* Report of the Independent Commission for World Wide Telecommunications Development (the Maitland Commission). Geneva, December 1985.

Jussawalla, Meheroo and Ebenfield, Helene. *Communication and Information Economics: New Perspectives.* New York: Elsevier Science Publishing Co., 1984.

Jussawalla, Meheroo, Lamberton, Donald M. and Karunaratne, Neil D. *The Cost of Thinking: Information Economies of Ten Pacific Countries.* Norwood, NJ: Ablex Publishing Co., 1988.

Katz, Raul Luciano. *The Information Society — An International Perspecitve.* Westport, CT: Praeger Publishers, 1988.

Kernan, Julie. *Our Friend, Jacques Maritain.* New York: Doubleday, 1975.

Kuhns, William. *The Post-Industrial Thinkers.* New York: Harper & Row, 1971.

Laurie, Peter. *The Micro Revolution: Living With Computers.* New York: Universe Books, 1981.

Lippmann, Walter. *Public Opinion.* New York: Harcourt, Brace and Co., 1922.

Machlup, Fritz. *The Production and Distribution of Knowledge in the United States.* Princeton, NJ: Princeton University Press, 1962.

Mackintosh, Ian. *Sunrise Europe: The Dynamics of Information Technology.* New York: Basil Blackwell, 1986.

Maddox, Brenda. *Beyond Babel: New Directions in Communications.* Boston: Beacon Press, 1974.

Martin, James. *The Wired Society.* Englewood Cliffs, NJ: Prentice-Hall Inc., 1978.

Mehra, Achal. *Free Flow of Information: A New Paradigm.* Westport, CT: Praeger Publishers, 1986.

McLuhan, Marshall. *The Gutenberg Galaxy.* Toronto: University of Toronto Press, 1962.

Miller, James G. *Living Systems.* New York: McGraw-Hill, 1977.

Muggeridge, Malcolm. *Things Past.* London: Collins, 1978.

Mumford, Lewis. *The Pentagon of Power.* New York: Harcourt Brace, 1970.

Nora, Simon and Minc, Alain. *The Computerization of Society.* Cambridge, MA: MIT Press, 1980.

Oettinger, Anthony and Weinhaus, Carol. *Behind the Telephone Debates.* Norwood, NJ: Ablex Publishing Co., 1988.

Oettinger, Anthony, Berman, Paul and Read, William. *High and Low Politics: Information Resources for the Eighties.* Cambridge, MA: Ballinger Publishing Co., 1977.

Papert, Seymour. *Mindstorms: Children, Computers and Powerful Ideas.* New York: Basic Books, 1980.

Pelton, Joseph. *Global Talk.* Rockville, MD: Sijthoff and Noordholf, 1981.

Pool, Ithiel de Sola, ed. *Handbook of Communications.* Chicago: Rand

McNally College Publishing Co., 1973.

———. *The Social Impact of the Telephone*. Cambridge, MA: MIT Press, 1977.

———. *Technologies of Freedom*. Cambridge, MA: Harvard University Press, 1983.

Read, William H. *America's Mass Media Merchants*. Baltimore, MD: Johns Hopkins University Press, 1976.

Reid, T. R. *The Chip: How Two Americans Invented the Microchip and Launched a Revolution*. New York: Simon & Schuster, 1984.

Ritchie, David. *The Binary Brain: Artificial Intelligence in the Age of Electronics*. Boston: Little, Brown and Co., 1984.

Robinson, Glen O. *Communications for Tomorrow: Policy Perspectives for the 1980s*. New York: Praeger Publishers, 1978.

Rubin, Michael R. and Huber, Mary T. *The Knowledge Industry in the United States: 1960–1980*. Princeton, NJ: Princeton University Press, 1986.

Sagan, Carl. *The Dragons of Eden*. New York: Ballantine Books, 1978.

Saunders, Robert and Wellenius, Bjorn. *Telecommunications and Economic Development*. Baltimore, MD: Johns Hopkins University Press, 1983.

Schiller, Dan. *Telematics and Government*. Norwood, NJ: Ablex Publishing Co., 1982.

Schiller, Herbert. *Communications and American Empire*. Boston: Beacon Press, 1971.

———. *The Mind Managers*. Boston: Beacon Press, 1973.

———. *Communications and Cultural Domination*. White Plains, NY: International Arts and Sciences Press, 1976.

———. *Information and the Crisis Economy*. New York: Oxford University Press, 1986.

Scientific American. "Communication." A special issue. September 1972.

"The Mechanization of Work." A special issue. September 1982.

———. "Computer Software." A special issue. September 1984.

Slack, Jennifer D. and Fejes, Fred, eds. *The Ideology of the Information Age*. Norwood, NJ: Ablex Publishing Co., 1987.

Smith, Anthony. *The Geopolitics of Information*. New York: Oxford University Press, 1980.

———. *Goodbye Gutenberg*. New York: Oxford University Press, 1980.

———. *Shadows on the Cave*. Urbana, IL: University of Illinois Press, 1973.

Stevenson, Robert L. *Communication Development and the Third World: The Global Politics of Information*. White Plains, NY: Longman Publishers, 1988.

Stonier, Tom, *The Wealth of Information: A Profile of the Post-Industrial Economy*. London: Thames Methuen, 1983.

Teilhard de Chardin, Pierre. *The Future of Man*. New York: Harper & Row, 1969.

Toffler, Alvin. *Future Shock*. New York: Bantam Books, 1971.

Tunstall, Jeremy. *The Media Are American*. London: Constable, 1977.

U. S. Congress, House of Representatives. *Options Papers*. Prepared by the staff of the subcommittee on communications of the Committee on Interstate and Foreign Commerce, 95th Cong., 1st sess. Committee Print 95–13 May 1977.

U. S. Department of Commerce. *The Information Economy,* 9 vols. Office of Telecommunications Special Publication 77–12, 1977.

Wiener, Norbert. *The Human Use of Human Beings: Cybernetics and Society.* Boston: Houghton Mifflin Co., 1950.

Weizenbaum, Joseph. *Computer Power and Human Reason.* San Francisco: W.H. Freeman and Co., 1976.

Zuboff, Shoshana. *In the Age of the Smart Machine: The Future of Work and Power.* New York: Basic Books, 1988.

Index

WILSON DIZARD is both a practitioner and a student of communications and information affairs. From 1951 to 1980, he served as a Foreign Service officer in the Department of State and U. S. Information Agency. His overseas assignments included Turkey, Greece, Iran, Pakistan, Vietnam, and Poland. Since 1965, Mr. Dizard has specialized in communications policy issues involving satellites, computers, radiocommunications, and international developments. He was a vice chairman of the U. S. delegation to the 1979 World Administrative Radio Conference in Geneva.

Mr. Dizard is currently a senior fellow at the Center for Strategic and International Studies in Washington, DC. He is also an adjunct professor of international affairs at the School of Foreign Service, Georgetown University.

His other writings include *The Strategy of Truth*, *Television: A World View*, and *Gorbachev's Information Revolution*, as well as numerous articles in scholarly journals and other publications.